A MATTER
OF TRUST

A MATTER OF TRUST

MI5 1945-72

Nigel West

WEIDENFELD AND NICOLSON
LONDON

Copyright © Westintel Limited 1982

First published in Great Britain by
George Weidenfeld & Nicolson Limited
91 Clapham High Street, London SW4

ISBN 0 297 78253 3

Printed and bound in Great Britain by Butler & Tanner Ltd,
Frome and London

Contents

Abbreviations

ASIO	Australian Security Intelligence Organization
BND	West German Security Service
BOSS	South African Bureau of State Security
BSC	British Security Co-ordination
CIA	Central Intelligence Agency
CID	Criminal Investigation Department
CIFE	Combined Intelligence Far East
CPGB	Communist Party of Great Britain
D-G	Director-General of the Security Service
DNI	Director of Naval Intelligence
DSO	Defence Security Officer
DST	French Security Service
FBI	Federal Bureau of Investigation
GRU	Soviet Military Intelligence
KGB	Soviet Intelligence Service
MI5	British Security Service
MI6	British Secret Intelligence Service
NATO	North Atlantic Treaty Organization
NKVD	Soviet Security Service
NSA	National Security Agency
OSS	Office of Strategic Services
PROD	Office of Production, National Security Agency
RCMP	Royal Canadian Mounted Police
RSLO	Regional Security Liaison Officer
SDECE	French Secret Intelligence Service
SIME	Security Intelligence Middle East
SIS	Secret Intelligence Service (MI6)
SLO	Security Liaison Officer
SOE	Special Operations Executive
UN	United Nations

Illustrations

Tables of MI5's Organization

POST-WAR DIRECTORS-GENERAL OF MI5

Sir David Petrie KCMG Kt CIE CVO CBE	1940–6
Sir Percy Sillitoe KBE Kt	1946–53
Sir Dick White KCMG KBE	1953–6
Sir Roger Hollis KBE Kt CB	1956–65
Sir Martin Furnival Jones Kt CBE	1965–72
Sir Michael Hanley KCB	1972–9
Sir Howard Smith KCMG	1979–81

POST-WAR DEPUTY DIRECTORS-GENERAL

Brigadier A.W.A. Harker CBE	1940–7
Captain Guy Liddell CBE MC	1947–52
Roger Hollis OBE CB	1952–6
Graham Mitchell CB OBE	1956–63
Martin Furnival Jones CBE	1963–5
Anthony Simkins CB CBE	1965–71

MI5 ORGANIZATION, 1945

Director-General: Sir David Petrie
Deputy D-G: Brigadier A.W.A. Harker
PA to D-G: Richard Butler

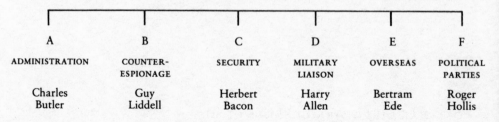

A	B	C	D	E	F
ADMINISTRATION	COUNTER-ESPIONAGE	SECURITY	MILITARY LIAISON	OVERSEAS	POLITICAL PARTIES
Charles Butler	Guy Liddell	Herbert Bacon	Harry Allen	Bertram Ede	Roger Hollis

MI5 ORGANIZATION, 1946

Director-General: Sir Percy Sillitoe
Deputy D-G: Guy Liddell
PA to D-G: Michael Suppell
Russell Lee

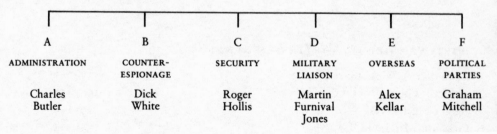

A	B	C	D	E	F
ADMINISTRATION	COUNTER-ESPIONAGE	SECURITY	MILITARY LIAISON	OVERSEAS	POLITICAL PARTIES
Charles Butler	Dick White	Roger Hollis	Martin Furnival Jones	Alex Kellar	Graham Mitchell

MI5 REORGANIZATION, 1953

Director-General: Sir Dick White
Deputy D-G: Roger Hollis

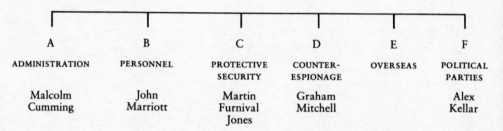

A	B	C	D	E	F
ADMINISTRATION	PERSONNEL	PROTECTIVE SECURITY	COUNTER-ESPIONAGE	OVERSEAS	POLITICAL PARTIES
Malcolm Cumming	John Marriott	Martin Furnival Jones	Graham Mitchell		Alex Kellar

MI5 ORGANIZATION, 1956–65

Director-General: Roger Hollis
Deputy D-G: Graham Mitchell*
         Martin Furnival Jones
PA to D-G: Walter Bell

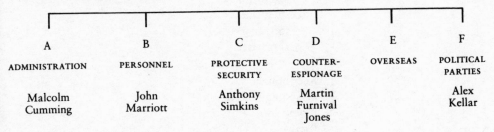

A	B	C	D	E	F
ADMINISTRATION	PERSONNEL	PROTECTIVE SECURITY	COUNTER-ESPIONAGE	OVERSEAS	POLITICAL PARTIES
Malcolm Cumming	John Marriott	Anthony Simkins	Martin Furnival Jones		Alex Kellar

* Retired 1963.

MI5 ORGANIZATION, 1965

Director-General: Martin Furnival Jones
Deputy D-G: Anthony Simkins
PA to D-G: Harry Stone

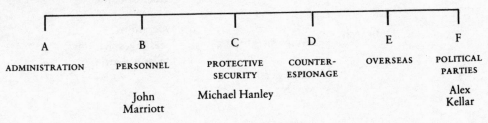

A	B	C	D	E	F
ADMINISTRATION	PERSONNEL	PROTECTIVE SECURITY	COUNTER-ESPIONAGE	OVERSEAS	POLITICAL PARTIES
	John Marriott	Michael Hanley			Alex Kellar

MI5's Internal Structure, 1953

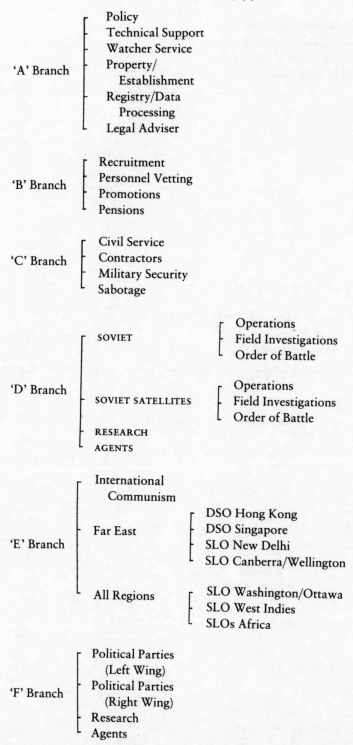

'A' Branch
- Policy
- Technical Support
- Watcher Service
- Property/ Establishment
- Registry/Data Processing
- Legal Adviser

'B' Branch
- Recruitment
- Personnel Vetting
- Promotions
- Pensions

'C' Branch
- Civil Service
- Contractors
- Military Security
- Sabotage

'D' Branch
- SOVIET
  - Operations
  - Field Investigations
  - Order of Battle
- SOVIET SATELLITES
  - Operations
  - Field Investigations
  - Order of Battle
- RESEARCH
- AGENTS

'E' Branch
- International Communism
- Far East
  - DSO Hong Kong
  - DSO Singapore
  - SLO New Delhi
  - SLO Canberra/Wellington
- All Regions
  - SLO Washington/Ottawa
  - SLO West Indies
  - SLOs Africa

'F' Branch
- Political Parties (Left Wing)
- Political Parties (Right Wing)
- Research
- Agents

1

TRANSITION

'The Security Service is, after all, a secret service
... this is part of its essence. Its cost is borne on
the Secret Vote and one must bear in mind
therefore that the number of parliamentary
questions which could be put to me with any
hope of an answer being properly answered is
very limited.'

HENRY BROOKE MP, *Secretary of State for the
Home Department, 1963*

When the war ended in Europe in May 1945 the British Security Service
was in the process of winding down its activities and returning a large
number of its personnel to civilian life. The reduction in the organization's size had actually begun in the summer of the previous year, as the
Allies had advanced towards the Rhine. The need for a large home
Security Service had diminished, and many of the counter-intelligence
staff had been attached to regular military units to supervise the liberation of the occupied areas.

Although counter-intelligence is a somewhat broad term, it does describe MI5's responsibilities which, since 1909, have been specifically
counter-espionage, counter-sabotage and counter-subversion in all
British territory. Counter-intelligence in other geographical areas has
always been dealt with by the Secret Intelligence Service (MI6).

Since November 1940 MI5 had been headed by a distinguished former
Indian police officer, Sir David Petrie. He had been brought out of
retirement in Egypt, at the age of sixty-one, to give the Security Service
the strong leadership it had lacked since the previous June, when
Churchill had sacked the original Director-General, Major-General Sir
Vernon Kell, and his Deputy D-G, Brigadier Sir Eric Holt-Wilson. The
organization had undergone a series of internal changes during that

period, but its fundamental structure of six Divisions had remained the same.

'A' Division, headed by Colonel Charles Butler, was the administrative department, and included such sub-sections as legal, transport, personnel and policy. A2 also provided experienced administrators for the supporting agencies, such as the GPO's telephone and letter interception units. The staff engaged on these duties had been drafted into the Services during wartime, so as to reduce union and other complications, but once the European war was over the responsibility for the interception of civil communications reverted back to the GPO's Special Investigation Branch. However A3, the transcription service, remained a direct Security Service section. Also nominally in 'A' Division was the all-important Registry which, by the end of hostilities, accounted for fully one third of MI5's strength. The department was traditionally female and labour-intensive in spite of the use of Hollerith punch-card sorters, an innovation of the Head of Registry, Reginald Horrocks. Horrocks had first joined MI5 in 1940 from Roneo, the business efficiency firm, but had stayed on after the war, ably assisted by his future successor, Harold Potter. Registry was generally an unpopular posting as the work was appallingly dull, even if it was of national importance. Registry girls were divided into three groups: filing clerks who operated the Nominal Indices, a card-index system linked to 'open' personal files and subject files which were available for any MI5 officer to request and examine; specially trusted girls who dealt with the top-secret Y Box Files; and the most exalted of all, the girls seconded to individual sections who kept guard over the 'Held Files', those considered too sensitive to leave lying around in Registry. Many members of this latter group showed considerable initiative and were rewarded by promotion to officer rank.

As we will see, 'A' Division was later to become highly technical and to acquire the services of a Scientific Adviser (A2) and to retain control over many 'technical sources'.

'B' Division, the principal counter-espionage department, was headed by Captain Guy Liddell. It included the famous B1(a) section, run by Colonel T.A. (Tar) Robertson, which had orchestrated the numerous double agents being used to deceive the enemy. Other 'B' Division sections included B1(b), an analysis unit interpreting intercepted Abwehr wireless signals, and several other important operational branches.

'C' Division, headed by Major Herbert Bacon, took charge of vetting and other defensive security work, whilst 'D', headed by Brigadier Harry Allen, maintained liaison with the regular military forces and appointed liaison officers to the other Services.

'E' Division, the province of Major Kenneth Younger,* oversaw the

---

* Later Labour MP for Rutherglen Division at the 1945 general election when Alex Kellar succeeded him.

activities of all aliens, both neutral, friendly and otherwise. E1 was headed by a veteran anti-communist, Millicent Bagot, and her section dealt with international communism. E2 maintained contact with the overseas representatives (called Defence Security Officers where there were British garrisons and Security Liaison Officers elsewhere). E3 under Courtney Young retained the Far East as a single geographical interest.

'F' kept surveillance on the two political extremes in the United Kingdom: F1 concentrating on the Communist Party of Great Britain (CPGB), F2 on the fascists. Both sections had operations and research sub-divisions, with F4 under John Bingham* running the deep-cover penetration agents.

Each Division was headed by a Director, a senior MI5 officer who had pre-war intelligence experience. These men, together with the Director-General, Sir David Petrie, and his Deputy D-G, Brigadier A.W.A. (Jasper) Harker, sat as the 'Directorate of the Security Service'. The exception to this was the head of 'F' Division, Roger Hollis, who only had the rank of Assistant Director. Hollis had joined MI5 in 1938 and therefore had little pre-war service. The Communist Party of Great Britain was his special concern, whilst the fascists were monitored by the other senior 'F' officer, Graham Mitchell, a former member of the Conservative Party's research department, who had also been a journalist on the *Illustrated London News*.

This, then, was the order of battle of MI5 in 1945. It maintained a headquarters in St James's Street, Mayfair, and used Blenheim Palace, in Oxfordshire, to house some of its administrative offices. It also ran a number of other smaller offices in London – in Regent Street, Piccadilly and Dolphin Square – where individual case officers could meet their agents.

During the war 'B' Division had also operated a small network of Regional Security Liaison Officers (RSLOs) attached to military districts in England, Wales and Scotland. It was their responsibility to discuss security matters with the Chief Constables in their area and build up good relations with the police forces in the provinces. The RSLOs, of which there were generally a total of eight, were disbanded in 1945 leaving background enquiries in the counties to the local Assistant Chief Constables and the Metropolitan Police's Special Branch. When the county forces developed their own Special Branches security enquiries were handled by them, except in Scotland where a single Regional Co-ordinator was established.

Surprisingly the greatest number of MI5 officers (aside from head-quarters' clerical staff) were overseas, as liaison officers with the Dominion or Colonial intelligence services, or posted to semi-independent

* Later Lord Clanmorris.

organizations, such as Security Intelligence Middle East (SIME), which was based in Cairo, or Combined Intelligence Far East (CIFE) in Singapore. Many other MI5 staff were seconded for duty with MI6, and in particular the Special Counter-Intelligence units, which were formed after the invasion of France to scoop up and 'turn' the German stay-behind agents.

These Special Counter-Intelligence operations gained increasing importance during the latter months of the war, when the code-breakers at Bletchley received less operational information from the now famous ULTRA intercepts, as the Wehrmacht and the SS fell back towards Germany and home territory, and made heavier use of land-lines. As a result wireless-orientated intelligence diminished and the Allied commanders at the front, particularly the 21st Army Group, were obliged to rely on the techniques of strategic deception which had been so successfully executed in the months leading up to D-Day.

Accompanying the first troops in each liberated area were joint British and American intelligence teams, armed with their 'Purple Primers'. These were ordinary school exercise books containing the names and addresses, or other identifying information, of enemy stay-behind agents. Each would be visited even as the local fighting continued and offered a simple choice: imprisonment and possible execution, or co-operation. Most opted for the latter and, in so doing, extended the Continent-wide network of 'controlled' double agents.

The information contained in the Purple Primers had been collated over the previous three years and was mainly the combined product of three separate organizations: the Radio Security Service, the B1(b) analysts and MI3, the German order of battle experts.

The Radio Security Service monitored all wireless transmissions and used direction-finding equipment to locate the sources of suspicious transmissions. Most stay-behind agents, equipped with radios, sent several test messages back to their German controllers before being overrun and this enabled the locations of suspects to be identified long before the front-line troops had arrived on the scene. Frequently radio intelligence coincided with details which had already been filed by the B1(c) officers, who had a vast store of knowledge on German intelligence techniques and personalities. As well as drawing on signals intelligence they had access to prisoner interrogation reports from MI 14, the Combined Services Detailed Interrogation Centres. All suspected Nazi agents and known enemy intelligence personnel were passed to MI 14 as soon as their identities had been verified. Delay between capture and first interview was kept to the minimum, thus enabling B1(b) to have the very latest information. Finally the accumulated material was passed to MI3, who constantly updated the Purple Primers.

Thus the Allies slowly took clandestine control of all the enemy's intelligence. As more networks were overrun, so the amount of intelligence escalated, providing further opportunities for strategic deception. The system proved to be especially successful during the last months of the war when the Luftwaffe were unable to verify their intelligence assessments by photographic reconnaissance.

Once an area had been liberated and the situation stabilized, MI5 staff had to help Field Security Wings obtain enemy intelligence documentation and vet prisoners in order to identify captured Abwehr or Sicherheitsdienst (SD) officers. MI5 also had to clear up any cases where British subjects were thought to have aided the enemy.

One of the first such 'clearing up' operations involved P.G. Wodehouse, who was interviewed in Paris shortly after the liberation by Edward Cussen, a former member of MI5's legal department.

Wodehouse had become notorious for a series of radio talks that he had given over German radio. He had been placed under house arrest during the occupation and had unwisely agreed to broadcast to England. The result of Cussen's interview with the author was a long statement describing in detail the events that led to the broadcasts, together with transcripts of the programmes themselves. It was decided that there were no grounds for prosecution, and Wodehouse promptly went to live in New York. It was a mistake that many were not prepared to forgive, and Wodehouse never returned to England.

Other British broadcasters on Nazi radio were less fortunate. The first to be arrested was John Amery, the black-sheep son of Leo Amery MP. Amery was intercepted by Italian partisans on 23 April 1945 whilst driving his Lancia Aprilia on the autostrada between Milan and Como. He was interned at the Tierney Internment Camp near Rome, where he was interviewed in May by Len Burt of MI5's 'B' Division.* Amery returned to London to face capital charges and, in November the following year, pleaded guilty to them. The judge, Mr Justice Humphreys, immediately questioned Amery's Counsel, Gerald Slade QC, to establish if the prisoner realized the consequences of his plea. Informed that he did indeed, Humphreys placed the black cap on his head and sentenced Amery to death. He was hanged at Wandsworth on 19 December 1945.

Amery's case had taken a long time to get to the Old Bailey, and in the meantime a second Nazi broadcaster, the equally notorious William Joyce, nicknamed Lord Haw-Haw, was arrested, tried and executed.

Joyce was caught attempting to cross the German frontier into Denmark near Wassersleben on 28 May 1945. He was challenged by a British officer, Captain A.A. Lickorish, who thought he recognized Joyce's familiar voice even though only a few words had been exchanged, and those had been in French. Joyce promptly put his hand into his coat

* Later Commander of Special Branch, 1946–58.

pocket to retrieve his papers (which identified him as 'Fritz Hansen'), but Lickorish's companion, an interpreter, misunderstood Joyce's sudden move and, thinking Joyce was reaching for a gun, shot him in the thigh. The wretched Lord Haw-Haw was taken to 2nd Army headquarters at Lüneburg for formal identification and interrogation by Jim Skardon of B2(a). On 16 June 1945 Joyce was flown back to London and appeared in the dock at the Old Bailey two months later. The trial lasted three days, at the end of which he was sentenced to hang. His appeal was dismissed on 18 December, and he climbed the scaffold at Wandsworth on 3 January 1946.

Norman Baillie Stewart, the celebrated 'prisoner-in-the-Tower' who had been court-martialled, cashiered and imprisoned in 1933, was next. He was arrested in May 1945 by American Counter-Intelligence Corps officers in Ault Aussee, Austria, who had used him as their interpreter. Baillie Stewart was transferred to a gaol in Brussels before being flown to England, late in 1945, to face trial on charges of treason at the Old Bailey. A search of his rooms in Austria however, by Reginald Spooner of MI5, established that the former Seaforth Highlander had changed his nationality in 1939, and he was therefore only found guilty of an infringement of the wartime Defence Regulations, a much lesser offence and one that did not carry a capital sentence. Baillie Stewart was sentenced to five years' imprisonment by Mr Justice Oliver on 10 January 1946.

There were many other similar 'turncoat' cases, many of whom had joined the Legion of St George, the so-called British Free Corps which had recruited British prisoners of war in Germany for service in an SS regiment on the Russian front. In fact none of the members, who volunteered after having met John Amery, actually saw any action beyond that found during numerous visits to SS brothels.

While MI5 liaison staff were sifting through the abandoned Nazi files, the French, Dutch and Norwegians were conducting post mortems into the wartime behaviour of certain of their countrymen. In France, where collaboration was widespread, especially amongst the civil police, the Direction de Surveillance du Territoire initiated a detailed investigation into those Resistance cells which had been penetrated by the Germans. Frenchmen suspected of betrayals were detained in the old Gestapo headquarters in the Rue de Saussaies and interrogated. Several interrogations confirmed the suspected guilt of an Englishman, Harold Cole, of complicity in the betrayal of Resistance networks.

Sergeant Harold Cole had deserted with funds from the Sergeant's Mess in the spring of 1940, when serving with the British Expeditionary Force in France. By December 1941 he had been arrested by the Brussels Abstelle and 'turned'; thereafter he had posed as a British escapee, denouncing each of his helpers as he passed down the PAT escape line which ran from Belgium, through occupied France over the Pyrenees. In 1942, having promoted himself to Captain, Cole infiltrated the PAT escape line again and effectively closed it down. After the war it was estimated that he had caused some 150 people to be arrested, of whom a large number had been tortured, and fifty had been known to have been killed. The French put a price on his head, as did MI9, the escape and evasion service, but he was not apprehended until late in the summer of 1945, when he was found in southern Germany, calling himself Captain Paul Mason and making himself indispensable to the American occupation forces. Soon after his arrest he was interviewed by Peter Hope of MI5, who had him returned to Paris for interrogation.

Cole, however, was an experienced survivor and, donning a convenient US Army tunic, escaped from custody. Some time later he was challenged in the Rue de Grenelle by two Gendarmes who suspected him of being a deserter. Cole drew a revolver and wounded one of them. The other returned his fire and shot Cole dead.

Cole was subsequently described by Reg Spooner of MI5 as the worst traitor of the war.*

When Clement Attlee came to power he learned from the Cabinet Secretary, Sir Edward Bridges, that the future of both MI5 and MI6 were under review by Sir Findlater Stewart, the Chairman of the wartime Home Defence Executive. Stewart, assisted by John Drew, took evidence from MI5, MI6 and a host of other wartime secret departments, and concluded in his secret report dated 27 November 1945 that Britain should retain its two separate intelligence organizations: MI6 for intelligence gathering abroad and MI5 for security at home. Most of Sir Findlater's attention was taken up by MI6, so that MI5 escaped detailed internal reorganization until 1953, but what Stewart did say about MI5 was:

The purpose of the Security Service is the Defence of the Realm and nothing else. It follows that the minister responsible for it *as a service* should be the Minister of Defence, or, if there is no Minister of Defence, the Prime Minister, as Chairman of the Committee of Imperial Defence. It had been argued that this would place an undue burden upon the Minister of Defence or Prime Minister, and upon the staff of the Cabinet Secretariat. But from the very nature of the work, need for direction except on the very broadest lines can never arise above the level of Director-General. That appointment is one of great responsibility, calling for unusual experience and a rare combination of qualities; but having got the right man there is no alternative to giving him the widest discretion in the means he uses to and the direction in which he applies them – always provided he does not step outside the law.

---

* Iain Garrow, *The Great Detective* (Frederick Muller, 1966).

It was an extremely apposite comment for Sir David Petrie was sixty-six and his successor had now to be chosen. Petrie's Deputy D-G, Jasper Harker, was only fifty-four, but his performance as Acting D-G during the crucial interregnum of Kell's departure and Petrie's appointment had been less than impressive. Those vital summer months of 1940 had proved that although Harker was a good administrator and socially very amiable, he was quite unable to provide leadership.

The next most senior officer was Guy Liddell, a veteran MI5 man whom Harker had appointed Director of 'B' Division in June 1940. Traditionally 'B' Division was the most senior branch of MI5 and so its head could hope for higher office, but Liddell was not considered a likely candidate for the very top although he was a possible deputy.

Guy Liddell's intelligence experience dated back to 1919 and his wartime record in MI5 had been exceptional. He had encouraged the formation of the double-agent exercise known as the double-cross system* and had taken an active interest in the developments made by the Radio Security Service. He was without question a brilliant intelligence officer, and he had recruited a number of outstanding brains into the office during the first twelve months of the war. But he had a regrettable choice in friends and was known to prefer the company of homosexuals, although he himself was not one. Long after the war he invariably spent Friday evenings at the Chelsea Palais, a well-known haunt of homosexuals.

If the general election of October 1945 had not elected a Labour administration it is arguable that Liddell might have been chosen to succeed Petrie, but with Attlee in Downing Street such a thing was impossible. Attlee, like most of his colleagues in the Labour Party, had deep reservations about the Security Service, probably (and understandably) fostered by the suspicion that MI5 had played a major role in the Zinoviev Letter scandal of 1924 which ensured a Tory victory at the polls the same year. Attlee did not feel he would be able to trust an internal candidate so he chose a reliable outsider, a police officer called Percy Sillitoe, to head the Security Service.

---

* See J.C. Masterman's *The Double Cross System in the War of 1939-1945* (Yale University Press, 1972).

2

SIR PERCY SILLITOE

I had always found it difficult to get down to facts with my MI5 colleagues. There was so much secrecy within secrecy. My colleagues were charming and amiable, conscientious and erudite, but sometimes when I was talking to one of them a glazed expression would come over his face; and I would try and make up my mind whether he was hiding information from me or whether he felt at a disadvantage because I had shown I knew more than he did. And on occasions I felt like a small boy unwillingly let into a prefects' pow wow ... for a sudden change of subject would take place just when I was beginning to be interested.

This appraisal was written by Derek Tangye* who served in MI5 from June 1940 to February 1950. It catches the flavour of caution and secrecy necessary even between colleagues. One of the more depressing aspects about working in the Security Service was the need to guard your tongue all the time, to talk to no one, to tell no one what you did, not even your wife. It encouraged the recruitment of rugged, independent originals. To lead such a team required equal strength of character.

In the foreword to Sillitoe's autobiography,** Attlee wrote:

A Director-General of MI5 needs very special qualities. He has to have the technical qualities required for intelligence work. He must be able to control a team of individualists engaged on important secret work. At the same time he has to have a very lively appreciation of the rights of the citizen in a free country.

Sillitoe's previous experience was limited to regular police work. He had originally joined the South African police in 1908 and, three years later, had transferred to the Northern Rhodesia police. He had remained in East Africa until 1923 when he had been appointed Chief Constable of Chesterfield. He had subsequently held posts in the East Riding of Yorkshire, Sheffield and Glasgow before moving to the Kent Constabulary in April 1943.

Sillitoe's appointment as Director-General of the Security Service, which he took up on 30 April 1946, heralded a number of changes within

* *The Way to Minack* (Michael Joseph, 1968).
** *Cloak Without Dagger* (Cassells, 1955).

MI5. The Deputy D-G, Jasper Harker, retired the following year, aged fifty-seven, and Guy Liddell was moved up to take his place. The prospect of having to work with 'a rozzer at the top' was simply too much to bear for some of 'B' Division's remaining staff. One officer with strong feelings on the subject was the head of B1(a), Colonel Tar Robertson. He resigned in protest and went to work for the Government Communications Headquarters at Eastcote. Liddell's assistant Dick White moved up to be the new Director of 'B' Division. White was later to consider resigning because of his frustration with Sillitoe, whom he thought supremely ignorant of intelligence matters.

When Sillitoe took over the Director-General's office in Leconfield House, overlooking South Audley Street, he found two major investigations in progress. Both were to have immense repercussions.

The first investigation had in fact been progressing since 5 September 1945 when a twenty-six-year-old Soviet cipher clerk named Igor Gouzenko failed in his attempt to sell his story to the *Ottawa Journal*. The newspaper thought he was a crank and suggested he go to the police. The following day Gouzenko and his pregnant wife tried to get an interview with the Canadian Minister of Justice, but were turned away. He was finally taken seriously when two Royal Canadian Mounted Police (RCMP) constables were called to Gouzenko's apartment, where the Soviet Assistant Military Attaché and three Embassy colleagues were found to be smashing down the door.

As it happened, most unusually, news of this none-too-remarkable event went to the Secret Intelligence Service (SIS) first. Under normal circumstances it would have been relayed instantly to the MI5 representative in Ottawa, Cyril Mills, but Mills was on his way back to England to be demobbed. In his absence the message went to the British Embassy in Washington, where it was received by Peter Dwyer, an MI6 officer. At the moment of its arrival Dwyer was representing MI5 in the American capital as well as his own organization.*

Dwyer promptly sent a coded message to MI6, London, where it was channelled to the desk of the head of Section IX, the Soviet department, H. A. R. (Kim) Philby. When it arrived Philby was in fact wrestling with another, similar problem in Istanbul. An apparently well-informed Soviet NKVD officer, Konstantin Volkov, had announced his intention to defect and had offered the names of some Soviet agents in England as an inducement for protection and help. The British Consulate-General sought London's advice, and the MI6 Chief, Major-General Sir Stewart Menzies, handed the case over to Philby. Philby was aghast at the

---

* It was not until 1947 that Dick Thistlethwaite, the first Security Liaison Officer, was posted to Washington as a permanent link between MI5 and his American opposite numbers.

prospect of being denounced and made plans to travel to Turkey immediately. Just as he was about to leave the Gouzenko telegram arrived.

Philby was quite unable to handle both cases, so he sent the Gouzenko file to his opposite number at MI5, the Director of 'F' Division, Roger Hollis. The way in which this transfer took place was to become a matter of considerable importance some years later. Philby went to see Menzies and obtained his approval for the Gouzenko case to be handed over to MI5. Philby then sent a demi-official letter to Hollis stating that the case was rather more his province than Philby's. That letter was to remain on Gouzenko's MI5 personal file and later cause much debate.

While Philby travelled to Istanbul, Hollis flew to Ottawa and was met there by Sir William Stephenson, the diminutive head of British Security Co-ordination, the New York-based organization which supervised British intelligence operations in the Western hemisphere. It was fortunate that the Mounties had consulted Stephenson, who was a Canadian citizen, because their initial instinct had been to hand Gouzenko back to the Russians. Stephenson immediately recognized Gouzenko and, more importantly, his stolen Soviet files, as excellent sources of intelligence, and had the defector transferred to a training camp on the shores of Lake Ontario which had been used by SOE during the war. Here, on the outskirts of the town of Oshawa, Gouzenko was interrogated at length by Stephenson, Hollis and the Mounties.

Gouzenko himself (now referred to by his code-name CORBY) was able to fill many of the gaps in the files he had stolen from the Soviet Embassy and identified more than twenty of the current Soviet Military Intelligence (GRU) code-names. Two were of particular importance to MI5. One was Kathleen (Kay) Willsher, a senior member of the British High Commission's Registry (with the GRU code-name of ELLIE), and the other was an atomic scientist, Alan Nunn May (code-named ALEK by the GRU).

None of these individuals were actually arrested until mid-February the following year, thus giving the FBI the opportunity to set up a surveillance operation on the home of Anatoli Yakovlev, the Soviet Consul-General in New York who, according to the CORBY papers, was the GRU *rezident* in the United States. Meanwhile, Nunn May (code-named PRIMROSE by MI5) had returned to England on 17 September and taken up an appointment at King's College in London. PRIMROSE was kept under constant surveillance, but at his first formal interview, on 15 February 1946, he told Len Burt that he had no knowledge of any leaks concerning atomic information. Five days later Burt confronted the scientist with the fact that he had failed to keep three appointments with the GRU outside the British Museum. Burt knew this to be the case because he and Reg Spooner had spent the nights of 7, 17 and 27 October in a room overlooking Great Russell Street waiting for him. This news took PRIMROSE completely by surprise and he promptly confessed to passing secrets to the Russians for a period of six months between February and August 1945. He was arrested on 4 March 1946 by Detective Inspector William Whitehead of the Metropolitan Police's Special Branch. As was their pre-war custom, MI5 always handed their cases over to Special Branch for arrest as they did not – and still do not – have any formal powers. Nunn May appeared at the Old Bailey on 1 May before Mr Justice Oliver. The trial lasted just one day, as Nunn May pleaded guilty, and he was sentenced to ten years' imprisonment.

The Nunn May case in London was followed three days later by the trial of Miss Willsher in Ottawa. She was sentenced to three years' hard labour.

Meanwhile, the FBI were pursuing the rest of an American network run by Yakovlev. Nunn May was later to provide important clues in this investigation when he identified various of his contacts from a film shot covertly by the FBI.

MI5's handling of the PRIMROSE case was judged to be a considerable success and incurred the gratitude of the FBI, who might otherwise have been unable to clear up their own atomic ring. The case was in stark contrast to the Volkov business which had been terminated by the Soviet diplomat's sudden disappearance. The SIS Head of Station in Istanbul, Cyril Machray, was mystified, and so apparently was Philby.

From MI5's point of view PRIMROSE was an indication of a Soviet espionage offensive and two counter-espionage officers from the B2 section of 'B' Division, Michael Suppell and Bob Hemner-Scales, were commissioned to write an appreciation of Soviet intentions.

Coincidentally another transatlantic investigation was also taking place during 1945-6. Sir Edward Travis's newly formed code-breakers at Eastcote had achieved considerable success with intercepted Soviet wireless traffic. The broken signals, code-named U-TRAFFIC, were providing fascinating insights into the exchanges between Moscow and Soviet diplomats overseas. The Americans were duplicating this effort with Operation BRIDE at the National Security Agency's decryption branch (known as PROD, for Office of Production) at Fort Meade, in Maryland. Co-operation in the field of decryption was later to be formalized in the UKUSA Agreement, a charter for co-ordinating the operations of Eastcote and Fort Meade. The joint target, of course, was Soviet signals traffic and the Americans had made their first advances in the field (with British assistance) in Australia. At the end of the war in the Pacific, an American intercept station at Shoal Bay near Darwin had by luck cut into some Soviet diplomatic wireless traffic. The results looked so promising that Courtney Young, MI5's Chinese-speaking Far East expert, was posted to Australia. As a consequence of the decrypted U-TRAFFIC, the Australian government received proof that the Soviets were operating several illegal spy networks and decided to create an Australian Security Intelligence Organization (ASIO). Sillitoe dispatched Roger Hollis to advise on internal structure and security procedures and, in March 1949, ASIO's first Director-General, Judge (Sir) Geoffrey Reed, was appointed.

An interesting insight into 'B' Division's assessment of Soviet espionage during this period can be obtained from *Handbook for Spies*,* the 'autobiography' of Alexander Foote, published in 1949, which was actually organized and written up by Courtney Young on his return from Australia. He based the book on fact.

Foote had turned up in the British Sector of Berlin in August 1947, having spent the previous eleven years working for the Russian NKVD. Born in Yorkshire, Foote had been recruited into Soviet intelligence whilst serving with the British battalion of the International Brigade in 1937. His two mentors were Wilfred Macartney, who commanded the battalion (having completed a prison sentence in England for espionage), and the political commissar Douglas Springhall (who was to be similarly convicted in 1943). Foote initially became a courier for the Communist Party of Great Britain, but he quickly graduated to more sophisticated work, including that of wireless operator for the Soviets' famous LUCY ring** in Switzerland.

On 20 November 1943 Foote had been arrested by the *Bundespolizei*, the Swiss Security Service. He was released the following September and made his way to the Soviet Embassy in Paris to report for further duties. From there he was ordered to Moscow, but was obliged to kick his heels in Paris until the following January to secure a flight. Once in the Russian capital Foote was put into training for a new mission to the United States. Instead he defected at the first opportunity, which he seized in Berlin.

Foote's interrogations in London were conducted by Courtney Young and other 'B' Division officers anxious to learn about the latest Soviet methods. Foote co-operated completely, encouraged by a promise of help with a government job. His debriefing covered every aspect of his life and offered crucial information about a possible Soviet agent living in England. When Foote had first joined the LUCY ring in 1938 he had been interviewed by a woman in St John's Wood and then instructed to make contact with a second Soviet agent code-named SONIA at the Post Office in Geneva. Both were apparently senior figures in the Soviet network. MI5 subsequently identified SONIA as Ursula Hamburger, *née* Kuczynski, the daughter of Professor Rene Kuczynski, a distinguished German

* Museum Press, 1949.
** Pierre Accoce and Pierre Quet, *The Lucy Ring* (W. H. Allen, 1967).

refugee then lecturing in economics at Oxford University. SONIA had married Rudolf Hamburger, a German architect, and both had gone to work as Soviet agents in Shanghai until 1935 when her husband was arrested and detained on a charge of espionage. She promptly fled to Switzerland, taking her two daughters with her, and set up home near Montreux. In February 1940 SONIA, being both a communist and a Jewess, became increasingly agitated about the prospect of a Nazi invasion of Switzerland and obtained British nationality by marrying another member of the LUCY ring, Leon Beurton, code-named JOHN. JOHN, like Foote, was a veteran of the Spanish Civil War and had also been recruited by SONIA's sister, Birgette Lewis, whom Foote recognized as the lady in St John's Wood. Foote reported that SONIA had left Switzerland for England in December 1940 and had been followed by JOHN in July 1942. JOHN's repatriation via Portugal had been facilitated by MI6, who thoughtfully provided him in Geneva with a forged British passport in the name of Miller. He then joined first the RAF and then the Coldstream Guards before settling down with SONIA.

MI5 traced SONIA and JOHN to a cottage in the village of Great Rollright, near Chipping Norton, late in August 1947 and paid them a visit with the local CID on the pretext of investigating SONIA's bigamous marriage. Was she, they asked, not still legally married to Rudolf Hamburger? SONIA denied the charge, although she freely admitted to having once worked as a Soviet agent. Both she and her husband claimed they had long since given up being active communists and were not in touch with the Soviets. The MI5 officer assured her he had not come to arrest them; he simply wanted their co-operation. They both refused and, shortly afterwards, took a holiday to East Berlin from which they failed to return.*

The full significance of SONIA's work was not to be realized until MI5 read Klaus Fuchs's statement of January 1950.**

The Director-General, Percy Sillitoe, agreed that Foote's experiences should be made public. Courtney Young would write the book and MI5 would supervise production, taking the opportunity to score a few propaganda points. In the conclusion 'Foote' is made to comment:

The obvious and important question is whether there is a Russian spy net at work in England at the present moment. On that point I have no factual evidence, and if I had I obviously could not give it here. On the other hand, it would be safe to say that the odds are definitely in favour of networks existing both in England and the United States.

Prophetic words indeed.

Again, Foote's case was a success from MI5's point of view, since he

---

* In 1977 she published her account of her activities, *Sonia's Rapport*, in East Germany.
** See page 33.

had provided a unique insight into the remarkable NKVD operation of LUCY, but it did not end happily for Foote. The 'government job' he ended up with was in the Ministry of Agriculture and Fisheries. He died a broken man on 1 August 1956.

Successful decrypts of Soviet wireless intercepts were now becoming more frequent. Comparison with the U-TRAFFIC summaries revealed that the British Embassy in Washington had been penetrated by a source code-named HOMER by the Russians. An investigation was launched, but it made little progress because of the paucity of clues provided by the intercepts. What MI5 did establish, however, was that the source was well-placed, probably of Second Secretary rank or above. This description covered a large number of people and it was more than two years before an unlucky slip in a U-TRAFFIC identified Donald Maclean.

Meanwhile another U-TRAFFIC intercept, in early October 1949, identified a further Soviet source. In America, the NSA's PROD had built on their earlier successes and had managed to reconstruct a mass of Soviet diplomatic messages which suggested that there was a further leakage of atomic secrets and that the two principal candidates were both distinguished nuclear physicists. The U-TRAFFIC summaries enabled the MI5 investigators to work out the location and dates of various meetings held between the source and his Russian case officer, and once the time-table had been completed it was sent to Dwyer, the MI6 officer in Washington. He then made a comparison between the time-table and the movements of the two scientists. His enquiries cleared one and pointed conclusively at Dr Klaus Fuchs.

To identify Fuchs as the Soviet source was one thing, but to obtain a conviction against him without disclosing the existence of the U-TRAFFIC material was quite another. By the middle of October 1949 only a minimal number of officers had been indoctrinated into the case: Dwyer in Washington (who was ending his tour of duty); the Director 'B', Dick White; his Assistant Director, John Marriott (a former Secretary to the wartime Twenty Committee); and the head of B2(a), Harry Hunter.

It was not in fact MI5's intention to arrest Fuchs for most of those concerned with the case suspected he might make a valuable double agent. They argued that a direct approach to him by MI5 would tip him off and certainly warn the Russians that their signals security was in need of improvement. Hoover, the FBI Director, would have nothing to do with this idea and became so convinced that Sillitoe would let Fuchs off that he sent Whit Lishman, the head of the FBI's anti-communist section, as his personal representative, to camp in Leconfield House until the arrest was made. Eventually it was decided that Wing-Commander Henry Arnold should also be told about Fuchs as he was MI5's Security

Officer at the Atomic Energy Research Establishment at Harwell, in Berkshire, where Fuchs was head of the Theoretical Physics Division with the rank of Deputy Chief Scientific Officer. Fuchs had arrived from Los Alamos to take up the post that June, so Arnold and his wife were able to befriend the scientist without arousing his suspicions. Arnold allowed the relationship to develop for two months, at the end of which time he brought up the subject of Fuchs's father, who had announced his intention of taking up a university professorship in Leipzig, behind the Iron Curtain. Arnold, of course, was perfectly well aware of this development since MI5 had been intercepting Fuchs's mail and tapping his telephone. Once Fuchs had mentioned his father, the way was clear for Arnold 'to seek further advice and get someone down from London to discuss the implications'. The man from London, who arrived on 21 December 1949, was Jim Skardon from B2(a).

Skardon went to work on Fuchs and on his third visit to Harwell, on 13 January 1950, Fuchs admitted that he had been passing secrets to the Russians since 1942, when he had been introduced to a Soviet intelligence officer by a colleague, Professor Jeurgin Kuczynski. Skardon reported this to his Director, Dick White, who in turn passed the news on to Bernard Hill, the Security Service's Legal Adviser. It was decided that a signed confession, under caution, would be the best possible course, so Skardon arranged for Fuchs to come to London on Friday 27 January to sign a formal statement.

Fuchs arrived at Paddington, where he was met by Skardon (whose B2(a) watchers were keeping an eye on the scientist every inch of his journey), and taken to Room 055 of the War Office, the MI5 'front' office. Fuchs signed his confession and then agreed to undergo a technical debriefing the following Monday at the hands of Michael Perrin, who had already been indoctrinated into the case by Dick White. Their session continued all day, by the end of which time Perrin and Skardon were satisfied that they had at least the basis for assessing the damage done. Fuchs then returned to Harwell, where he remained until 2 February when Perrin called him to a further debriefing session in London; but instead of talking to Skardon and Perrin, he was confronted with Len Burt who arrested him.

Fuchs's trial took place at the Old Bailey on 10 February 1950, before Lord Justice Goddard. He pleaded guilty to passing information on four occasions between 1943 and 1946. He was sentenced to fourteen years' imprisonment. No mention was made of any intercepted Soviet signals and all concerned promoted the idea of the defendant spontaneously confessing to Wing-Commander Arnold. At the time no one in 'B' Division could explain why Great Russell Street had been so completely devoid of loiterers on the three nights they knew that the GRU had agreed to meet Fuchs. Fuchs himself had certainly not been tipped off, but had genuinely decided to cut his ties with the Russians. But how did the Soviets know this? Why had there not been a Soviet diplomat on hand? The answer was that the MI6 representative in Washington during Dwyer's investigation had been Kim Philby. Once in Wormwood Scrubs Fuchs agreed to a further debriefing session with Skardon and recalled in detail every meeting he had ever had with his Soviet contacts.

The first was known to him only as ALEXANDER and they had met four times in London. Fuchs went through a batch of Soviet diplomatic passport pictures and identified ALEXANDER as Simon Kremer, Secretary to the Soviet Military Attaché and a known GRU officer. When ALEXANDER had left England at the end of 1941 he had passed Fuchs on to a woman who turned out to be Jeurgin Kuczynski's sister, SONIA. Fuchs had met her in Banbury, a convenient location half-way between his work in Birmingham and her radio station at 50 George Street, Oxford. At his last rendezvous with SONIA in October 1943, shortly before he was due to go to America, Fuchs had received instructions on how to meet his new case officer, whom he would know as RAYMOND. On 11 May 1950, Fuchs successfully spotted RAYMOND in a film covertly shot by the FBI. The man he picked out was Harry Gold, who was arrested in Philadelphia by the FBI on 23 May.

Fuchs's account of his work for SONIA was a painful reminder to 'B' Division of their failure to obtain any information from her when they had confronted her in August 1947. They now realized that they had inadvertently stumbled on Fuchs's one-time case officer who was unquestionably still operational. Furthermore, at the time of MI5's visit to her cottage, she had recently reactivated Fuchs as a spy.

In June 1946 Fuchs had returned to England to take up his post at Harwell and had been instructed by RAYMOND to resume contact with his GRU case officer by attending a rendezvous at Mornington Crescent tube station, in north London, at exactly 8pm on the first Saturday of each month. In fact Fuchs ignored the instructions because of the Canadian spy scandal, but early the following year decided it was safe to begin passing secrets again. Assuming the Mornington Crescent meeting place to be out of date, he tried to find Jeurgin Kuczynski. He failed because Kuczynski had been recruited into the Office of Strategic Services (OSS) in 1944 and had moved to the United States, where he was acting as economic adviser to George Ball (later the US Under-Secretary of State).* Instead Fuchs approached a member of the Communist Party of Great Britain who put him in touch with SONIA. She had just one further meeting with him at which she gave him details of a new rendezvous, the saloon bar of a pub in north London, The Nag's Head at Wood

* Later Kuczynski joined his sister in East Germany.

Green. It was here that Fuchs met the last Soviet officer he was to deal with before his arrest.

The Fuchs case closed one particular phase of MI5's operations, since it was the last one to develop from signals intelligence. No doubt Philby's suitably caustic comments on Soviet signals security were taken to heart by Moscow.

In spite of Fuchs's guilty plea and the briefest of trials at the Old Bailey (it lasted less than an hour and a half), MI5 were severely mauled by the press for not having spotted Fuchs earlier. When Parliament returned Attlee declared on 6 March (after a briefing from the Director-General): 'I do not think there is anything that can cast the slightest slur on the Security Service. Indeed, I think they acted promptly and effectively as soon as there was any line they could follow up.'

It would, however, only be fair to point out that other British intelligence organizations were not immune from troubles of their own at this time. On one memorable occasion in May 1948 the Security Service had actually had the opportunity of rescuing MI6 from their plight over the particularly embarrassing fiasco of Colonel Tasoev.

Colonel Tasoev, the head of the Soviet Reparations Mission in Bremen, in north Germany, was also a Russian intelligence officer. Although Bremen was in the American Zone of Occupation MI6 had targeted him as suitable for subornment. Early in May, Tasoev was 'lifted' in Bremen and flown to England, but within a matter of days the operation misfired. Instead of being grateful for having been helped to defect, Tasoev announced that he wished to return to his colleagues in Bremen. This development was particularly awkward because MI6 had scored what they believed was a propaganda victory by announcing on 6 May that Tasoev had been granted political asylum in England at his own request. A further complication was the anger of the Americans, who resented MI6 operating on their territory without advance warning, contrary to agreement.

MI6's first problem was to find a secure home for Tasoev, who had become increasingly vocal in his demands to see a diplomat from the Russian Embassy in London. In desperation they turned to MI5, who arranged to have him put in a cell in Hammersmith police station while Sir Stewart Menzies, the MI6 Chief, made up his mind about what to do. Some MI6 officers suggested that he be taken on a flight over the North Sea and encouraged to leave the aircraft without a parachute, while the 'moderates' proposed that MI6 should cut its losses and simply hand him back to the Russians. Optimistically they argued that the Soviets, having been suitably embarrassed, would hush the matter up.

Such optimism was ill-founded for Tasoev was a deliberate 'plant' right from the beginning, as Menzies discovered when he opted to return the defector to Germany. Tasoev was bundled aboard a special flight to

Berlin on 20 May and driven straight to the Russian Commandantur. However, instead of keeping quiet, the Soviets issued a long statement early in June indignantly accusing the 'British Secret Services' of kidnapping one of their officers. Whereupon MPs asked questions of the Foreign Secretary, Ernest Bevin, in the House of Commons. The exchanges were relatively light-humoured until the veteran communist MP for West Fife, William Gallacher, suggested that Bevin evidently 'knew as much about MI5 as he did, and that was damn all'. The Foreign Secretary, no doubt bemused at having to answer questions which would have been better directed at the Home Secretary or the Prime Minister, retorted that since Gallacher was a communist he probably had more dealings with MI5 than the Minister did. And with that the affair was dismissed, though the memory of Colonel J. D. Tasoev would long remain in the minds of both MI5 and MI6.

The 1950s were to herald many changes in the organization of the Security Service, not the least of which was a significant alteration in its status within the Whitehall structure, in apparent contradiction to Sir Findlater Stewart's recommendations of November 1945. MI5 had not moved into shared accommodation with the Secret Intelligence Service, MI6.

MI5 had by now made the transition from its wartime role. Blenheim Palace had been returned to the 10th Duke of Marlborough, and the London 'office' had become Leconfield House, on a rather more permanent basis than anyone had anticipated. The building was not entirely suitable, even though steel grilles had been placed behind what remained of the bricked-up ground-level windows. One curious feature of the property were the gun-ports on the south-west corner, pointing up Curzon Street towards Hyde Park. These had been installed in 1940 when the HQ London District had anticipated a street by street battle for Mayfair with Nazi parachutists. A decade later the British leftist press suggested that the loop-holes were manned night and day in case a mob should try to storm the building. In fact the single remaining gun-ports had long since been blocked up and the room behind was a communications centre, filled with teleprinters, not machine-guns.

MI5's staff had also undergone something of a transformation since their wartime days, a change highlighted by the appointment of Percy Sillitoe by the incoming Labour government. By early 1950, with the prospect of three further years ahead until the Director-General reached retiring age, Dick White, for one, was actively canvassing to find outside employment. He had been appalled by the former policeman's lack of professionalism and love of publicity. Sillitoe had attended trials at the Old Bailey and had on several occasions conducted press conferences, despite pleas for discretion from his new Personal Assistant, Russell Lee.

Some of the old-stagers had departed and some new talent had been recruited. Two well-known 'office' figures had left: Captain Derbyshire (known to everyone as 'Derby') and Max Knight. Knight commanded considerable respect for his pre-war operations against the Communist Party of Great Britain which, in 1938, led to the conviction of Percy Glading on charges of spying for the Russians, and against pre-war fascists, which resulted in Anna Wolkoff being imprisoned in 1940 and Captain Archibald Ramsay MP being detained under Regulation 18b.

Not all of Knight's operations were a success though, and MI5 had experienced considerable embarrassment over what became known as the Greene Affair.

Benjamin Greene was a member of the famous Berkhamstead family which had produced such distinguished men as his first cousins, the writer Graham Greene and the Director-General of the BBC, Sir Hugh Greene. He had served briefly on Ramsay MacDonald's staff as his Private Secretary and was an active member of the Labour Party, occasionally making speeches at Party Conferences. He was also an active Quaker, which had brought him into contact with many German refugees. One such refugee had been Harald Kurtz, a nephew of Queen Mary's and an MI5 stool-pigeon. Shortly after Kurtz's arrival in England, he had been introduced to Max Knight, who at that time headed the B5(b) section of 'B' Division. Kurtz was desperately short of money, in spite of his royal connection, and agreed to go to work for MI5. His job was to play the part of a Nazi sympathizer and report any suspicious characters to B5(b).

Kurtz took to his new role with alacrity and denounced several dozen people as potential Fifth Columnists, who were promptly interned under the Aliens Acts. He was then himself sent to Kempton Park internment centre to report on any subversive influences among the detainees and was regarded as a very successful stool-pigeon. However, one of his 1940 reports concerned a certain Benjamin Greene, who was arrested and detained in Brixton the same month. Normally this would have been the end of the matter, but the Greene family were mystified by his arrest because Benjamin was a pacifist, rather than a fascist, and was certainly not disloyal to the Crown, although he had been vocal in his criticism of Chamberlain's administration.

Greene's first attempt to get released ended when the Courts ruled his Writ of Habeas Corpus invalid. His family, and in particular his brother Edward Reginald, were undeterred and sought the advice of Oswald Hickson Collier & Co., a well-known firm of City solicitors.

Hickson, through contacts in MI5's legal department (which was almost entirely staffed by City-based solicitors and barristers), discovered that Benjamin Greene had been arrested on evidence provided by a Security Service informant, one Harald Kurtz. Edward Greene took this news to his brother, who denied ever having been 'subversive' with Kurtz, although he recalled the German refugee introducing himself and asking for a loan. It was then that Edward Greene recalled that shortly after his brother's detention he had had a similar experience. Kurtz had called on him at his office, offered his sympathies and then asked for financial help 'so he could emigrate to Brazil'. He had been shown the door after only the briefest of interviews.

The Greenes now took up the case in earnest, having hired a private detective to find the MI5 agent, no easy task. The detective failed, but by coincidence Edward Greene suddenly bumped into Kurtz in 1941 outside the Café Royal in Regent Street. The MI5 man had appeared embarrassed, but Greene pretended to be very friendly and invited Kurtz to lunch the following day, at Simpson's in the Strand. Kurtz agreed and overnight Hickson and Greene prepared a trap for the 'stoolie'. At the end of their meal, and suitably fortified, Kurtz again repeated his offer to try to help with Benjamin's case. Edward Greene immediately took him up on it and accompanied Kurtz to Hickson's office, which was not far away. Inside, Hickson was waiting with a stenographer and proceeded to confront Kurtz with his evidence. Had not Greene in fact been detained on Kurtz's testimony? At first the refugee blustered, but he quickly succumbed under cross-examination. He agreed that he had lied about Greene and signed a statement to that effect.

Naturally, this was something of an embarrassment for B5(b), and Knight arranged for Benjamin Greene's release. The case was not yet over, for Greene pursued the matter by sueing for wrongful arrest and managed, in January 1942, to get Kurtz named in the House of Lords as the mischievous MI5 informant, thereby 'blowing his cover'. Nevertheless, the case was lost, on the grounds that the Secretary of State had acted reasonably by accepting MI5's word that Greene was a danger to the security of the country. Kurtz was later employed as an interpreter at Nuremberg and wrote several successful biographies including *The Empress Eugenie*.*

Thereafter Max Knight's position in MI5 was somewhat undermined and his frequently voiced opinion that the Soviets had managed to penetrate the Security Service went unheeded. During the early 1950s Knight devoted more and more time to his naturalist talks for the BBC, leaving the business of running agents to his deputy, John Bingham, who operated from a flat in Exhibition Road, South Kensington. On Knight's retirement Bingham became head of F4, the 'F' Division section running agents inside the Communist Party of Great Britain.

When Churchill won the 1951 general election he learned that the

---

* Hamish Hamilton, 1964. Perhaps not coincidentally Graham Greene gave the name 'Kurtz' to a villainous character in *The Third Man* (Bodley Head, 1950).

out-going Prime Minister, Attlee, had commissioned the Cabinet Secretary, Sir Norman Brook, to prepare a secret review of the Security Service. Brook's report, which he submitted in March 1951, proposed a major change in the existing arrangements.

I recommend that the Security Service should in future be responsible to the Home Secretary. I believe that it would be helpful to the Director-General of the Security Service to be able to turn to a senior Permanent Secretary for advice and assistance on the policy aspects of his work and on his relations with other Government Departments; and that he would receive from the permanent head of the Home Office support and guidance which the Prime Minister's secretariat is not in a position to give.

Brook then added, as if to reassure MI5 about their lost status:

The Prime Minister would doubtless continue to send for the Head of the Security Service from time to time, to discuss the general state of his work and particular matters which might be of specially close concern to him. And on matters of supreme importance and delicacy, the Head of the Service should always be able, at his initiation, to arrange a personal interview with the Prime Minister.

While the new Home Secretary, Sir David Maxwell Fyfe, was considering this proposal, MI5 suddenly obtained a dramatic break in their prime investigation.

Having obtained a conviction in the case of Fuchs, 'B' Division decided to re-examine all the information they and the Americans had accumulated on the Soviet source known as HOMER. The new analysis revealed that HOMER had been in the habit of visiting New York twice a week and that, in September 1944, his wife had been expecting a baby. Now, eight years later, this profile was found to fit Donald Maclean, the former First Secretary in Washington and then head of the Foreign Office's American Department. Maclean was immediately placed under B2(a) surveillance, with the agreement of the Foreign Office's Head of Security, George Carey-Foster. The head of 'B' Division's B2 section applied for and obtained the necessary Home Office warrant to tap Maclean's telephone at his home in Tatsfield, on the North Downs.

There now followed a long period of B2(a) surveillance, during which time Maclean was never spotted with any Soviet contacts. After Maclean's departure much fuss was made over the fact that surveillance on the diplomat was limited to London and as soon as he had climbed aboard his train home in the evenings the watchers turned in. But the movement of Russian Embassy officials was restricted to a limited distance around London (as it still is), and it was thought unlikely that Maclean's contact would risk drawing attention to himself by breaking the travel rule. In addition the watchers believed that extending the surveillance operation into Surrey would alert Maclean.

The difficulties facing B2 at this point were considerable. There was only flimsy circumstantial evidence against him and the prospects of catching him red-handed (the ideal solution) were receding. Indeed, most of those indoctrinated into the case felt they probably had the wrong man. (It was only much later that MI5 were to learn of Maclean's erratic behaviour and breakdown in Cairo.)

In such cases the Security Service have to rely on straightforward confrontation and permission for such an interview was finally given by the Foreign Secretary, Herbert Morrison, on Friday, 25 May 1951. Accordingly, the necessary notices were dispatched to Washington, so that the FBI and the CIA could be informed. Maclean was to be interviewed by Dick White and the B2 on Monday 28 May.

On the appointed Monday, Maclean failed to appear for work and Mrs Maclean telephoned the Foreign Office to report that her husband had been missing since Friday. Carey-Foster conveyed this news to the Deputy D-G, Guy Liddell, who was aghast. A certain 'Roger Styles' had dined with the Macleans the previous Friday evening and had then left, taking the diplomat with him. 'Roger Styles' was Guy Burgess, and his hired Austin A70 was found on the dock in Southampton. To date Burgess, also a diplomat, had never even come under suspicion of being a Soviet spy.

The man Liddell turned to for help in unravelling the mystery of Burgess's involvement was Anthony Blunt, a former personal assistant to Liddell when the latter had been the wartime Director of 'B' Division. Blunt, who was then Director of the Courtauld Institute, agreed to accompany a pair of B2(a) watchers to Burgess's flat in Chester Square and give them access. This would circumvent the necessity of applying for a search warrant through Special Branch. Blunt also gave the MI5 men some assistance in searching the flat.

The flat proved to be a gold-mine of information. Burgess had left a mass of incriminating papers, enough to keep B1 and B2 occupied for many months. While the watchers pored over the contents of a trunk found under the bed, Blunt was busy pocketing letters from Burgess's desk which, if found, would have compromised both himself and Philby.

The sudden departure of Burgess had taken everyone at Leconfield House completely by surprise, and a 'damage control' exercise was promptly launched by White and the B2 to investigate the backgrounds of the two missing men and to identify the source of the obvious warning they had received.

The implications of Maclean's escape and Burgess's defection were enormous. News of the disaster quickly reached the newspapers and the FBI Director, Hoover, summoned Sillitoe to Washington to explain what had gone wrong. Not surprisingly the subject was an awkward one for MI5 because the FBI had not been kept entirely in the picture during the latter stages of the HOMER investigation. Hoover's aggressive behaviour over Fuchs had confirmed 'B' Division's opinion that Hoover had no idea of how to conduct a delicate intelligence operation. The arrival of his personal representative, Lishman, at Curzon Street at that time, had been interpreted as an insult. Now the situation was rather more embarrassing because the proposed espionage coup by MI5 had collapsed into a fiasco. The full extent of the disaster was, however, concealed. When the FBI asked for the exact date on which 'B' Division had targeted Maclean, MI5 lied and put the date back a fortnight.

This face-saving cover-up was treated with caution in Washington and the Director-General was requested to give a rather fuller account of the affair. Sillitoe therefore arranged to fly to the United States on 11 June 1952. The prospect of the 'honest copper' attempting to deceive the Americans filled 'B' Division with alarm, so Liddell suggested that an indoctrinated representative, Arthur Martin, should accompany the Director-General. Sillitoe agreed, but insisted that they would both make the journey under their own names. At the time there seemed little point in raising objections to this plan, although the officer selected by Liddell to go with Sillitoe reported misgivings to his Director, Dick White. In any event the two MI5 men asked BOAC to allow them onto the aircraft before the rest of the passengers, thus avoiding milling around in the departure lounge. Needless to say, the plan went wrong.

When the Director-General's car drove onto the tarmac, it was spotted by several waiting Fleet Street photographers, who had been tipped off by staff at the airport. When BOAC discovered that the names of Sillitoe and his companion had been leaked, they made a half-hearted attempt to alter the passenger list, which merely served to confirm to the eager journalists that something fishy was going on. The following day the *Daily Express* published a picture of Sillitoe emerging from his limousine at Heathrow and the caption speculated on the identity of the 'Mr Martin' accompanying him.*

When Sillitoe finally arrived in Washington, he briefed the FBI Director and the Director of Central Intelligence, General Walter Bedell Smith. It is unlikely that either of the Americans believed MI5's version of the Burgess and Maclean affair, but they were unable to catch their Allies out in a lie.

Back in London all those involved in the HOMER case agreed that there had been a tip-off, but who had been responsible? The candidates were few, but one in particular had actually drawn attention to himself. From Washington Philby had sent a telegram to his Chief at MI6, Sir Stewart Menzies, expressing his astonishment at the news of Burgess's

* See picture no. 5.

departure. This had been followed up, two days later, with a more thoughtful letter detailing various actions on the part of Burgess which Philby had, 'upon further reflection', considered suspicious.

The MI5 officer who received the Burgess case file was Arthur Martin, the same 'B' Division representative who had been selected to nurse Sillitoe through his American trip. Martin had first become involved in intelligence whilst serving as an NCO with the 53rd Special Wireless Service in North Africa. At the end of the war Martin, who had by now received a commission, liaised between MI5 and the Radio Security Service which, since May 1941, had been under MI6's control. While Martin began indoctrinating himself with the Burgess file, his secretary sifted through the papers found under Burgess's bed.

One particular set of documents caught her eye. They were unquestionably official Treasury appreciations and she recognized the handwriting on them, which did not belong to Burgess. She was convinced some papers in the same handwriting had passed over her desk only recently and she backtracked through her paperwork until she found what she was after ... a routine security form signed by one 'J. C. Cairncross', a Treasury official.

Cairncross was immediately put under B2(a) surveillance in the hope that he would contact his Soviet case officer when news of Burgess's disappearance was revealed as a defection, but in the meantime a further lead had appeared.

The Burgess dossier included all the information MI6 had on him, including Philby's recent letter to Menzies which simply did not ring true. Martin reported his feelings to Dick White. White asked him to return the following day and, when he did so, he was in for a surprise. Not only did Philby already have a large 'held' personal file, but it revealed that MI5's veteran pre-war anti-communist in E1, Millicent Bagot, had made an entry concerning her suspicion of Philby. Her main comments related to Philby's suspected membership of the Communist Party of Great Britain at Cambridge, and then his membership of the right-wing Anglo–German Fellowship. The first contradicted the second. Even more inexplicable was a memo on the HOMER investigation from Philby, which proposed drawing a comparison between the list of candidates made by MI5 and the descriptions of various alleged Soviet agents in England given to MI5, in January 1940, by the Russian defector, Walter Krivitsky. This did not seem to fit with Philby's later letter to his Chief. White gravely told Martin that he shared his doubts about Philby's letter to Menzies, which he considered completely out of character, and said he would visit MI6 to discuss the matter further.

The result of that meeting was a cable recalling Philby to London. As soon as he arrived, he was summoned to Broadway, where he was received by one of the Deputy Directors of Intelligence, Air Commodore

James Easton. Easton told Philby that MI5 were anxious to see him immediately and the two of them drove over to Curzon Street, where the Director of 'B' Division began a formal interrogation. At this preliminary session Philby denied knowing Maclean and outlined his long-standing friendship with Burgess.

Neither White nor Martin were impressed by the interview and a second meeting was arranged a few days later. On this occasion the emphasis was placed on Philby's own record, as opposed to his relations with Burgess and Maclean. The session served to prove Philby's guilt from the Security Service's point of view, an opinion which was voiced privately to the Americans. A letter followed from the Director of the CIA, Bedell Smith, to Menzies, boldly stating that Philby should not return to Washington. Menzies had little alternative but to ask for Philby's resignation which, with evident reluctance, he did on 19 September 1952.

But Philby was not to get off lightly. His 'commuted' pension, totalling some £4,000, would be paid in stages, thus ensuring Philby's future cooperation. He would receive half as a lump sum and the rest would be paid in four half-yearly payments. Philby did not demur.

In parallel, the B2 investigation on Cairncross was providing few rewards. A letter intercept disclosed a rendezvous with a Soviet contact, and B2(a) made elaborate arrangements to trap whoever met him. Unfortunately Cairncross turned up and waited impatiently for his contact, but no one else appeared.

Faced with a possible repetition of the Burgess and Maclean defection, B2 was ordered to confront the suspect with the evidence against him and Arthur Martin was assigned the task. Cairncross appeared embarrassed that his handwriting should be on the Treasury papers and admitted that perhaps unwisely he had given them to Burgess. Martin cautioned him that such an unauthorized disclosure might well result in prosecution, only to be told that since none of the documents were classified, there had been no breach of the Official Secrets Acts.

Bearing in mind that Burgess had not been conclusively proved a Soviet spy, Cairncross's comment was perfectly true. No crime had been committed and B2 were reluctant to challenge him with his abortive meeting. Instead the B2(a) surveillance was continued, and MI5 watchers had the frustrating task of seeing Cairncross depart to a lecture post in the United States.

There now followed a detailed reconstruction of Philby's past. If, as 'B' Division thought, Philby was indeed a Soviet agent, it was vital to establish the starting date of his work for the Russians. The investigation continued until October, when MI5 felt they would be able to interrogate Philby with some hope of success.

The interrogation, which took the form of a judicial enquiry, was conducted at Leconfield House in November 1951. Menzies had given his consent to the idea and had telephoned Philby to tell him to come to London. Then both men had made their familiar way across St James's Park to Curzon Street. Bernard Hill, the Legal Adviser, took over from there and introduced the MI5 inquisitor, Helenus Milmo. Milmo was a King's Counsel and a former wartime member of B1(b). For much of the war he had acted as the link between B1(b) analysts and the CSDIC interrogators at Ham Common. He had spent the previous month at Leconfield House familiarizing himself with Philby's case and had been assisted by Martin, who had become something of an expert on Philby.

No one who attended the hours of questions which followed believed in Philby's innocence. He was patently guilty, but he was not prepared to admit it. Nevertheless, the performance served its purpose. Sir Stewart Menzies, Philby's boss, accepted the MI5 verdict and retired prematurely the following year. His successor at MI6 was Major-General Sir John (Sinbad) Sinclair, who had been the Director of Military Intelligence for the last year of the war. The Philby case, however, was not entirely closed. Jim Skardon was given the opportunity to coax a confession from Philby, and when Sinclair was appointed, he too conducted a formal interview, but neither achieved any progress, chiefly because there was nothing remotely approaching admissible evidence against Philby. Philby himself was a sufficiently skilled operator to know it.

At this point the Philby case was suspended, pending the discovery of further evidence, and Philby himself became a journalist. Courtney Young, Dick White, Guy Liddell and Arthur Martin all called on Anthony Blunt to enlist his help, but he was unwilling to volunteer anything except surprise. The matter was to rest there for a further ten years.

In the meantime, security procedures throughout the Civil Service were tightened up and the concept of 'Positive Vetting' introduced. As all the observers commented, after the defections of Burgess and Maclean, neither could have stood even the most cursory examination of their backgrounds. The fact remains, however, that up to 1948 a youthful connection with the Communist Party of Great Britain had never been enough to debar officials from secret work. In March 1948 Clement Attlee had been the first Minister to announce that known communists and fascists would be relieved of duties 'vital to the security of the State'. Information from the Security Service of this nature would be presented to the individual civil servant's Minister, who would then confront the person concerned with the allegation and move him to a less sensitive post. If the civil servant denied the charges, he could refer the matter to three special advisers who would adjudicate.

The 1951 Positive Vetting procedure was a further development of this system and its catchment was much larger. Instead of relying on the Security Service to offer advice on suspects, it required all civil servants who had 'regular and constant access to the most highly classified defence information' and those who had 'access to the more highly classified categories of atomic energy information' to submit to Positive Vetting. These people had to prove their eligibility for a security rating which widened departmental consciousness of security. As of January 1952, security was not a private matter between MI5 and a Minister, with MI5 having to justify their case to the three special advisers. Everyone who fell into the qualifying category would be examined and this automatically included everyone of the rank of Under-Secretary and above.

The loop-hole, of course, was the phrase 'regular and constant'. This implied that people with only occasional access to secrets would escape Positive Vetting and this, as we shall see, is exactly what happened. Nevertheless, in 1952, the Security Service were reasonably satisfied with what they had achieved. They had also managed to avoid having to execute the vetting procedure themselves. All the relevant departments were to establish security departments, which were to be responsible for the vetting of internal staff; it was not a particularly sophisticated procedure, but it was judged to be more effective than leaving everything to MI5. The candidate received a questionnaire in which he or she was asked to give a full curriculum vitae and declare any present or past sympathies with communist or fascist organizations. Finally there was a box for the names and addresses of two character referees. When the departmental security unit received the completed questionnaire, a copy was forwarded to 'C' Division which made a routine check in the Nominal Index in Registry. Once the candidate and his referees had passed this hurdle, the department sent a standard confidential letter to the referees. If the references were satisfactory, the candidate underwent an interview with a security investigator and finally his name was recommended for clearance. When this procedure was instituted there was naturally a huge backlog of people requiring clearance so the concept of Provisional Clearance crept into the system, thus enabling existing staff to continue their duties without interruption.

The glaring disadvantage of the procedure was the lack of field investigations, the background checks carried out by specially selected staff. At first these were required if a candidate fell at one of the hurdles, but they were not an intrinsic part of the system. Indirectly the Security Service can be held responsible for this defect because, although it was the only governmental organization remotely qualified to carry out Positive Vetting field checks, it resisted doing so and received support for this stand from the Civil Service, who believed only departmental officials should meddle into their colleagues' affairs. One prevalent argument was that security was too important to leave to the experts and that, if MI5 retained overall responsibility for security, there would be even more departmental apathy on the subject. It slowly dawned on officials that certain personal problems laid an individual open to black-mail or could place him in such a position that he became greedy for money. Such people could become security risks because of their un-satisfied desires which others might prey upon. Homosexuality, alcohol-ism, indebtedness were just such problems. But it was not until 1956 that the Conference of Privy Councillors formally included 'character defects' in the list of barring qualifications. In their Report the Privy Councillors highlighted the threat from the Communist Party of Great Britain:

... one of the chief problems of security today is thus to identify the members of the British Communist Party, to be informed of its activities and to identify that wider body of those who are both sympathetic to Communism or susceptible to Communist pressure and present a danger to security. Thereafter steps must be taken to see that secret information is not handled by anyone who, for ideo-logical or other motives, may betray it.*

Although MI5 welcomed the introduction of departmental security units, their shortcomings became evident quite quickly. The Positive Vetting questionnaires rarely revealed any communist connections and on the very few occasions field enquiries did expose a liar, a debtor or a drunk (or sometimes a combination of these misfortunes) very little was ever done about it. Indeed, sometimes the Security Service were not even informed. The security units themselves conformed to no general organ-izational pattern so every department had its own internal structure, each with its own complex range of command structure for MI5 to deal with. From time to time 'C' Division seconded one of its own staff to a department to beef up its arrangements, but such moves were often misinterpreted and resented. Initially at least security training was non-existent, the departmental investigators being in the main retired Colon-ial police officers. Only later did MI5 offer courses on the subject.

The departmental security units were a mixed bunch. The Admiralty, for example, did not even introduce a separate security branch until the end of August 1961, by which time at least three Soviet agents had done untold damage. On the other hand the Foreign Office and the Atomic Energy Authority, which had already suffered badly through the cases of Burgess, Maclean, Fuchs and Nunn May, were much more efficient. The Foreign Office's Security Department was already in operation under George Carey-Foster and a parallel unit was set up at the Common-wealth Relations Office under Sir Philip Vickery, a former Director of the Indian Intelligence Bureau. For their part the Atomic Energy Autho-rity had offered their chief security job to Guy Liddell, Sillitoe's Deputy D–G. These three departments led the field by insisting on Positive Vetting procedures being conducted every five years (as opposed to the

* Report of the Conference of Privy Councillors (HMSO, 1956).

usual once-and-for-all policy) and whenever a civil servant was a candidate for promotion.

In practical terms the only useful results from the inauguration of the Positive Vetting procedures emanated from the check with the Security Service's Registry. Registry had always been the foundation of MI5's activities and now its performance was impressive, or at any rate more impressive than the checks made at the departmental level, for it did turn up some surprising information. But as we will see, a number of fairly obvious security risks slipped through the net, including John Vassall, Harry Houghton, George Blake and Frank Bossard. It was only after these cases had come to light that the whole Positive Vetting system was reviewed and field investigations made a routine feature of every application.

The need for Positive Vetting checks on all those engaged in sensitive jobs was clear to all Western intelligence agencies by the 1950s. So in March 1951 the relevant British, American and French agencies came together to form the Tripartite Security Working Group as all were anxious to adopt a common system. MI5 were represented at these talks by the Washington Security Liaison Officer, Harry Stone. The other British delegates were Sir Philip Vickery, from the Commonwealth Office, and Sir Robert Mackenzie from MI6. Whatever the hopes of this group, it was eventually to become clear that the Positive Vetting system, as originally applied, rarely identified unsuitable security clearance candidates and was never to pinpoint a spy. The whole procedure had been introduced far too late. The majority of security breaches in the 1960s were to be traced to individuals who had been cleared, although patently ineligible.

A random encounter, not careful checking, was to produce MI5's one case of any significance between the end of the first stage of the Philby case in November 1951 and Sillitoe's retirement in May 1953.

On 25 April 1952 a B2(a) watcher was returning home to Kingston-upon-Thames; as he got off the bus he spotted a Soviet diplomat in conversation with another man on a street corner. The watcher recognized 'Third Secretary' Pavel Kuznetsov instantly because he had often been assigned the task of trailing the diplomat to and from the Russian Embassy and his flat in Holland Villas Road. He now kept the two men under surveillance while they had lunch and afterwards, while they sat on a park bench in Canbury Gardens overlooking the River Thames. It appeared to the watcher that the younger man was drawing sketches for the GRU officer. When the two men parted, the watcher followed the second man to his home in Elborough Road, Southfields, and made a note of the address. The following day it was discovered that he was William Martin Marshall, aged twenty-four, and that he was known to

Registry. He was currently employed by the Diplomatic Wireless Service and was based at Hanslope Park. The previous December he had returned from a twelve-month tour of duty at the British Embassy in Moscow, where he had worked as a cipher clerk.

Marshall's National Service record showed that he had been demobbed in 1948, after serving three years with the Royal Corps of Signals, part of which he had spent in Palestine and Egypt. He had then been recruited by the Diplomatic Wireless Service and, after a brief stay in Ismailia, had been posted to Moscow where he had evidently been cultivated by the Russians. Now a B2(a) surveillance operation was launched. On 19 May Marshall met Kuznetsov on Wimbledon Common and had dinner with him at a hotel afterwards. On 12 June Marshall again met Kuznetsov, this time at an afternoon gathering of the British–Soviet Friendship Society at Holborn Hall. The following morning he was trailed to a rendezvous in King George's Park, Wandsworth, but Kuznetsov did not turn up. Instead Marshall visited two hotels in Putney and a café, and then went home. Later the same afternoon Marshall returned to King George's Park, but only stayed long enough to check that Kuznetsov was not already there waiting for him. He repeated the exercise half an hour later and, finally, at half-past seven, spotted Kuznetsov sitting on a bench.

While the two men sat in conversation, a combined team of watchers and Special Branch men kept observation from behind some shrubs. Then, without warning, the watchers suddenly found themselves surrounded by uniformed police officers. A local resident had spotted what she had regarded as suspicious behaviour and had telephoned Scotland Yard. The senior Special Branch officer present, Detective Chief Inspector William Hughes, explained the situation to the milling constables, but the game was up. Hughes walked up to Marshall and Kuznetsov as they were about to leave the park and arrested them both. Initially Kuznetsov pretended not to know Marshall and claimed diplomatic immunity. In such cases the claimant has to be searched, in order to establish his credentials, and on this occasion Kuznetsov was found to be carrying a roll of twenty one-pound notes. Both men were taken to Wandsworth police station, where Kuznetsov was able to prove he was indeed a Soviet diplomat with the rank of Second Secretary. When this was queried (for the watchers knew him to be Third Secretary), he insisted he had recently been promoted. Kuznetsov was released, but Marshall was found to be carrying classified information from Hanslope Park in his wallet. It consisted of notes written on a sheet of paper. Examination of his diary showed no less than eight meetings with the Russian and a note of Kuznetsov's telephone number, Park 7851. Faced with this incriminating evidence, Marshall contradicted Kuznetsov and admitted having known him for some time. In his statement Marshall described visiting the

Russian Embassy in London, shortly after his return from Moscow, to hand in a pass. It was this initial contact which led to Marshall's recruitment.

Marshall was tried at the Old Bailey in June 1952 and was found guilty of obtaining and communicating secrets. The judge, Mr Justice Barry, took note of the jury's recommendation of leniency and sentenced him to five years' imprisonment. Once the trial was over, the Foreign Office assumed that Kuznetsov would discreetly return to Moscow, but instead the Soviet Chargé d'Affaires delivered a protest about Kuznetsov's treatment at the hands of the police at Wandsworth. His detention and search were illegal, he claimed. Astonished, the Foreign Office requested his withdrawal and, on 17 July, MI5 watched him slip aboard the Polish vessel *Jaroslav Dabrowski* at the London Docks.

Sillitoe planned a quiet retirement, running a sweet shop in Eastbourne, and the remainder of his term proved comfortably uneventful.* In anticipation of a peaceful future he initiated a popular Security Service tradition, the Director-General's final tour. Six months before his scheduled departure, Sillitoe embarked on a round-the-world tour to say his farewells to MI5's overseas representatives. However, before he set off on his odyssey he announced the name of his successor, Dick White.

Sir Percy Sillitoe had been in charge of MI5 from 1946 to 1953. During that time MI5's sole success had been the uncovering of William Martin Marshall. The defection of Igor Gouzenko in Ottawa had led to the capture of Alan Nunn May, and clever detective work by signals intelligence had led to the arrest of Klaus Fuchs. The defection of Alexander Foote had offered greater insights into NKVD tactics, but all these intelligence gains paled into insignificance when compared to the harm done by the departure of Maclean and Burgess and the suspension of Philby.

Sillitoe had not been a popular choice inside MI5 and he had failed to lose his plodding policeman's image. However, when one considers that Burgess, Maclean and Philby had all been professionals, Sillitoe would probably not have minded being called unprofessional.

* In fact the retired Director-General was to be lured away from Eastbourne to hunt diamond smugglers for de Beers.

3

SIR DICK WHITE

Dick White had joined MI5 in 1936, having been introduced to Guy Liddell by Malcolm Cumming. White had soon become Assistant Director of 'B' Division and had then gone on to become its Director, so that it was not entirely unexpected that he should have received promotion to the most senior post of all, for up to 1953, 'B' Division (counter-espionage) had long been considered the most senior branch and much was demanded of its top echelon.

Guy Liddell, who had been Sillitoe's Deputy D-G, might at first glance have seemed the most likely candidate for the post, but he had already been passed over by Attlee and was known to have counted Anthony Blunt and Guy Burgess amongst his friends. He was moreover soon due to retire. As a retirement job, he was going to replace Kenneth Morton Evans as the Security Adviser to the Atomic Energy Authority.

Whilst Sillitoe made his farewell tour, Dick White took on the role of Director-General and Roger Hollis, a year older than Dick White, but with two years' less service, was appointed his deputy. Since the war, Hollis had set up the Australian Security Intelligence Organization and had returned to head 'C' Division. It did not pass unnoticed that, although most of the old hands found Sillitoe impossible to work with, Hollis had made a special effort and developed a reasonable relationship with him.

White's tenure as Director-General was to be short, but in his three brief years from 1953 to 1956 he was to make considerable changes in MI5's internal structure. A graduate of Christ Church, Oxford, and the universities of Michigan and California, White possessed a formidable brain and was a thorough professional. He was also determined to turn MI5 into a more professional organization, especially in the way new-comers were selected.

If 'B' Division was the most senior, arguably the second most important was 'F', which focused its attention on the Communist Party of Great Britain and other allied extremist groups, and generated the majority of Registry's files. F4 had mounted several CPGB penetrations in the late 1940s designed to repeat the successes masterminded during the 1930s by Max Knight. However, instead of relying on the flair of a natural intelligence officer to recruit suitable agents, advertisements had been placed in the Situations Vacant columns of *The Times*. One placed in June 1949 read:

Applications are invited from girls of good education for pss in London with good prospects and possibility of service abroad for periods; age 18-30; must be able to type; shorthand also required for some vacancies; minimum initial salary £5 p.w. - Write Box O. 706, The Times, EC4.

One such girl was Betty Gordon who spent the next ten years in the CPGB, the British–Soviet Friendship Society and even took a job on *Soviet Weekly*. She was befriended by such senior CPGB figures as Harry Pollit and Betty Reid and kept F4 supplied with a stream of intelligence. No doubt the case officers concerned were trying to emulate Max Knight's famous pre-war Woolwich Arsenal operation* which took his principal agent, Olga Gray, more than nine years to crack. The subsequent Official Secrets trial at the Old Bailey in 1938 had led to the conviction of Percy Glading, a veteran communist activist.

White's reorganization took special account of the importance of recruitment, training and vetting, and established an entirely new Branch to deal with personnel. The concept of Divisions was abolished, and Branches were introduced. Under the new order 'A' remained administration, led by Colonel Malcolm Cumming, an MI5 veteran who joined the office in 1934 and had actually been responsible for introducing Dick White to Guy Liddell. His predecessor, Colonel Charles Butler, had been in the office since 1926 and reached his retiring age in March 1950. Sillitoe had simply promoted his long-time Assistant to the post of Director 'A'.

The most significant development was the introduction of a new Branch devoted entirely to personnel, 'B', a reflection of MI5's new professionalism in a move designed to prevent a further Burgess-type embarrassment. Once the Fleet Street bloodhounds had got started on that diplomat's career they had turned up all kinds of unsavoury tales. However, one they did not learn was that Burgess had been a frequent and welcome visitor to MI5, particularly to Guy Liddell's office. Burgess had also attended Security Service training seminars which were held from time to time at Worcester College, Oxford, where J.C. Masterman was Provost.

In consequence of its new standing 'B' was placed in the hands of John Marriott, a solicitor and graduate of King's College, Cambridge, who had been recruited into MI5 in 1940 for wartime service and had stayed ever since. (His brother, Richard Marriott, was a senior BBC admini-

---

* See Nigel West, *MI5: British Security Service Operations 1909-1945* (Bodley Head, 1981).

strator and had originally started the BBC's Monitoring Service way back in 1936.) During the war John Marriott had worked as Tar Robertson's deputy in B1(a) and had therefore liaised closely with White for many years.

'C' was regarded by some as the most junior of the Branches, since it was a dull post, best suited for bureaucrats with tidy minds and an acceptable social presence. It was usually 'C' Branch officers who had the greatest contact with the public and Whitehall, so the public relations role of 'C' was one of its principal functions. In Hollis's place at 'C' was a former Slaughter & May solicitor, Martin Furnival Jones. 'C' Branch was concerned with protective security and divided its responsibilities into C1 (Civil Service Security), C2 (Contractors), C3 (Military) and C4 (Sabotage).

The biggest changes in White's proposals concerned 'D' Branch, which was to take on the old 'B' Division responsibilities of counter-espionage. The Branch was divided into D1 (Soviet), D2 (Satellite Countries and China), D3 (Research) and D4 (Agents). The senior section, D1, was further divided into D1(a), D1(b) and D1(c), being Operations, Field Investigations and Soviet Embassy order of battle. The new Director of 'D' Branch was Graham Mitchell, formerly Hollis's number two, and the old 'F' Division expert on fascist organizations. 'E' remained the overseas Branch. It employed the largest number of people and was headed by a former Indian Army officer. It will come as a surprise to many people to learn that MI5's entire counter-espionage department was staffed by less than thirty officers between 1945 and 1972.

'F' retained its political parties charter and was modernized under its new Director, Alexander Kellar. Kellar's promotion was a significant one, as his previous work had been in 'E' Division. Just a year older than White, Kellar was typical of the new breed of MI5 man. He had read law at Edinburgh University and had for a time been President of the National Union of Students. After graduating from Edinburgh he won a visiting fellowship and travelled to Yale and Columbia, where he studied international law. He was called to the Bar in 1936 and had been recruited into the Security Service in 1941, along with several other members of the Middle Temple. His appointment to 'F' marked the end of the 'seconded Army officer' system which had prevailed since the organization's first days in 1909. It was under Kellar's direction that 'F' completed a vast survey of CPGB affiliations and sympathizers at Oxford and Cambridge Universities.

The only case of direct concern to 'F' Branch which actually came to Court during this period was that of a twenty-seven-year-old petty criminal named John Clarence. The case had begun early in September 1952 when Clarence, a long-time member of the Young Communist League and, more recently, the CPGB, had volunteered his services to a

Soviet diplomat named Barabanov at the Russian Consulate. Apparently Clarence had offered to undertake anything, but Barabanov put him to work selling Soviet literature at Marble Arch. In January 1953 Clarence was interviewed informally by Chief Inspector Ward and Detective Inspector Rhodes of Special Branch. Clarence told Ward and Rhodes that Barabanov wanted him to spy on Russian émigrés, but a check on his past behaviour showed Clarence to have been rather less than reliable. He had been sentenced to twelve months' imprisonment in Portsmouth in November 1946 for larceny and on his release had enlisted with the Royal Signals. Whilst on leave in October 1951 he had been found wandering in France, in a uniform of his own design, claiming to be the Duke of Clarence on a special mission. He had spent the next three months in hospital where a psychiatrist had diagnosed him as schizophrenic and had him discharged from the Army.

After Ward and Rhodes had seen Clarence, he had obtained a civilian job in the Army as quartermaster's clerk in the 464 Anti-Aircraft Regiment stationed at Whitley Bay in Northumberland. The job only lasted for four months, but it enabled Clarence to gather military intelligence of mobilization contingency plans, concerning anti-aircraft sites in the area. Probably nobody would ever have known that he had acquired such information, but some twelve months later, in October 1954, he mislaid a briefcase containing his notes. The case had been found by a stallholder in Catford Market and handed in to the local police. The station sergeant had searched it and found a number of papers inside. Ominously, one piece of paper was headed 'Embassy, Soviet Union'. Special Branch was called in and it was learned that Clarence was already in police custody on a charge of obtaining property by false pretences. Chief Inspector Ward took a statement from him and charged him with four offences under the Official Secrets Acts.

Clarence's trial opened at the Old Bailey on 17 December 1954 before Mr Justice Hilbery. Clarence pleaded not guilty and conducted his own defence while the Attorney-General, Sir Reginald Manningham–Buller, and Mr Christmas Humphreys prosecuted. All the evidence was heard *in camera*, including Harry Pollit of the CPGB who was subpoenaed to appear as a witness for the defence.

The trial lasted four days, at the end of which Clarence was found guilty and sentenced to five years' imprisonment.

This relatively harmless affair was conducted against a background of important developments abroad, including territories which came under MI5's jurisdiction. The main trouble spot was South–East Asia, where the French were losing the war for Indo–China, and in May the following year they were defeated at Dien Bien Phu. The Dutch too were finding their colonies recalcitrant, and Britain was coming under pressure in Kenya, Malaya and Borneo.

'E' Branch's major overseas centre was Singapore, where the Commissioner-General for South-East Asia was Malcolm MacDonald, Ramsay MacDonald's son, who had been the British High Commissioner in Ottawa at the time of Gouzenko's defection. Attached to his staff in Phoenix Park, Singapore, were three separate British intelligence departments: the MI6 Station, headed by James Fulton, a former 21st Army Group Intelligence officer, whose deputy was a former SIME case officer destined to be the future Chief of MI6, Maurice Oldfield; the Psychological Warfare section known as the Foreign Office Information Research Department under John Rainer and Alex Peterson; and the MI5 unit under a former Indian police officer. One further contributor to the local scene was the American CIA Station Chief, Bob Jantzen.

Anglo–American relations were at their worst in the region during this period, although the local personalities generally got on well together. The State Department's policy was anti-imperialist and the local CIA personnel had not been limited to a liaison role. The British had assumed, wrongly as it happened, that under the 1946 joint agreement the CIA would not deploy their Clandestine Services Division against British interests. Because Malaya and Borneo were British territories they came under MI5's jurisdiction. The MI6 Station in Singapore directed their attention to the neighbouring countries of Burma, Cambodia and Vietnam, where Britain did not have a direct defensive role.

MI5's local man in Singapore was their Defence Security Officer from E3, Keith Way, a former Indian police officer who worked under the Director of Intelligence for Malaya. Way liaised with the local police, headed by a former City of London Police Commissioner, Colonel Arthur Young, and in particular with his Special Branch, and generally directed operations. One source of trouble was the CIA-backed 'Asia Foundation', a covert propaganda operation in Singapore based on 'Radio Free Europe' lines. Its CIA-nominated Chief, an Irish–American named Pat Judge, was on less than friendly terms with MI5, who knew his gigantic budget could buy influence at even the highest levels. Co-operation between Britain and America at this time was later summed up by Joseph Smith, the Singapore CIA Station's Deputy Chief, in the following terms:

There were two schools of thought about liaison with the British. One was that it was a rare and beautiful thing to be nurtured with every care, because the British were the more sagacious in the business, with a long and remarkable tradition of success. The other was that it was a waste of time, the British officers were a bunch of supercilious snobs toward whom we should show an equivalent disdain ... as a result of being briefed by both schools of thought, however, I arrived at my post with a formula for guiding my conduct that went something like this: our liaison with the British is one of our greatest assets; don't tell the bastards anything important.*

At first the MI5 staff in Malaya was limited to the Director of Intelligence and Way (who was later succeeded by Guy Maddocks), but late in 1952 Arthur Martin, the 'B' Division investigator who had handled the Burgess and Philby cases, was posted to Singapore. He proceeded to write a highly critical report on the performance of the Malay Special Branch, and was promptly posted to Kuala Lumpur as Director of Intelligence and Commissioner of the Special Branch, replacing Keith Way as E3's local representative during the Malayan Emergency.

During this period the other major trouble spot for 'E' Branch was Kenya where the Mau-Mau terrorists had begun their murder campaign. MI5's Security Liaison Officer in Nairobi during the early stages of Mau-Mau was Walter Bell, a former MI6 officer who had been recruited into MI5 by Sillitoe in 1949. In 1952 he was transferred to New Delhi and replaced by a former Indian police officer named Macdonald.

Apart from the Emergency in Malaya and the Mau-Mau in Kenya, White found his 'E' Branch was becoming more involved in an Australian case that promised to develop into another Gouzenko.

The case began in February 1951 when Vladimir Mikhaelovich Petrov was appointed Soviet Consul at the Russian Embassy in Canberra. Within four months of his arrival a part-time Australian Security Intelligence Organization informant, code-named BAKER, had befriended him and had been quickly recruited as a full-time agent. BAKER was a Polish refugee, Dr Michael Bialoguski, and was run by George Richards, the Deputy D-G of ASIO. For the past six years BAKER had acted as a communist sympathizer, becoming a familiar face at meetings of organizations of the Left.

Gradually Bialoguski built up Petrov's trust, providing a sympathetic ear to Petrov's complaints about his Ambassador, Lifanov. In May 1953 Petrov was about to be recalled to Moscow, but ASIO were now gaining confidence that Petrov was preparing to defect and they arranged for Dr Bialoguski to diagnose some eye trouble for the Soviet diplomat so as to prevent him from leaving Australia. In fact Petrov's eye complaint was only a minor one, but Bialoguski recommended a stay in hospital. Petrov duly accepted the doctor's advice and escaped his scheduled return to Russia.

Shortly after Petrov's release from hospital, Lifanov was replaced by an even more disagreeable man, Ambassador Generalov, whose wife quarrelled with Mrs Petrov. Petrov was now openly discussing defection with Bialoguski, unaware of the latter's dual role. Petrov started nego-

* *Portrait of a Cold Warrior* (Random House, 1976).

tiations to buy a farm near Sydney and, just to ensure he did not change his mind, ASIO tape-recorded him confirming Monday, 5 April 1954, as the date on which he would complete his farm purchase and defect.

Petrov had chosen that day because, unknown to ASIO, a replacement had been appointed to take over from him. Also unknown to ASIO was the fact that Mrs Petrov was a senior Soviet intelligence officer with twenty years' experience, and Petrov had deliberately delayed telling her of his plans. In the end, Petrov left Canberra for the last time on Saturday 3 April and delivered himself to Bialoguski together with a stack of documents removed from the Embassy.

When the news of Petrov's disappearance broke, Mrs Petrov was placed under guard at the Soviet Embassy and arrangements were made to fly her back to Russia on 18 April. This incensed Australian public opinion, which was treated to daily pleas from husband to wife.

On the appointed day the Soviet Second Secretary, Filipp Kislitsyn, supervised Mrs Petrov's removal to Sydney Airport. She sat in the back of a fast Embassy limousine, wedged between two 'diplomatic couriers', Karpinsky and Zharkov. A huge crowd had gathered to watch and there were wild scenes as the foursome walked towards a BOAC Constellation. The mob surged forwards as Mrs Petrov approached, and her two escorts began to panic. They seized Mrs Petrov by both arms and propelled her towards the aircraft steps. Mrs Petrov, incensed by her escorts' behaviour, angrily tried to push them away. To the onlookers it represented a classic scene. Three Russian bullies dragging a defenceless woman back to Moscow against her will. There was uproar, and a considerable propaganda coup for the West.

Eventually the plane took off on its flight to Darwin, the first refuelling stop, but even then ASIO had not given up hope of persuading Mrs Petrov to stay in Australia. The BOAC crew had been briefed and, once airborne, Mrs Petrov was provided with a newspaper filled with details of her husband's appeals for her to remain. Each time she visited the toilet, feigning sickness, a stewardess would talk to her in Russian. Eventually, a tearful Mrs Petrov agreed she wanted to stay, and the pilot, Captain J. Davys, sent a prearranged signal to Darwin. When the plane landed, at half-past five in the morning, State police officers climbed aboard and, after a struggle, disarmed Karpinsky and Zharkov. Both were carrying Walther automatics. Mrs Petrov was escorted to the airport building, where she was handed a telephone to speak to her husband, whom she believed dead.

Petrov and his wife were reunited and given new identities, those of Greek immigrants named Cronides, and in May 1954 testified before a Royal Commission set up to investigate Soviet espionage in Australia. There followed a number of conferences between Charles Spry, the former Australian Director of Military Intelligence who had replaced Sir

Geoffrey Reed as Director-General of ASIO in June 1950, and representatives of MI5, amongst whom was the new Director of 'E' Branch, Graham Mitchell, and Dick Ellis who had acted as a link between the Australian Secret Intelligence Service (ASIO's overseas counterpart) and London following his retirement from MI6. Petrov was a singularly well-informed member of the MVD, the forerunner of the KGB, and was able to provide many of the missing details about the defection of Burgess and Maclean. He described their journey from Paris to Moscow, via Berne and Prague, and confirmed that both had been working for Russia since leaving Cambridge. He was, however, unable to identify the source of the tip-off to Burgess.

The Petrov case was to have severe repercussions in Australia, where the Menzies government achieved an unpredicted victory over the Labour Party at the Federal elections, and there were accusations of 'another Zinoviev Letter' from the Australian Left.

The Petrov case not only provided firm evidence of a sustained espionage offensive by the Russians, but the information they had produced threw new light on the U-TRAFFIC material and made Philby seem a likely Soviet source. Bill Harvey, of the FBI's Office of Security, had written a comprehensive report for Hoover in 1951 on what he saw as Philby's duplicity, and Jim Angleton, of the CIA's Counter-Intelligence Division, had also submitted a critical report to his new Chief, Allen Dulles. Angleton was almost a protégé of Philby's, having served with him in OSS at the wartime Section V headquarters in St Albans. He knew Philby well, and had extended a warm welcome to him in Washington when Philby had been appointed the MI6/CIA liaison officer there in October 1949.

MI5 had already reached the same conclusion, and the Director-General now confirmed that he had 'totted up the ledger and the debits outnumber the assets'. This remained strictly secret, even when Philby's name was raised in the House of Commons on 25 October 1955. Word of Philby's 'third man' activities had reached Colonel Marcus Lipton MP via a Fleet Street journalist, but because of the lack of any evidence which could be used in a Court of Law, the Foreign Secretary, Harold Macmillan, was obliged to say that he had 'no reason to conclude that Mr Philby has at any time betrayed the interests of this country, or to identify him with the so-called "third man", if indeed, there was one.' Lipton's question had been prompted by a newspaper anxious to link Philby's name to the scandal before the long-awaited government White Paper was published in November, a mere four years after the defection of Burgess and Maclean. But where had the newspaper and Lipton got Philby's name from? Lipton himself hinted that it had originated from MI5, but the truth is somewhat different. In fact the name had been mentioned by the CIA Station Chief in Berlin, who had been determined to curry some favour with a local journalist and, at the same time, 'blow' Philby once and for all, since the British seemed reluctant to do so. The CIA Station Chief in Berlin, appointed by Dulles at the end of 1954, was Bill Harvey, the former FBI man whom Philby had once pulled off Burgess in Washington, after Burgess had drawn an obscene caricature of Mrs Harvey; the same man who had reported Philby to Hoover in 1951.

Harvey's blatant tip caused considerable embarrassment for White, because as Director-General he was the official who had earlier 'sold' the 4,000 word White Paper to the Prime Minister, although the briefing document had been prepared by his Director of 'D' Branch, Graham Mitchell. The Security Service were in an impossible position for, although certain 'D' Branch personnel were sure Philby, and possibly Blunt, were involved in tipping off Burgess, they simply could not offer any evidence. Indeed, until Petrov's testimony, it had been impossible to state that the missing diplomats Burgess and Maclean were even in Russia at all.

In fact, far from damaging Philby, Harvey had actually helped him, for Macmillan had no option but to publicly exonerate a traitor for lack of evidence. More than ten years later, in Moscow, Philby described the incident as 'the happiest day of my life'.* An unmentioned gulf now split MI5/CIA relations; ironically, it was not caused by MI5's refusal to do anything about Philby (they had, after all, obtained his departure from MI6), but rather because the maverick Bill Harvey had actually made proof much harder to obtain. Meanwhile, Philby continued to work as a journalist.

What made the breakdown in relations all the more galling was that, in spite of his extraordinary behaviour, Harvey was a brilliant intelligence officer and was at that moment conducting a highly successful joint operation with Berlin's MI6 Station headed by Peter Lunn, who had also previously served in Vienna. Another MI6 officer, Colonel Grimshaw, was specially assigned the task of supervising the British contribution to this new plan, code-named PRINCE, and he was provided with a Russian-speaking deputy, named George Blake, to help assess the intelligence product.

PRINCE had its origins in Vienna five years earlier. At that time Vienna had still been an occupied city, governed by British, Soviet, American and French military authorities. The Russians had been headquartered in the old Imperial Hotel, and most of their communications had been sent by a land-line to Moscow. MI6 had succeeded, in an operation code-named CLASSIFICATION/LORD, in tapping the cables carrying all the Soviet traffic and in monitoring their messages. The project had been a complete success, although one aspect of it had

* *Daily Express*, 15 November 1967.

departed from the original plan. The Russian cable lay under a busy road, so MI6 had had to build a tunnel to the right spot. This had meant the purchase of a secure base from which to work, and a shop had been bought and covertly managed by the MI6 Station in Vienna. The cover for the shop had been a textile importing business, which the intelligence officers involved had been confident would not greatly distract them from their more pressing task. But suddenly English tweed had become the rage in Austria and MI6 found themselves with a commercial success on their hands, which attracted considerable attention. Much to their embarrassment they had had to close the shop down and establish the MI6 officer in charge in a sumptuous private house instead. Thereafter he was known inside MI6 as 'the gallant major who lived like a LORD'.

The success of CLASSIFICATION/LORD in 1950 led to PRINCE, a similar, though more ambitious attempt to tap Soviet communications in Berlin in 1955. The location was an American radar station in the West Berlin suburb of Rudow, directly across the border from the Russian Air Force base at Schoenefeld. A chart of all the Berlin telephone lines had been acquired by the CIA and it was agreed that, once the Americans had built the tunnel, installation of the equipment necessary to monitor and record the Soviet communications undetected would be provided by the local MI6 Station. The tunnel, which extended 1,400 feet into East Germany, was completed on 25 April 1955, at an estimated cost of $25 million. Nevertheless, everyone was sure that the investment in 'Harvey's Hole' would prove worthwhile. The MI6 technicians completed their part of the arrangement, and the flow of intelligence began. The sheer size of the unprocessed raw material was staggering; most of it was recorded on tape and then shipped to the United States for analysis. The voice recordings were flown to London where the MI6 Controller of German Stations, Andrew King, had established some 250 specially recruited Russian émigrés in a large office in Chester Terrace, Regent's Park, to translate the material. By coincidence it was learned that the Secretary of State for War, Mr John Profumo, lived in the house next door, so he was discreetly let in on the secret.

King was provided with an American deputy and together they prepared transcripts of the most interesting intercepted Soviet telephone conversations. The only lines monitored on site were the police and engineering cables which might give advance warning of discovery.

The tunnel continued to provide valuable data for eleven and a half months, when the Russians broke into it on Saturday, 21 April 1956, and sealed off the American end. The Russians then invited the press to come and inspect this undeniable evidence of American espionage.

News of the collapse of PRINCE was to have a special impact in London, where both MI5 and MI6 were having troubles of their own. Two days earlier, on 19 April, an unauthorized MI6 operation had gone badly wrong, and a retired Royal Navy diver, Commander Lionel (Buster) Crabb GM OBE RNVR, had disappeared. His mission had been relatively straightforward: he was to dive off HMS *Vernon*, the Navy base in Portsmouth Harbour, and carry out an underwater survey of the hull of a Soviet cruiser, the *Ordzhonikidze*. The cruiser and her two destroyer escorts were moored alongside the South-West Jetty awaiting the return of the Soviet premier, Nikita Khrushchev, and Marshal Bulganin, who had arrived the previous day on a goodwill visit to England and were ensconced in Claridge's.

Crabb's mission had been requested by the Admiralty, and in particular the Director of Naval Intelligence (DNI), Rear-Admiral John Inglis, who thought that the underwater inspection would yield important information. Here it is necessary to outline briefly MI6's post-war internal structure. The various MI6 Heads of Station around the world reported to their individual Station Controllers in London. They in turn were subordinate to the four regional Directors of Production: Europe, headed by a former Parachute Regiment officer; Middle East, headed by George Young; Far East and Latin America, headed by James Fulton; and all extraneous areas and operations, headed by Andrew King. These four officers were responsible for all of MI6's intelligence gathering operations and, having acquired it, they distributed it among the nine Requirements sections: Political, Military, Navy, Air, Counter-Intelligence, Economic, Press, Government Communications Headquarters and Scientific.

Inglis's request had been received by the head of MI6's Merchant Navy section, who operated from the MI6 London Station, located in the Vauxhall Bridge Road. He accepted the mission, but insisted that the DNI make his request in writing, just for the record. This he duly did, and the mission was given the go-ahead by the head of the London Station, Nicholas Elliott, although through an oversight Foreign Office approval for the operation was neither sought nor granted. In fact there was nothing particularly unusual in the mission. When British warships had visited Soviet ports the sea had sometimes appeared to be alive with frogmen.

Buster Crabb was a veteran diver who had taken part in many such operations, both during the war, when he was based in Gibraltar, and afterwards. In spite of his advancing years and his excessive consumption of cigarettes and alcohol, Crabb was still arguably the finest frogman in England. He had completed countless similar missions and was full of enthusiasm for this job. He slipped into the water from HMS *Vernon* shortly after seven on Thursday morning and, after a brief return to the jetty to add an extra lead weight, was never seen again.

When Crabb was seriously overdue, it was assumed that he had got into difficulties and had perhaps been swept out to sea and picked up by a vessel which was not equipped with a radio. MI6 first realized the game was up when the Admiralty reported receiving a message from the senior Soviet naval officer, Rear-Admiral Kotov, mentioning the fact that a diver had been spotted on the surface, close to the three warships. The complaint had originally been received by the Chief of Staff to the Commander-in-Chief Portsmouth, Rear-Admiral Philip Burnett. Burnett denied all knowledge of a diver, but routinely informed the Admiralty.

MI6 anticipated an unholy row and the same day arranged to have Crabb's belongings removed from the Sallyport Hotel where he had been staying. The Director of MI5's 'A' Branch, Malcolm Cumming, was telephoned and he agreed to try to help. He contacted the head of Portsmouth CID, Detective Superintendent Lamport, and instructed him to visit Crabb's hotel and remove any evidence of Crabb's stay there. Lamport went straight round to the Sallyport and presented the proprietor, Mr Edward Richman, with his warrant card. On that authority he tore four pages from the visitor's book and signed a receipt for them. Alongside Crabb's name and address was that of his MI6 companion, 'Bernard Smith', and his address: 'Attached Foreign Office'. This was the second occasion in which MI6 had been saved considerable embarrassment by MI5's intervention: the first being the Colonel Tasoev fiasco in May 1948.

MI6 were apparently confident that, as MI5's timely help seemed to have been successful, the whole affair would remain secret, and the Admiralty issued a brief announcement concerning the loss of Crabb ... in Stokes Bay, out in the Solent. The Russians, however, had other ideas, and on 4 May the Embassy in London sent a curt Note to the Foreign Office and then leaked the contents to the press. In essence, they asked whether in the light of the Admiralty's announcement Rear-Admiral Burnett had lied when he had dismissed the idea of a frogman in Portsmouth Harbour. Now the floodgates opened.

On 9 May the Prime Minister, Sir Anthony Eden, made a statement to the House of Commons, saying that 'what was done was done without the authority or the knowledge of Her Majesty's Ministers. Appropriate disciplinary steps are being taken.'

The disciplinary action Eden referred to was an enquiry into the affair headed by Sir Edward Bridges, the former Cabinet Secretary and the retiring Permanent Secretary at the Treasury. All the parties involved gave their evidence orally to Bridges who then prepared a written statement. The MI6 controller, who had suffered a minor heart attack on the day of Crabb's dive, was given very sympathetic treatment by Bridges who viewed the operation in a surprisingly favourable light.

The MI6 Chief, however, fared much worse, in part because he completely failed to support his own staff. Major-General Sir John Sinclair had succeeded Menzies four years earlier and would normally have been expected to retire in May 1962. Eden was livid at the embarrassment heaped on him by the Russians and decided to replace Sinclair. Traditionally, the post was in the gift of the Foreign Secretary, but on this occasion the entire Defence Cabinet concurred with the view that a stern rebuke should be delivered to MI6, and they should be provided with a really experienced intelligence officer who would ensure that this blunder was the last of its kind.

But who was the right candidate? The choice was somewhat limited by the nature of the job. The Deputy Chief of MI6 was a former RAF officer, Air Commodore Sir James Easton. He had joined the Secret Intelligence Service in 1945 as Deputy Director (Air), in succession to Air Commodore (Lousy) Payne. The appointment of Deputy Director (Air), matched by similar posts for the other Services, had been created by Menzies to reduce Service criticism of MI6's wartime distribution of intelligence. Easton was well regarded and was later knighted in the Birthday Honours that very year, but Eden, like Attlee in 1945, was not prepared to promote an insider.* Instead his candidate was the Director-General of the Security Service, Sir Dick White.

Dick White had only spent three years in office as Director-General of MI5. During that time there was much activity abroad, in Kenya against the Mau Mau, in Borneo and Malaya against communist insurgents, and in Australia Petrov had been persuaded to defect. There was, however, little activity in England, except for the capture of John Clarence; the Philby affair was also still no nearer solution.

White was now an MI5 officer of some twenty years' standing and had made a reputation for himself in Whitehall for his professional approach to his job and his successful reorganization of the office. Evidently he had also won the Prime Minister's trust in the three years he had held MI5's top job.

---

* Easton remained in MI6 for a further two years and in 1956 was appointed British Consul-General in Detroit. He was succeeded by George Young.

4

SIR ROGER HOLLIS

When it became clear that the Soviets had shut down the Berlin tunnel and switched off the PRINCE source, it was a severe blow. What with the PRINCE closure and the Crabb fiasco occurring so closely together, MI5 and MI6 were reduced to a low ebb. To add insult to injury it was decided to give the Americans all the credit for PRINCE and to keep the part Britain had played a secret.

White recommended that his Deputy D-G, Roger Hollis, should be promoted to the post of Director-General and this was approved by the 'Three Wise Men', the Permanent Under-Secretaries' Committee which in theory made the appointment. The Prime Minister gave his consent and Hollis then gave his old job to the Director 'D', Graham Mitchell. This left another senior vacancy and Malcolm Cumming was appointed Director 'D' from 'A' Branch.

Roger Hollis had spent his early working years in the Far East with British American Tobacco. He had then returned to England to join MI5 in 1938. After two years studying the Communist Party of Great Britain and the Comintern he had been promoted to Assistant Director rank. He had also joined Lord Swinton's wartime sub-committee monitoring the growing Soviet activity in London. After the war he had been one of the few officers from the pre-war era who could tolerate Sillitoe. It was his successful relationship with Sillitoe that had led to Hollis's appointment as Deputy D-G in 1952.

The first case that Hollis had to deal with as Director-General was that of Anthony Wraight, a Flying Officer then stationed at RAF Halton. Wraight had joined the RAF in January 1953 and had graduated from Cranwell in July 1955; his first posting was to RAF Chivenor, where he flew Hawker Hunters. Less than a year later he was writing to the Society for Cultural Relations with the USSR. He was also in touch with a Soviet intelligence officer named Solovei, who worked at the Russian Embassy under Soviet Film Agency cover.

Wraight's first visit to the Soviet Embassy in Kensington Gardens on

15 March 1956 coincided with his signing the normal RAF officer's book of standing orders, one of which required officers to report any contact with Soviet officials to their Commanding Officer. When Wraight's intercepted mail to Solovei was eventually traced back to him at RAF Halton in October, he was invited to attend an interview at Room 055 to receive a lecture from MI5 and Wing-Commander John Smith of the RAF Provost Marshal's Department. During the course of the interview, which took place on 25 October, Wraight denied knowledge of the 'report all Soviet contact' rule and said he had not signed the relevant order. The Flying Officer was given a verbal warning about the dangers of corresponding with the Russians and was sent back to his Station.

Five days later, on 30 November, MI5 received confirmation from Wraight's Commanding Officer that the pilot had indeed signed the relevant order. Smith and an MI5 officer promptly went down to Halton and confronted Wraight with his lie. He was warned that he might be court-martialled for his lapse, but before any further action could be taken Wraight disappeared. On 2 December he booked a ticket to Berlin and two days later he was in the Soviet Zone seeking political asylum. This was by no means the end of the affair, as we shall see, but at the time it seemed that the Security Service had let a Soviet spy slip through their fingers. The RAF arranged a thorough search of West Berlin for him, but it was too late. It was an embarrassing start for Hollis.

Apart from a propaganda broadcast from East Berlin the following January nothing more was heard from Wraight until 24 November 1959, when he walked into the American Embassy in Moscow and asked to be repatriated to England. He duly arrived at London Airport on 14 December and was interviewed by George Smith of Special Branch. In fact Smith, MI5 and Group Captain H.D.A. Bisley of the RAF Provost Marshal's Department questioned Wraight eight times before the end of the year. Opinion divided over exactly what to do about him because he was not prepared to admit to espionage, although he agreed he had been thoroughly debriefed while he was behind the Iron Curtain. Eventually, on 18 February 1960, Wraight was arrested at his parents' home at 35 Marine Parade, Brighton, by George Smith. On 1 April he was sentenced at the Old Bailey to three years' imprisonment by Mr Justice Donovan (himself a former RAF pilot).

A review of the West's intelligence assets in 1956, when Hollis became Director-General, would have presented a depressingly bleak picture. The gloom had lifted briefly in 1954 with the defection of Peter Deriabin in Vienna when Deriabin had warned that there were two KGB agents, code-named PETER and PAUL, operating within the West German counter-intelligence service, the BND. But it was five years before Heinz Felfe and Hans Clemens were positively identified, despite the launching of Operation DROWZY to find the two.

There was in fact only one agent of any importance active in the Soviet intelligence camp, Lieutenant-Colonel Peter Popov of the GRU. Popov had volunteered his services to the CIA in Vienna in 1953 by dropping a note into an American diplomat's car. He had been assigned a CIA case officer, George Kisvalter, who had himself been born in St Petersburg before the Revolution, had joined the CIA's Soviet Russia Division in 1952 and spoke fluent Russian, French, German and Italian. Popov provided a mass of GRU intelligence, including the cryptonyms of 370 Soviet 'illegals' in the West. The first such code-name caused great excitement when it was discovered to be the agent's real name, spelt backwards. It was, however, the only such lucky break. In 1955 Popov returned to Moscow for six weeks' leave and was then posted to East Germany. These moves left the CIA without a means of communication, so Popov simply handed a letter, explaining the situation, to a member of a British military mission, who happened to be touring East Germany. The British officer passed the envelope to the MI6 Station in Berlin, housed at the Olympic Stadium Buildings, and in due course the letter found its way to Kisvalter. The MI6 case officer who had been entrusted with the letter was named George Blake, of whom more was to be heard later.

Once contact had been re-established Popov resumed his regular meetings with Kisvalter. On one occasion Popov disclosed that he was about to send an 'illegal' to New York, a girl using an American passport 'lost' by a tourist in Poland. This news was given to the FBI by the CIA, with misgivings from the CIA officers concerned, and the Soviet spy was placed under heavy surveillance when she arrived in New York. The operation succeeded in panicking the girl, who returned to Moscow saying she had been 'blown' from the moment she arrived at Idlewild. A KGB investigation ensued and Popov was ordered back to Moscow. A CIA officer from the US Embassy in Moscow, Russell Langrelle, was appointed the local case officer, but both he and Popov were arrested on 16 October 1959 on a Moscow bus surreptitiously passing messages. Langrelle claimed diplomatic immunity and was released, but Popov was executed by being thrown live into a furnace before an audience of his GRU colleagues.

The FBI bore the brunt of the blame for Popov's demise, but they had themselves organized two important successes in the United States. The first was to suborn a member of the Polish mission to the United Nations, Joseph Sizmonic, who spent twelve months feeding the FBI with information and then defected with two suitcases full of secret documents.

The second case, which concerned MI5, was that of a Czech cipher clerk named Tisler, who worked in the Czechoslovakian Embassy in Washington. The FBI built up Tisler's standing in the Embassy by giving him interesting items of intelligence, so much so that his success was recognized and he was recalled to Prague for promotion. This development was not what Hoover had in mind, so Tisler's replacement was denounced as a spy and expelled. Tisler returned to Washington to work for another year. When the time came for Tisler to leave, he emptied the Czech Embassy of all its records, dropping them out of a window in the middle of the night to waiting FBI agents. At dawn Tisler calmly walked out of the front door and 'retired' with a new identity.

Tisler's information, code-named ARAGO, was extremely valuable, and one item concerned Colonel Oldrich Prybl, the Czech Military Attaché in London since May 1954. Prybl had met a forty-two-year-old electronics engineer named Brian Frederick Linney at a reception in London in 1955. Prybl and his wife had asked the Linneys to join them at a concert after the reception and the Linneys had accepted. Two years later Prybl renewed their acquaintance and recruited Linney as an agent. By this time Linney had separated from his wife and had joined an aerospace company in Shoreham, Sussex, which held several classified contracts for the RAF. Linney began his work there in January 1957 and was one of several keyholders with access to the steel cabinet where the firm kept their secret documents. Many of them related to the radar project he was engaged on. Others were routine development papers on the Rolls-Royce Avon engine. MI5's 'C' Branch, then headed by Martin Furnival Jones, warned Linney's employers in an attempt to isolate him from any important strategic information and arranged for an MI5 officer to join the staff. Despite intensive surveillance on Linney himself and his home in Charmandean Road, Worthing, the watchers never spotted him meeting Prybl. In fact on one occasion the watchers followed Linney to what was evidently planned to be a rendevous, but neither Prybl nor his Czech assistant turned up. On 27 May 1958 a representative of 'D' Branch visited Linney at work and challenged him to explain his relationship with Prybl. The electronics engineer was so deeply shocked by the confrontation and what he mistakenly believed to be MI5's firm evidence that he admitted everything, stating that he had received £500 as payment and had only seen the Czech nine times since their first meeting. MI5 called in Inspector Cecil Nason of the West Sussex police to take a statement and it was this which formed the basis of his prosecution at Lewes on 18 July.

Linney pleaded guilty to five offences under the Official Secrets Acts and was sentenced by Mr Justice Cassels to fourteen years' imprisonment. If Linney had only known MI5's source was in Washington and kept quiet, he might well have escaped prosecution for lack of evidence.

In the following March the Americans were to begin tapping yet another Iron Curtain source; information obtained was to develop into what the British Security Service regarded as their finest post-war investigation.

The case originated in Berne when the American Ambassador, Henry J. Taylor, received a typewritten letter postmarked Zurich. Inside was an envelope addressed to the Director of the FBI. The Ambassador handed the letter and enclosure to the CIA Station Chief, who opened it and photographed an offer of intelligence from Poland, typed in German, from someone signing himself 'Sniper'. This was to be the first of fourteen letters from 'Sniper' detailing Polish and Soviet intelligence operations in the West. It was then decided that the case should be handled by the CIA's Berlin Station, still headed by Bill Harvey, who had survived the row that followed when Hoover was told his mail had been opened by the CIA.

The CIA analysts at Langley in the United States concluded that 'Sniper' was not a Russian, had typed on a machine of Eastern European manufacture, and had used paper with Eastern watermarks. None of this information was conclusive, but it was enough for the CIA to impart selected items to MI5 and the Swedish Security Service, then headed by Commodore Henning.

According to 'Sniper' a senior Swedish Air Force officer, who had once been a CIA agent, had been recruited by the Russians when serving in Moscow as the Swedish Air Attaché. The records were checked and it turned out that Colonel Stig Wennerstrom, the Swedish Air Attaché in Moscow between 1948 and 1951, had indeed consented to carry out minor intelligence missions for the Americans. He had subsequently served as Air Attaché in Washington between April 1952 and March 1957. When 'Sniper' named him he was the senior officer in the Air Force section of the Swedish Command's headquarters at the Ministry of Defence in Stockholm. His case was given to Otto Danielsson of the Swedish Security Police, who arranged, on 10 November 1959, for a telephone tap to be installed at Wennerstrom's villa in Djursholm, outside Stockholm. Danielsson's investigation continued until the autumn of 1961, by which time the evidence against Wennerstrom was irrefutable. He was then transferred to a less sensitive post in the Swedish Foreign Ministry, where he remained until his arrest on 20 June 1963. Under interrogation Wennerstrom admitted to having spied for the last fourteen years and then attempted suicide. Eventually he identified all his Soviet case officers, two of whom were still in Stockholm. They were duly expelled and in May the following year he was sentenced to hard labour for life.

In the autumn of 1959 the 'Security Adviser' at the British Embassy in Washington was a relatively junior 'D' Branch officer. In fact Walter Bell of 'E' Branch, an old friend of Guy Liddell's who had previously served with MI6, had been scheduled to go, but when Hollis replaced White, he asked for Bell to become his Personal Assistant. The change of appointment caused a furore because of Bell's relative lack of service in MI5 (he had represented MI5 in Nairobi and New Delhi) and because he had excellent contacts in the United States. In 1935 Bell had been posted to New York by MI6 as their 'Assistant Passport Control Officer' and had later joined British Security Co-ordination, where he had established a close relationship with the fledgling OSS. MI6 had appointed him their link with OSS in London during the war and afterwards he had returned to Washington as First Secretary. There was, indeed, an even better reason to send Bell to Washington: his wife Katherine was the daughter of General Carl Spaatz, the wartime commander of the American Air Force in Europe. In spite of all of this, and with notice of just one day, the officer from the D1(a) (Soviet Operations) section, packed his bags and left for Washington instead.

It was therefore 'D' Branch which first received 'Sniper's' information that the KGB were operating a spy in the British Admiralty. The name supplied did not appear in the Navy List, but further information was forthcoming: the agent, whose name began with the letter 'H', had been recruited whilst serving at the British Embassy in Warsaw. This narrowed the field considerably and pointed to an ex-Master-at-Arms, Harry Houghton, a fifty-three-year-old clerk at the Port Auxiliary Repair Unit in Portland, Dorset. He had served in Warsaw as the Naval Attaché's clerk from July 1951 to October 1952 and appeared to fit 'Sniper's' description of the Soviet spy.

Once Houghton had been identified by D1 as the Soviet source, the case was passed to Jim Skardon of D2 for surveillance. The watchers took up their positions in the spring of 1960 and continued their operation for more than a year. The Washington SLO's successor in D1 was Charles 'Elton', an expert on Soviet espionage married to a former MI5 officer and agent, Ann Glass.

Surveillance on Houghton led to the identification of his mistress, Ethel (Bunty) Gee, and, in June 1960, to a Soviet 'illegal' operating under the cover-name of Gordon Arnold Lonsdale. Confirmation of Lonsdale's address in Regent's Park caused considerable embarrassment at Leconfield House. In October 1956 a Canadian of the same name had enrolled as a mature student on a course at London University's School of Oriental Studies. One of his fellow students had been attending under his cover-name of Charles Elton! Enquiries with the Security Service of the Royal Canadian Mounted Police revealed that Lonsdale had been issued with a Canadian passport in January 1955 and had given an address in Burnaby Street, Vancouver. The fact that Lonsdale was an 'illegal' was firmly established by a listening station set up in 636, the flat next door to his, on the sixth floor of the White House, overlooking Regent's Park. It later became clear that he had a regular rendezvous with Houghton on the first Saturday of each month, and the watchers attended a further five of these meetings, in July, August, November,

December and January. In September and October Lonsdale was absent abroad.

Towards the end of August 1960 Lonsdale was followed to the Midland Bank in Great Portland Street, where he entrusted a briefcase and steel box to the Safe Deposit. The D2 watchers correctly assumed that both these items might contain espionage paraphernalia and, accordingly, Special Branch obtained a search warrant, which was served on Lonsdale's bank manager, Mr Len Easter, by Superintendent George Smith on 24 September. Both the briefcase and the steel box were examined by MI5 and found to contain, amongst other things, a Ronson table lighter which concealed a one-time pad and a radio schedule. Smith returned the briefcase and box to the bank, warning the manager to say nothing about the search warrant to his client, and then waited for Lonsdale to collect his belongings.

This he did on 24 October, carrying them on a shopping tour of the West End. He then went by underground to Ruislip Manor station, where he alighted and walked to a private house in Cranley Drive.

The occupants were Peter and Helen Kroger, formerly of 18 Penderry Rise, Catford. Kroger, apparently, ran an antiquarian book business from a room in the Strand, and a check was made on his background while Skardon drove through the neighbourhood looking for a suitable observation post. One house, on the corner of Cranley Drive and Courtfield Gardens, was ideal. It overlooked the Krogers' bungalow and was approached from Courtfield Gardens, out of view of the target property. The electoral roll revealed that a Mr and Mrs W.S. Search owned the house in question and, by chance, Mr Search's name appeared in the Security Service's Registry. As well as having served in the RAF, he was currently working in Birmingham as an aircraft engineer. Part of his work on gas turbine engines was classified and he had signed the Official Secrets Acts. Skardon telephoned Mrs Search and arranged to visit her on Friday 4 November.

Skardon made no mention of the Krogers when he spoke to Mrs Search, and she agreed to allow his watchers to use her front room and her daughter's bedroom over the weekend.

The following day Lonsdale held his usual meeting with Houghton, this time at The Maypole public house in Surbiton. After a discussion in Houghton's car and a drink in the pub the two men parted, and the next afternoon Lonsdale reappeared at Ruislip.

The surveillance continued until the first Saturday in January 1961, when Houghton and Gee were arrested by Superintendent George Smith moments after having passed a carrier bag to Lonsdale in Lower Marsh, outside the Old Vic Theatre on the South Bank of the Thames. The three agents were driven to Scotland Yard and Smith sped over to Ruislip to arrest the Krogers. The bungalow in Cranley Drive turned out to be a

veritable treasure trove of ingenious Soviet-made espionage paraphernalia. Even when, some two months later, the house was released by
Special Branch so the Krogers' solicitors could take an inventory, false
passports and well-concealed bundles of currency kept turning up in the
unlikeliest places. A short-wave transmitter was found under the kitchen
and, even though the garden had already been excavated, another transmitter was dug up by the new owners in 1980.

Houghton and Gee were very shocked at their arrest, but Lonsdale
remained the true professional he was until he spotted the Krogers at
Bow Street police station, shortly after they had been charged under the
Official Secrets Acts. At this stage D2 still had no idea of the Krogers'
real identity, and they were obviously unwilling to help. Both they and
Lonsdale refused to have their fingerprints taken, and it was only after
the Magistrates Court had ordered them to comply that the FBI were
able to identify Peter and Helen Kroger as Morris and Lona Cohen,
American subjects of New York City. They had been wanted by the FBI
since 1951 on suspicion of being accomplices of the Rosenbergs, the
atom spies who had been arrested and executed in the aftermath of the
Nunn May case ten years earlier.

When the five 'Portland spies' appeared at the Old Bailey in March
1961 before the Lord Chief Justice, Lord Parker, all pleaded not guilty.
After a trial of six days they were all convicted without, incidentally, an
acceptance of Houghton's offer to turn Queen's Evidence. Houghton
and Gee received fifteen years; Lonsdale twenty-five, and the Krogers
twenty each. After sentencing, Lonsdale was approached by MI5 and
asked if he would consent to being interviewed. He agreed, and his
former fellow-student (still working under the cover-name of Elton)
conducted the interrogation. By the end of it Lonsdale had identified
himself as a Soviet officer, Conon Molody, but was convinced that
Houghton had been an MI5 agent who had been sucked into a trap the
previous January. Although that was not the case, Elton declined to
disabuse him of the idea.

Houghton had first suggested co-operating with MI5 during his trial
when he passed a note to them via his Defence Counsel, Mr Henry
Palmer. In it he alleged that he knew of three further Soviet case officers
other than Lonsdale, two being known to him as NIKKI and JOHN.
He also maintained that the Russians had boasted to him of having
already penetrated the Polaris base at Holy Loch and of receiving secret
information on such subjects as mines, radar, fire control and the nuclear
submarine HMS Dreadnought. As was their custom, the Security Service
declined Houghton's invitation, but he was interviewed on 18 and 23
May in prison after his appeal had been dismissed. On these two occasions Houghton continued to lie so MI5 advised the Admiralty, on 13
June, that Houghton could not be relied upon.

The case was in general regarded as a success, but in many respects it was inconclusive. D2 harboured a suspicion that the three Soviet agents, Lonsdale and the Krogers, had been deliberately discarded, possibly to draw attention from another operation, or perhaps to build up the reputation of a double agent.

The 'Portland spies' were not arrested until after 'Sniper', whose fourteen letters had been the initial source for the case, had defected.

Late in December 1960, he had turned up in West Berlin with his mistress and was met by a CIA case officer, Howard Roman. 'Sniper' turned out to be Michal Goleniewski, a high-ranking Polish Military Intelligence officer who had also informed on his colleagues to the KGB. The CIA wasted no time putting their latest star on a USAF plane to Washington. At Edwards Air Force base, he was discreetly transferred to a private car and driven straight to Ashford Farm, a sixty-eight-acre estate overlooking the Choptank River in Talbot County, Maryland. The twenty-six-room mansion, operated as a safe-house by Peter Sivess and his wife Ellie, was to become the CIA's principal receiving station for defectors and was arguably the most secret place in the whole of the United States.

Although Goleniewski had not brought any documents with him, he had left some three hundred photographs of documents in Warsaw and the CIA Station in the Polish capital was given directions to the right tree. The pictures were developed and turned out to be extremely valuable, particularly to MI5. One vital piece of evidence provided by 'Sniper', for example, was the fact that an MI6 officer in Berlin had betrayed details of the few agents MI6 were running in Poland. Although Goleniewski could not name the traitor, he did offer enough details for MI6 to narrow the field down to one man, George Blake.

Blake's case was handled jointly by MI6 and MI5 who ran the London end of the surveillance on Blake. Blake's first contact with British Intelligence had been in November 1943, shortly after his escape from Occupied Holland. He had joined the Royal Navy and anglicized his Dutch–Jewish family name of Behar by deed-poll to Blake, as his mother and sisters had done. In May 1944 he was recruited into SOE after a short spell in Naval Intelligence. His work for the Naval Intelligence Department in Holland and Germany after the war had marked him out as a thoroughly professional intelligence officer and, in 1947, he had been invited to join MI6. Blake agreed and spent three years at Downing College, Cambridge, learning Russian. In September 1948 he had been posted to the MI6 Station in Seoul under the diplomatic cover of Vice-Consul, where he was arrested and interned in June 1950 by the North Koreans. Blake had remained a prisoner, along with the rest of the British Legation staff, until April 1953. He had then been released and flown to London via Peking, Moscow and Berlin. After a period of leave to recover from his ordeal, Blake (now engaged to be married to a former MI6 secretary) had been offered the post of Deputy Director (Technical Operations) at the MI6 Station in Berlin. He accepted and began work there in April 1955 under the local Head of Station, Peter Lunn. After a tour of duty lasting four years Blake returned to London in April 1959. He spent the next eighteen months at MI6 headquarters in London before being posted abroad again, this time to the Middle East Centre for Arab Studies, a language school based at Shemlann near Beirut and run by the British Foreign Office.

When Goleniewski's information* was examined by MI6 in London, it explained a number of incidents which had occurred during Blake's four-year tour in Berlin, including Popov's execution by the KGB and the Russian closure of PRINCE. One of Blake's principal agents in Berlin had been Horst Eitner, code-named VICTOR. In October 1960 the West German counter-intelligence service had arrested him on suspicion of working for the Russians, as well as the British and West Germans. All these incidents added up to an unacceptable amount of coincidences and losses.

Sir Dick White, now the MI6 Chief, was satisfied that the weight of evidence against Blake would justify a confrontation. A signal was sent to the MI6 Head of Station in Beirut, Nicholas Elliott, and he passed a message to Blake offering a promotion. Would Blake care to fly to London after Easter to discuss it?

The ploy worked, and Blake arrived in London on 3 April 1961. The following morning Blake reported to White, who told him he would have to answer certain questions. He was then introduced to a senior MI6 officer and Terence Lecky, who accused him directly of being a Soviet agent. Blake denied the charges, and eventually the interrogators broke off for lunch. As soon as Blake left the building, he was trailed by the MI5 watchers who observed Blake's evident distress. At one point he walked up to a telephone kiosk and then apparently changed his mind at the last moment. Minutes later he repeated the exercise. Clearly Blake was in a state of panic and could not decide whether to ask his Soviet contacts for rescue. The watchers reported this incident to the MI6 interrogators who used Blake's indecision with tremendous effect. Soon after his return to MI6 headquarters Blake confessed to having been a Soviet agent since his conversion in Korea in 1950.

Blake subsequently signed a statement which was given to White. He in turn authorized it to be given to Louis Gale, a senior Special Branch detective. They arrested Blake and drove him straight to Bow Street police station where he was charged with breaches of the Official Secrets

* Goleniewski later claimed to be the last of the Romanovs and campaigned to be recognized as the Czar, but despite this eccentricity his information was judged to be of the highest quality.

Acts. The wording of the charges cited various offences since 1 September 1953.

Blake was tried at the Old Bailey on 3 March 1962. The Lord Chief Justice, Lord Parker, sentenced him to a record forty-two years' imprisonment, stating that Blake's espionage had rendered much of this country's efforts completely useless.

The successful breaking-down of Blake became a text-book model for other counter-intelligence staff, but it did not mark the end of the KGB's attempts to penetrate the British Intelligence Services.

5

KAGO'S REVELATIONS

'I feel it is right to warn the House hostile
intrigue and espionage are being relentlessly
maintained on a very large scale.'

HAROLD MACMILLAN
14 *November 1962*

The first months of 1962 certainly appeared to have been eminently
successful for MI5, and this was the high point of Hollis's tenure
at Curzon Street. There were, however, grounds for a cautious re-
evaluation of the counter-intelligence scene. When this was later forced
on the Security Service, it revealed some disturbing aspects to the cases
of Blake and the 'Portland spies'.

The initial post mortem on the Portland case was made by a formal
tribunal of enquiry, consisting of Sir Charles Romer, a former Lord
Justice of Appeal, Sir Harold Emmerson, a former Permanent Secretary
at the Ministry of Labour, and the recently retired Vice-Admiral Sir
Geoffrey Thistleton-Smith. None had any first-hand experience of intelligence work, but in spite of this apparent handicap the resulting Romer
Committee Report made interesting reading. For example, it revealed
that Portland naval base had been unaware of misconduct by Houghton
whilst he was stationed at the British Embassy in Warsaw (he had created
a thriving black-market side-line); that Houghton had been denounced
by his ex-wife, but no notice had been taken of the allegations; that
Houghton had been reported as a security risk twice in 1956. Having
severely criticized the Admiralty, the Report singled out MI5 and Special
Branch for particular praise, much to the delight of Hollis.

There was, however, to be a second examination of the case, which
raised some serious doubts. Although Lonsdale had agreed to a 'friendly'
interrogation by Charles Elton, he had given away very few operational
secrets. He was unquestionably a professional intelligence officer, but

was he quite as important as was at first thought? He was in quite a different league to Colonel Abel, whom the FBI had arrested in New York in August 1957.

Rudolph Ivanovich Abel had been betrayed to the Americans by his alcoholic Finnish assistant, Reino Hayhanen, whom he had ordered back to Moscow for lack of discipline. Hayhanen had known exactly what this meant and defected to the American Embassy in Paris on 4 May 1961. The cases of Lonsdale and Abel were similar, in that both were Soviet 'illegals', but the former was of a much lower calibre. The contrast between them operationally could not have been greater. Abel was discreet and security-conscious; Lonsdale was a flamboyant womanizer and always short of money. Abel's cover was that of a quiet photo-grapher and artist; Lonsdale was something of a spiv, constantly involv-ing himself in get-rich-quick projects which invariably went wrong. He had a substantial overdraft at his bank and was often pursued by hire-purchase collectors. One vending-machine firm, of which he was a director, the Automatic Merchandising Company Limited, actually folded in March 1960 with debts of £30,000. Was Lonsdale's arrest really such a coup, or would he have drawn attention to himself eventually? One of his fellow directors in another venture, Peter Ayres, said later that he thought Lonsdale's frequent trips abroad were suspicious and assumed that he was a spy working for the British. In June 1961 an East German defector, Captain Gunther Maennel, told the CIA that two of his colleagues, Armin Grosz and a trade official operating under the cover-name of 'Eric Hills' (code-named HALTER), had really run the Krogers and had been able to escape to East Germany.

Under this kind of critical examination the arrest of the Krogers appeared less of a coup. Their fingerprints had been distributed world-wide by the FBI and their photographs had been discovered in Abel's apartment in New York. They would have been identified the moment any police officer arrested them, whatever the offence. What all four cases, Lonsdale, Abel and the two Krogers, had in common was that all were later repatriated to the USSR without completing their prison sentences.

This somewhat depressing analysis was forced on MI5 by yet another Soviet defector, Anatoli Golytsin. Golytsin remains, even today, by far the most controversial figure in the world of intelligence, and his impact on Western counter-intelligence in December 1961 was dramatic.

The Golytsin case began in 1954 in Vienna, when Peter Deriabin, the GRU defector from Vienna, compiled a list of possible future defectors. He had placed Golytsin high on his list because he was unpopular with his colleagues and his wife, Svetlana, was known to be difficult. However, before an attempt could be made to subvert Deriabin's candidate, he was recalled to Moscow and was not given another foreign posting, according to the CIA computers. In fact Golytsin spent six years at KGB headquarters before adopting a new identity, that of Anatoli Klimov, and a counter-intelligence job at the Russian Embassy in Helsinki.

Golytsin's defection astonished everyone, including the CIA. One day he simply turned up on the doorstep of the CIA Station Chief's home in Helsinki and announced he wanted asylum in America for himself, his wife and his daughter. To dispel any suspicions the CIA might have about him, he delivered the complete KGB order of battle at the Helsinki Embassy and promised to identify Soviet 'illegals' and their agents around the world. His details were found to be accurate, and the Golytsin family were flown to a USAF base in West Germany before arriving in Washington and Ashford Farm.

What Golytsin had to offer was well prepared. He claimed that he had spent many months accumulating information about KGB operations in the West, and he now began to produce them. What he told the CIA was to have an impact on every Western intelligence service and create a fundamental split in the counter-intelligence community.

Initially there were suspicions at Langley that Golytsin was an *agent provocateur* in the classical mould. He required constant attention and was undoubtedly the most demanding guest Ashford Farm had ever had to deal with. He treated his CIA Soviet Bloc Division debriefers as idiots and frequently appeared paranoid. One of his conditions for co-operation, for example, was that he should never come into contact with anyone who spoke Russian. He argued that a Russian speaker would inevitably have learnt the language from a native, and that meant he was tainted. What his CIA hosts found particularly trying was his habit of making traps for his debriefers, testing them to see if they were merely concealing the fact that they understood Russian. He saw KGB everywhere and, judging by the number of people he denounced, he was quite justified.

For their part, the CIA were less than polished in their handling of someone whom they initially regarded as a top-grade, but temperamental, defector who suffered from paranoia and delusions of grandeur. Instead of providing AE/LADLE (his CIA code-name) with stimulating conversations on his intellectual level, they simply left him alone to brood in-between debriefing sessions. Virtually his only companionship was with CIA guards who, to put it mildly, were not selected for their drawing-room manners.

In spite of this insensitive treatment Golytsin never ceased in describing the files of agents and operations he had spotted in Moscow. He revealed the existence of the SAPPHIRE network in Paris, which consisted of Soviet agents in the French intelligence organization SDECE and denounced a member of General de Gaulle's Cabinet, Jacques

Foccart.* This item of information was considered so sensitive that President Kennedy wrote personally to General de Gaulle to inform him. SDECE dispatched a senior French military intelligence officer, General Temple de Rougemont, to Washington in secret to question AE/LADLE further. De Rougemont interrogated him for three days, at the end of which time he was forced to admit that the defector appeared to have incredibly secret information about SDECE and its internal structure. SDECE had been completely reorganized in 1958, yet the KGB had the very latest details of its personnel. To make matters worse, Golytsin boasted that security in Paris was so lax that new NATO plans were in Moscow within forty-eight hours of them being printed in Paris. To prove that particular point, Golytsin submitted to a test to identify genuine and specially prepared NATO documents. He spotted all the fakes. A fictionalized account of the affair was described by Leon Uris in *Topaz*,** in which Golytsin is referred to as 'Boris Kuznetov'. It resulted in the SDECE representative in Washington, Philipe de Vosjoli, deciding to remain in the United States rather than return to Paris at the end of his tour of duty.

Golytsin also named a Canadian Ambassador, Herbert Norman, as a long-term communist and KGB agent. Norman killed himself in Cairo before he could be interviewed.

Golytsin's knowledge of KGB agents in England seemed so extensive that, early in March, it was decided in London to send two senior counter-intelligence officers to Ashford Farm to listen to him. The man chosen by MI6 was the head of CI4, the Soviet espionage section, a graduate of Worcester College, Oxford, who had joined MI6 from the Ministry of Information in 1943. MI5 sent Arthur Martin, who had been the head of D1 since January 1960. Both men were appalled by what Golytsin told them: Philby was indeed a long-term agent and was one of a Ring-of-Five operated by Yuri Modin, whose particular speciality was running homosexual agents. Golytsin was uncertain of the identities of all the Ring-of-Five's members, but he supplied all their code-names and certain anecdotes concerning them. The two British officers listened open-mouthed. George Blake was a long-time ideological convert; a spy in the Admiralty was providing photographs of top-grade NATO documents; a senior civil servant in London had become the mistress of a Yugoslav diplomat and had been photographed in a compromising situation. The defector had learned of some of the cases whilst serving in the KGB's Northern European section, a geographically orientated unit taking in Scandinavia, the Low Countries and Great Britain. Other

---

* Foccart, who was alleged to be a Soviet spy code-named COLUMBINE, later successfully cleared his name by winning three libel actions in France.
** William Kimber, 1968.

cases had been presented to him as training lessons and Golytsin had managed to link some of the case histories with the particular geographical sections which had handled them, even though many of the details and code-names had been altered.

This litany of penetration sent Martin and the MI6 officer back to London to report to their respective chiefs, Roger Hollis and Dick White. Their joint conclusion was that a special committee should be formed from both organizations to investigate Golytsin's claims. In the meantime AE/LADLE would be given the Security Service code-name KAGO, and the working party would use the next code-name on the Joint Intelligence Committee's list, which happened to be FLUENCY. Thus the Fluency Committee was born.

The Fluency Committee began its work with a review of a case of Soviet penetration known to it, that of Philby. Philby was living in Beirut at this time, working as a journalist. The MI6 Head of Station in the Lebanon was Nicholas Elliott, an experienced counter-intelligence officer whose career had begun in Tar Robertson's B1(a) section in 1940. He had subsequently joined Section V of MI6 and had been their representative in Istanbul from 1942 to 1945. At this stage there was little prospect of headway in the case, although it was later decided to make Philby a formal offer of immunity from prosecution in exchange for his full co-operation. This option must have appeared even more attractive to Philby following Blake's heavy sentence in May 1962. As we shall see, Philby accepted the offer of immunity.

The question of Philby's guilt had already been established to MI5's satisfaction, so KAGO's evidence was treated as simply one more score against him. KAGO provided no direct proof, so the case against Philby was little advanced in court-room terms, and those who had watched his performance under Milmo's hostile cross-examination knew that another attempt would fail. The CIA too had been confident of Philby's duplicity and reluctantly acknowledged the difficulty of bringing a case before a jury. The FBI undoubtedly found MI5's chronology of events before the escape of Burgess and Maclean difficult to swallow. It later transpired that Hoover had ordered surveillance on Philby as soon as the defection of Burgess had become known. On one occasion the FBI had followed him into the Virginia countryside and had seen Philby move into some tree cover close to the road. He had appeared to reach up into a tree as though he was emptying a dead-letter drop and had then suddenly changed his mind, moved quickly towards some cover and relieved himself. The FBI were convinced they had actually watched Philby leave a message for his Soviet case officer, but when they had searched the branches of the tree for a concealed hiding-place they had found nothing. They had concluded that Philby had been receiving a message rather than leaving one. They also knew that Philby would simply claim that he had stopped his car and walked to the spot to relieve himself. There was no proof that he had any other motive.

KAGO had been unable to help the Fluency Committee over Philby, so attention was turned to the spy in the Admiralty. MI5 had been aware of a leak of NATO documents from the Naval Intelligence Department and a regular naval officer was already under investigation by a D1 officer. There was, however, the alternative possibility that KAGO was an *agent provocateur* and that he was simply discarding unwanted cards; this view was argued by the Deputy D-G, Graham Mitchell, who mistrusted KAGO.

The D1 officer had joined MI5 in 1951 and had been educated at Rugby and New College, Oxford. He had recently joined D1 from F1(a), the section concerned with monitoring the Communist Party of Great Britain. His task now was to identify the Soviet agent from among the 1,500 people, servicemen and civilians, who worked at the Admiralty. On 4 April 1962, immediately after Martin's return from Washington, the Director-General sought an interview with the First Lord of the Admiralty, Lord Carrington, who was informed that there was a strong possibility of the existence of a KGB spy in the building; he was also told that an investigation was underway. The next step was for the newly appointed Director of Naval Security to be informed of the situation. The incumbent, since the previous August, had been Colonel John Macafee RM, a tough no-nonsense former Commanding Officer of the Royal Marine Commandos. The division of labour was straightforward: the D1 officer would carry out the external investigation, Macafee would search every desk in the Admiralty. This kept him and his only assistant up almost every night for several weeks, as the searches could only be conducted once the staff had gone home in the evening.

The investigation which began in April continued throughout the summer, but it failed to identify the spy. Then, fortuitously, further details of the elusive spy appeared from America, this time from an FBI source code-named FEDORA. FEDORA was a Soviet official at the United Nations building who, for a period of six years, had been feeding the FBI secrets from the Soviet mission to the UN. He revealed that the KGB's spy in the British Admiralty was a homosexual who had originally been blackmailed into service whilst in Moscow. This news was sent straight to D1, and eventually a name was put to the profile: William John Christopher Vassall, who lived in Dolphin Square and was a clerk in the Fleet Section of Military Branch II, the secretariat of the Naval Staff of the Admiralty, and a former Assistant Private Secretary to the Civil Lord of the Admiralty, the Hon. Thomas Galbraith MP.

Vassall had served in the British Embassy in Moscow as a clerk to the Naval Attaché and had returned to London in June 1956. Since that date he had had hundreds of secret documents pass over his desk. Worse still, he had been trained as a photographer by the RAF during the war. The DI visited Hood House in Dolphin Square and, with the aid of Vassall's neighbour, established a listening post in the flat next door. A team of watchers covered his journeys to and from work on the number 24 bus, and his desk at the Admiralty was searched. In spite of these steps Vassall proved a difficult subject, and the DI consulted with the Director of 'D' Branch, Martin Furnival Jones. The DI was convinced that, since it was known the Admiralty spy was using a camera, a search of Vassall's flat would reveal some evidence of his espionage. This took place one afternoon early in September 1962, and everyone waited tensely for the news from 807 Hood House.

The operation was a success. Vassall's Exakta camera was found, along with various items of espionage paraphernalia. Orders were given to Special Branch to arrest him and, on 12 September, Vassall was intercepted leaving work by Superintendent George Smith. He admitted to spying for the Russians and described how he had been blackmailed for seven years. As soon as he had been charged at Bow Street, he was asked for the keys to his flat so a search could be made. Vassall surrendered them and was later told that his camera had been found, as had several photographic films which had been concealed in a specially constructed bookcase. The spy never knew that in fact it had all been discovered already.

The details of his case revealed an appalling lack of security, both in Moscow, where he had been 'befriended' by a Pole employed in the Embassy named Mikhailsky, and at the Admiralty in London, where no precautions had been taken to prevent office staff taking documents home for the night. Even worse, Vassall had been cleared for access to classified material, but the check carried out on him had been absurdly superficial.

Vassall pleaded guilty at the Old Bailey later that year and was sentenced to eighteen years' imprisonment. The government came in for severe criticism, especially since the prosecution of Vassall had followed so closely on that of Blake. Under considerable public pressure the government agreed to an enquiry into the case, the second such enquiry that year, and appointed Sir Charles Cunningham to head a tribunal, consisting of two other senior civil servants. This move subjected the government to further criticism and in November the Prime Minister, Harold Macmillan, set up a second enquiry, with formal powers, under Lord Radcliffe, a High Court judge. All three of its members had had first-hand intelligence experience. Lord Radcliffe had served in the Ministry of Information throughout the war, and for the first two years had been the Chief Press Censor, heading the Press Censorship Division. This had involved close liaison with MI5. Field-Marshal Sir Gerald Templer's entire career had been built on his intelligence work. He had served as Lord Gort's Director of Military Intelligence in the British Expeditionary Force in France and Belgium in the early part of the war and had been appointed Director of Military Intelligence at the War Office in 1946. The third member of the tribunal was the former Labour MP for Grimsby, Kenneth Younger, who had been the wartime Director of 'E' Division, the MI5 department responsible for the supervision of all aliens.

The Radcliffe Tribunal took evidence from virtually everyone involved in the case except, of course, the original source of the information which led to Vassall's arrest, KAGO. Much to the dismay of MI5 there had been some speculation in the press concerning the source, and a somewhat 'leaky' politician had hinted at the involvement of a defector to Chapman Pincher, the *Daily Express* journalist. As was his custom, Pincher checked this with Colonel Leslie (Sammy) Lohan, the Secretary of the 'D' Notice Committee, who in turn passed the disturbing news to the Legal Adviser, Bernard Hill.

MI5 were appalled at the politician's indiscretion and equally concerned that further talk of a mysterious defector would jeopardize their access to KAGO. So as to prevent further discussion on the subject, it was agreed privately that Pincher would have to endure only the most superficial of cross-examinations by the tribunal. There was also another reason for seeing that Pincher was let off lightly. Earlier the previous year he had reported to Rear-Admiral George Thomson, the then 'D' Notice Secretary (and Lord Radcliffe's successor as the wartime Chief Press Censor), that he had made an important contact at the Russian Embassy. Thomson assumed that this was merely Pincher covering himself in case he was spotted by MI5 wining and dining with a KGB officer, but he did mention the matter to the Legal Adviser. There was no comment from MI5, but shortly afterwards Pincher brought the subject up again with Thomson and suggested that he, Pincher, might be able to help MI5. This was again passed on to the Legal Adviser, who was obliged to inform his colleagues in 'D' Division. Would they care to take up Pincher's offer? Opinion differed sharply. On one side were the officers who took the view that 'D' Division's knowledge of the Soviet set-up was so inadequate that they should take every opportunity to improve it, especially when the proposed agent was known to MI5. The other view was that Pincher had always been intrigued by the Security Service and that this was an attempt by him to learn something of its methods and personnel.

In the end a compromise was reached. The D1(a) would interview Pincher at Room 055 and listen to his story. If he was genuine he would be recruited, but always kept at arm's length. This decision was endorsed by the entire Directorate because of the 'No Contact' with journalists rule in Standing Orders. The D1(a) then held a meeting with Pincher and behaved in a perfectly straightforward manner, even abandoning the standard practice of adopting a cover-name. The net result was that each impressed the other. Pincher thought he had been signed on as an MI5 agent, whilst it was reported to Stewart, one of the D1(b) Soviet experts, that the journalist might have a useful contact after all. Pincher spun out his link with the D1(a), but it became obvious that there was no possible advantage to retaining him as a 'window' into the Soviet camp and he was given a gentle brush-off. Nevertheless, at the time of the Radcliffe Tribunal he was still in touch with D1.

Two of Pincher's Fleet Street colleagues received rather less generous treatment from Lord Radcliffe. Brendan Mulholland and Reginald Foster were both imprisoned for contempt (six months and three months respectively) when they refused to name their sources. MI5 suspected that these sources were less than reliable. Percy Hoskins, the veteran Fleet Street crime correspondent, involved himself in a somewhat similar tangle. In one of his articles, he claimed that clues to Vassall had been found among Lonsdale's belongings. Lord Radcliffe found that this allegation was without foundation, but newspapers seemed perfectly willing to invent plausible links between the two cases in the absence of any official guidance. In Hoskins's case his speculation was based on a conversation with a police officer who knew nothing whatever about KAGO. Lord Radcliffe concluded his Tribunal's Report with some harsh words for Fleet Street.

The 'senior civil servant' mentioned by KAGO had in the meantime been identified as Miss Barbara Fell, a forty-four-year-old Assistant Overseas Controller of the Central Office of Information with more than twenty-three years' experience and an OBE to her credit. In the spring of 1959 she had become the mistress of the Press Attaché at the Yugoslav Embassy, Smiljan Pecjak, and, for a period of seventeen months, had been lending him documents classified as confidential. The case was to be a major success for MI5's resident interrogator, Tony 'Healey'.

Healey was an experienced Security Service officer, having joined Courtney Young's staff at CIFE in Singapore after the war. After two tours of duty in Malaya, Healey was posted briefly as Security Liaison Officer, Hong Kong, before returning to Curzon Street. Shortly after his return Skardon was transferred to take charge of the watchers, thus creating a vacancy for the post of interrogator. Marriott's first choice for the job had declined the offer, so Healey got the job instead and went to work on Miss Fell.

The interrogations took place over a three-week period at her parents' home in The Boltons, West Kensington. She admitted having lent Pecjak several Foreign Office briefings, which she had considered innocuous, and remembered an occasion in June 1959 when she might have been photographed with her lover. Nevertheless, she had certainly not been blackmailed into betraying secrets and was unaware that any photographs had been taken. She was formally cautioned by Chief Inspector Stratton of Special Branch on 30 September 1962 and the following month he served her with a Summons alleging breaches of the Official Secrets Acts. She pleaded guilty on 7 December 1962 and was sentenced to two years' imprisonment.

Within twelve months of his defection KAGO had confirmed the guilt of two MI6 traitors and helped identify two other KGB sources in England. But this was to prove to be only the beginning of his revelations.

In spite of the magnificent results the CIA had obtained from KAGO, they were to discover that the defector had rather more in mind for himself than simply being a source of information.

KAGO's escape to the West in Finland had been just one stage in an elaborate plan that he had spent years developing. His betrayal of KGB networks around the world was also part of a grander scheme which involved building a special intelligence research department to combat the KGB, with a budget of $30 million. KAGO's debriefings gradually developed from relatively simple exchanges of information to long diatribes against the Kremlin's ambition of world domination, tinged with an element of paranoia. The defector interpreted the Agency's lack of interest in his plans as evidence of their naïvety and demanded to make his views known to senior politicians, including the President. The CIA were naturally unwilling to have their prize recruit thus exposed and used delaying tactics to postpone his unrestricted contact with the outside world. As soon as KAGO realized that his debriefers were humouring him and had no intention of participating in his scheme, he became less co-operative.

Control of the CIA switched in the autumn of 1962 from Allen Dulles to John McCone, and the new Director of Central Intelligence had no desire to spend American tax-payers' dollars on what some in the Agency saw as a one-man crusade against the KGB. In the aftermath of the Bay of Pigs disaster of the previous April, the American intelligence community were anxious not to provoke the Moscow leadership or provide them with more propaganda fodder. When this overly cautious attitude was communicated to the increasingly temperamental KAGO, he became even more belligerent and eventually only communicated with the Director of Counter-Intelligence, Jim Angleton, and his assistant, Raymond Rocca. Only these two men, in his opinion, displayed any deeper understanding of the Soviet problem.

Angleton was then forty-five years old. He was the son of a senior National Cash Register Company official and had been educated at Malvern College in England, Yale University and Harvard Law School. In 1943 he joined OSS, the forerunner of the CIA, and was posted to the

OSS X-2 counter-intelligence staff at St Albans where he met Kim Philby, then head of the Iberian department of Section V of MI6. Angleton proved to be a rarely gifted intelligence officer and, when he was stationed in Italy in 1944, he was, aged twenty-seven, the senior intelligence officer in that theatre.

When KAGO was passed into the care of Angleton, he moved out of Ashford Farm and was established in a suburban home on the outskirts of Washington. He had been provided with a new identity, that of 'John Stone', and a full-time CIA driver/bodyguard. He was, however, less than satisfied and decided to move to England. The CIA discouraged this idea for as long as possible, but by the spring of 1963 they were unable to prevent him from leaving. It was a move that MI5 welcomed.

KAGO's comments to Martin and MI6 had led to the creation of the Fluency Committee, as we have seen, and in the meantime the Committee had come to some very disturbing conclusions.

The basis of KAGO's philosophy was that the KGB had the skill to penetrate the West's secret departments and manipulate their counter-Soviet operations. According to KAGO there was not a single such organization in the world that had escaped this attention. The cases of Burgess, Maclean, Philby, Blake, Wennerstrom and Felfe were all evidence of the Soviet offensive. Yet there had been no suggestion to date that MI5 itself had been a target.

The Fluency Committee took the apparently logical view that if the Secret Intelligence Service and the Foreign Service had been penetrated, then surely the Security Service would also have been a target. If one was to follow this negative argument, then there was circumstantial evidence to support such a disagreeable contention. Unlike most countries, Britain had not received any defectors. On its own this fact could mean nothing, bearing in mind that the CIA were generally recognized as having very substantial funds available for covert operations such as financing defectors. But there were other pieces of the jig-saw, such as MI5's unsatisfactory record with Soviet double agents. The success of the double-cross system during the last war had led MI5 to believe that they were skilled handlers of double agents. In fact it was the proud boast of B1(a) that they had only lost one double agent, an Abwehr officer code-named ARTIST. He had been trapped by the Gestapo in 1944 and murdered. After the war B2 and later D4 launched a similar double-cross operation against the Russians, but the results had been disappointing. Most had followed the same pattern. A patriotic Englishman would be approached by a KGB or GRU officer and made an offer of recruitment. Sometimes there was a financial inducement, on other occasions blackmail was involved. The person concerned would then contact the Security Service and be assigned a case officer, thus coming 'under control'. The agent would then build up a relationship with his Soviet handler which had a two-part advantage to MI5, according to the text-books. The first was the positive identification of a hostile Soviet Bloc intelligence officer; the second was the opportunity to feed Moscow with specially prepared information, thus either deceiving them or simply causing them to waste valuable time which might otherwise be more profitably spent.

This first advantage was important to MI5 because of the organization's very limited resources. The combined forces of the KGB and GRU in London were always judged to be in excess of 150 intelligence officers. With such an excessive number it was obviously impossible to keep surveillance on them all, so if even a small proportion were tied up in worthless exercises, it enabled MI5 to deploy its forces more effectively. It was also believed that of the 150 intelligence officers only about six were actively engaged in the recruitment and running of important agents. The question was, which six? With some hundred decoys moving around the town every day of the week, it was an impossible task. But according to KAGO, the Soviets actually capitalized on these counter-measures, turning them to their advantage.

Experience gained during the war gave MI5 even more cause for worry. After the collapse of Germany most of the Abwehr's case officers were shipped to MI5's interrogation camp at Ham Common to undergo a thorough programme of debriefing. The object had been to identify unknown Nazi sources in England and hear an account of the double agents from the other side's point of view. Some Germans had co-operated, others had refused to answer any questions, but one lesson had been learnt: case officers who suspected their agents had been 'turned' invariably failed to tell anyone. This was not just a matter of currying favour with the enemy, but rather an arrogant reluctance to openly admit that someone on the other side had got the better of them. There were countless wartime examples of double agents apparently achieving the impossible or being in two places at once. This had happened in spite of the most rigorous supervision and could not be avoided. Yet when these blunders had happened there had been no response from the other side. In fact in 1943 the Twenty Committee had authorized an operation (involving MI5's double agent SCRUFFY) designed to convince the Abwehr that MI5 were so clumsy at running double agents that there was little danger of one surviving undetected. To the amazement of all concerned the Abwehr had registered nothing and had continued the contact without any attempt to turn the double agent into a 'triple'. This had so alarmed B1(a) that the case had been hastily abandoned.

KAGO's theory was depressingly simple. A KGB agent in London would approach someone confident that the recruit would report the matter to MI5. When the subject responded positively and began supplying information, the KGB officer would do one of two things: he would either use the double agent to identify the MI5 case officer involved (a useful exercise to establish MI5's internal structure), or he would make it known to the agent that the agent was being run by MI5 and use him to recruit the MI5 case officer. Thus appeared the spectre of MI5's case officers themselves becoming agents rather than admit to a higher authority that they had been 'blown'. What made this latter course so unpalatable was the fact that, according to the files, no case officer had ever reported being approached by the opposition in such a manner. KAGO was convinced that such techniques were standard practice, although he was unable to be specific about individual cases. Certainly MI5 had its share of arrogant young case officers anxious to demonstrate their prowess at the intelligence game.

If KAGO's theory was correct, then it would explain MI5's lack of success with double agents and the reluctance of potential defectors to entrust themselves to a Security Service they knew to be thoroughly penetrated. It would also explain the uneasy feeling that some had about MI5's post-war 'successes'. In the case of Brian Linney, Prybl had failed to keep the rendezvous at which both were to be arrested. The surveillance on Lonsdale and the Krogers had been vastly time-consuming (and they were all to be swapped eventually, Lonsdale for Greville Wynne in April 1964 and the Krogers for Gerald Brooke in July 1969). Moreover, there had already been a suspicion that a more senior Soviet 'illegal' had completely evaded capture in the Lonsdale–Kroger episode. And there were other examples: in 1951 Burgess had clearly received a warning about Maclean's impending interview with MI5 and John Cairncross's contact had failed to show for his rendezvous. There were some nagging doubts about the Vassall case too. Six days before George Smith arrested him, his Soviet case officer, Nicolai Karpekov, had fled the country. Had he been tipped off?

KAGO's ideas were taken so seriously that the Fluency Committee decided they should take up the offer that the CIA had turned down. He was accordingly invited to England and told that his help would receive the recognition the Americans were so reluctant to give.

'John Stone' (KAGO's new alias) sold his CIA-supplied house in Arlington, Virginia, and embarked in New York for a transatlantic voyage with his wife and two daughters. He had given his German Shepherd guard-dog and his television set to a fellow Soviet defector.

When KAGO and his family arrived at Southampton he contacted the two members of the Fluency Committee he had met at Ashford Farm. It had been agreed that initially at least KAGO would fend for himself and tour the country staying at hotels selected by him. Every few days he would telephone Arthur Martin and arrange a meeting to discuss a particular case. For the sake of security no one would know KAGO's exact location. There was also another reason for this somewhat over-elaborate procedure. By the summer of 1963 MI5 had accumulated much more evidence of a Soviet agent working within their ranks.

At this point we must go back to the previous year and follow other developments that were taking place in parallel to the KAGO case.

Almost a year before KAGO's unexpected defection in Finland another well-placed Soviet source had volunteered information to the Americans and had been politely turned away. The source was a self-confessed GRU officer and his approach was so blatant that the CIA concluded that he must be an *agent provocateur*. The British, however, decided to take him up on his offer, which was somewhat indiscreetly made to an English tourist, and thus began the case of Lieutenant-Colonel Oleg Vladimirovich Penkovsky, code-named ALEX.

Penkovsky was not entirely unknown to either MI6 or the CIA as he had been posted to Ankara in 1955 as Assistant Military Attaché. On his return to Moscow he had made various unsuccessful attempts to contact Western intelligence organizations, but it was not until 1960 that he had been contacted by Greville Wynne, one of MI6's many agents operating under business covers. A number of British businessmen who regularly travelled within the Soviet Union were encouraged to keep their eyes open and then to attend a debriefing session on their return to England. Wynne, who had some wartime experience with MI5, had been recruited by two senior MI6 officers and encouraged to build up his firm's trade with the USSR. In 1956 he had played the part of a decoy in a joint MI6/CIA operation to assist the defection from Odessa of a certain Major Kuznov.

In April 1961, Penkovsky arrived in London to lead a Soviet trade delegation. The party, which consisted of six senior Russian officials, booked into the Mount Royal Hotel near Marble Arch, where MI6 had arranged a suite of rooms on the floor above the delegation's. Here Penkovsky underwent a lengthy debriefing at the hands of the CIA and MI6.

The CIA had been brought back into the operation for a number of reasons, not the least being their willingness to finance it. The head of the Soviet Russia Division of the CIA at the time was Jack Maury and he assigned George Kisvalter to the case with the code-name ALEXANDER. As it happened Kisvalter was already in London picking over the bones of Blake's confession in an attempt to establish whether he had been responsible for Popov's arrest.

When Penkovsky was ushered on 20 April into the converted hotel suite he was introduced to his four debriefers, although only the two Americans could actually speak Russian. Kisvalter chaired the meeting, the first of many, and Penkovsky delivered copies of Soviet training manuals, some ten thousand photographs of military documents and details of the very latest missile systems. The volume of information was gigantic and much of it was of direct interest to MI5 as well as MI6 and the CIA. For example, ALEX gave personal biographies of every GRU officer he had come into contact with and dozens of others who were known to his family. Kisvalter had the information sent to Washington where Maury gave it the highest classification of secrecy and, unusually, distributed it under a single code-name. The debriefing continued until 6 May 1961 when the delegation returned to Moscow.

MI5's participation in the operation was limited to keeping ALEX's delegation busy with tedious visits to factories in the Midlands and occasionally taking the opportunity to offer interesting subjects for the single member of the delegation who had been equipped by the GRU with a miniature camera. The reward for 'C' Branch's efforts was a new insight into the Soviet order of battle at the London Embassy. ALEX was able to identify all the GRU officers and give their real names, including the GRU *rezident* in London, Karpekov, who was listed as a Counsellor; his deputy, Colonel Pavlov; the Air Attaché, Colonel Konstantinov, and the Assistant Naval Attaché, Lieutenant-Commander Ivanov. This provided 'D' Branch with a complete picture of the *rezidentura* which remained accurate for some months and was later, as we will see, the cause of a major political scandal in England, resulting in the fall of Harold Macmillan's government.

As well as detailing dozens of GRU operations and naming staff, ALEX also produced some remarkable documents for the West's counter-intelligence experts. Among them was the transcript of a lecture given by Lieutenant-Colonel Prikhodko, a GRU officer who had worked at the United Nations in New York under diplomatic cover between 1952 and 1955. His lecture, entitled 'Characteristics of Agent Communications and Agent Handling in the USA', gave a fascinating insight into current GRU methods and field-craft.

The debriefings were continued later in May when Wynne visited ALEX in Moscow and was handed dozens of exposed Minox films. As a back-up Penkovsky was also assigned an MI6 case officer from the Moscow Embassy, Roderick Chisholm, who operated under the diplomatic cover of Second Secretary. He had, of course, been instantly identified by the KGB as a career MI6 officer (he had previously served in Germany and Singapore), so his wife Janet invariably acted as a courier whilst taking her children for walks in the afternoon.

In July 1961 ALEX made a second trip to London, this time to attend the Soviet Industrial Exhibition. On this occasion he was booked into the Kensington Close Hotel, only walking distance from his Embassy, and the debriefings were conducted at a rented flat in Coleherne Court in the nearby Old Brompton Road. Two months later ALEX was again in the West, this time visiting an exhibition in Paris. More 'safe-houses' were prepared and the debriefings continued.

The ALEX case began to go sour in January 1962, when it became obvious that his apparently casual encounters with Janet Chisholm had been monitored by the KGB. He reported that further meetings would be too dangerous and fell back on an elaborate series of dead-letter drops. This prearranged system relied on ALEX secreting his messages in hiding-places and then informing his case officer that they were ready for collection. This he did by telephoning the homes of CIA contacts twice and then hanging up after an agreed number of rings. The case officer would then check a particular lamp-post on the Kutuzov Prospect for a tell-tale black mark, which indicated that ALEX had completed his 'drop' successfully, and empty the hiding-place. So as to reduce the possibility of interference by the KGB, no dead-letter drop was used more than once and the entire operation was only conducted once a month. ALEX was also instructed to give advance warning of his visits to the West via a system of apparently innocent tourist postcards mailed to MI6 cover addresses in London. It was this latter system that ALEX used on 12 January 1962 to call off further direct meetings, although on the occasions that he met Janet Chisholm at official diplomatic receptions, such as the Queen's Birthday on 31 March 1962, which they both attended, and the Fourth of July celebration at the American Embassy, more valuable rolls of film passed hands.

By the summer of 1962 KGB surveillance on ALEX had intensified to such a degree that he advised that Wynne be withdrawn from Moscow a day earlier than planned. It was later established that at their final meeting, at the Ukraina Hotel, their conversation had been taped. In spite of the KGB's by now obvious surveillance, ALEX continued to fill his dead-letter drops until one final abortive visit to an American Embassy reception on 5 September. ALEX failed to identify any of his CIA contacts and retained his packet of films. Before he could defect he was arrested by the KGB on 12 October. (The exact date of his arrest has never been disclosed. Some Western intelligence officers believe it may have taken place ten days later, on 22 October 1962.) News of ALEX's arrest did not leak out until Wynne had been intercepted in Budapest on 2 November. Wynne was arrested after a cocktail party at his mobile trade exhibition. A pair of specially constructed vehicles were to be used to smuggle ALEX out to the West by road. A Soviet passport with all the correct authorizing stamps had been forged in the United States to enable ALEX to visit Hungary once he had shaken off the KGB in Moscow.

The escape plan had only the remotest chance of success, but the attempt had to be made so as to prevent ALEX being interrogated. He would have no alternative but to describe the extent of his work for the CIA/MI6 and would thus reduce its value. Wynne's case was less important in intelligence terms because he had never seen ALEX's material and therefore was not in a position to compromise any of it. As it turned out the Russians appeared to disbelieve that ALEX could possibly have passed the quantities of intelligence he admitted to, which enabled Fort Meade to continue decrypting the GRU signal traffic. That, however, was a doubtful consolation for his loss and that of Wynne. To compound the disaster, Popov's execution was announced the very next month, in December. The statement in the Soviet press simply stated that an infantry officer, 'Lieutenant-Colonel P', had been shot for treason, as a spy of the American intelligence service. In the aftermath of the arrests of ALEX and Wynne no less than eight American and British diplomats were declared *persona non grata* and expelled.

A four-day show-trial was duly held in the Soviet capital in May the following year with the world's press invited to inspect and photograph a display of MI6/CIA spy paraphernalia. The result was, of course, a foregone conclusion. Penkovsky was sentenced to death and confiscation of his property; Wynne to eight years' imprisonment. Eleven months later Wynne was exchanged at Checkpoint Heerstrasse in Berlin for Gordon Lonsdale.

Once Wynne had been flown back to Northolt the CIA began work on their release of *The Penkovsky Papers*,* a full account of ALEX's work. The man chosen to write the book was Frank Gibney from *Time* magazine who received much help from George Kisvalter which, for security reasons, had to remain unacknowledged. Mention of the NSA's success with the GRU signals was also omitted. The translation of all ALEX's messages was entrusted to Peter Deriabin, the GRU defector from Vienna. Wynne felt that he should have been asked to edit the book and subsequently published his own version, *The Man From Moscow*,** in spite of objections from MI6.

Between the moment of ALEX's first encounter with the CIA in April 1961 and his execution in May 1963 several important events had taken place in the intelligence world. The question facing MI5, MI6 and the CIA was: were they all linked? According to KAGO they were.

One of the more inexplicable aspects of ALEX's case was the fact that he himself believed he had come under suspicion following a meeting with Mrs Chisholm on 6 January 1952. If that was the case, why did the KGB wait for a further nine months before closing in? One argument took the view that because of ALEX's seniority and his powerful political connections the KGB were determined to develop an unassailable case. Alternatively, ALEX was simply being over-sensitive to routine KGB surveillance on foreigners. Nevertheless, there remained the ugly suspicion that in the latter part of his active life ALEX might have been

* Doubleday, NY, 1965.
** Hutchinson, 1967.

used either by the GRU or the KGB as a double agent. Purveyors of that particular line also suggested that the whole characterization of Penkovsky was an elaborate deception, with the added twist that he is still alive and living the life of a Soviet hero.

6

ENTRAPMENT

The ALEX case had provided excellent dossiers for MI5 on each of the members of the GRU *rezidentura* at the Embassy in Kensington Palace Gardens. Each officer had been described in detail, as had his family in Russia and his individual shortcomings. ALEX's information also provided what 'D' Branch considered a splendid opportunity to mount an operation aimed against the GRU. The particular target within the London *rezidentura* was Lieutenant-Commander Eugene Ivanov, mentioned by ALEX as a man who loved a good party. His knowledge of Ivanov dated back to the Military Diplomatic Academy in Moscow where they had been students together. Even before ALEX had been apprehended by the KGB, MI5 began their new operation.

Ivanov's diplomatic cover was that of Assistant Naval Attaché and he had been recognized by 'D' Branch's order of battle unit as an intelligence officer when he first arrived in London on 27 March 1960. ALEX's confirmation also suggested that he might be a profitable target, so the watchers began tailing him. Almost immediately he led them to a house at 17 Wimpole Mews. The electoral roll revealed it to be the home of Stephen Ward, a society osteopath who ran a surgery close-by in Devonshire Street. Ward's name was completely unknown to Registry, so discreet enquiries were made which revealed that he had many prominent friends, including the third Viscount Astor. Ward had a reputation for providing Astor and his friends with girls. Astor was well known to MI5 and had several contacts within the organization because he had served during the war in the Naval Intelligence Department under Admiral John Godfrey. Astor had been Godfrey's representative on the secret Thirty-One Committee in Beirut which had consisted of all the British intelligence organizations with interests in the Lebanon. They included the Inter-Service Liaison Department (the MI6 cover), Security Intelligence Middle East, the Naval Intelligence Department and the deception experts from Brigadier Dudley Clarke's unit. The principal role of this committee had been to mislead the enemy and provide Nazi agents with bogus information.

The prospect of using Ward's female 'assets' as a route to Ivanov was too good to miss, so D1(a) decided to approach the osteopath with a view to recruiting him as an agent. The scheme 'D' Branch had in mind was entrapment, with defection as the ultimate objective. Ivanov would either be compromised and blackmailed or else simply persuaded to defect. The lever to be used was Ivanov's family in Russia: his father-in-law, Aleksandr Gorkin, was Chairman of the Soviet Supreme Court. What made Ivanov even more vulnerable was the fact that his wife's oldest sister, Irena, was married to the Air Attaché in London, Colonel Konstantinov, who also happened to be a member of the GRU *rezidentura*. This combination was hard to resist, and a D1 officer using the cover-name 'Woods' telephoned Ward at his consulting rooms posing as a man 'from the War Office' and arranged to lunch with Ward on 8 June 1961. During the meal Woods asked Ward about Ivanov. Ward described meeting him the previous January and agreed to co-operate. After lunch Ward invited Woods back to tea at his mews house and there he met a young girl who had evidently recently moved in. When he returned to Leconfield House, Woods described his interview with Ward. While they had been talking they had been served tea by a girl who was, in his opinion, the most beautiful he had ever clapped eyes on. Unfortunately he had failed to catch her name. Although the D1(a) officer, Woods, had some reservations about Ward himself, he became Ward's case officer. The girl's name was Christine Keeler.

There was a certain degree of urgency about the whole entrapment operation because if ALEX was apprehended by the KGB, he might well name Ivanov under interrogation as a candidate for entrapment by MI5. This would result in Ivanov being recalled to Moscow and 'D' Branch losing the opportunity to suborn him. In fact the case progressed well, with Ward reporting to Woods by telephone on 10 July with some dramatic news. Ward announced that he had spent the previous weekend with Christine Keeler at his cottage on Lord Astor's Cliveden estate in Buckinghamshire and they had been visited on Sunday by Ivanov. During the course of the afternoon Ivanov had asked Ward to try to find out if the British government intended to arm West Germany with atomic weapons. Ward also mentioned that the house-party at Cliveden had included John Profumo, the Secretary of State for War, and his wife. In fact Profumo later began an illicit affair with Christine Keeler, having first met her whilst she was swimming naked in Lord Astor's pool late on Saturday evening. This item of news failed to reach 'D' Branch until January the following year when quite a different source volunteered it.

Profumo's unexpected appearance on the scene threatened to wreck the entrapment of Ivanov, so 'D' Branch asked Special Branch to run a check on Ward and Keeler. A week later Special Branch replied that neither had a police record and the Wimpole Mews address was not known as a 'disorderly house', either by the Vice Squad or the CID at Marylebone police station.

In spite of this reassurance 'D' Branch believed Profumo's appearance at Cliveden might jeopardize the Ivanov operation and Hollis agreed. He decided that rather than talk to Profumo direct, he would pass on a message through the Cabinet Secretary, Sir Norman Brook, and this he did the same day, on 31 July. Brook did not have a suitable opportunity to warn Profumo of MI5's interest in Ivanov and Ward until 9 August 1961. Profumo thanked him for the warning saying that he had only met Ivanov twice, once at Cliveden and once at a reception at the Russian Embassy. He suggested that a similar warning be given to another of his Cabinet colleagues whom he knew was on friendly terms with Stephen Ward.

Brook then told Profumo of MI5's intention to 'turn' Ivanov and asked for Profumo's help. Profumo understandably declined the Director-General's request. The Cabinet Secretary did not press him and merely reported the result of the interview to Hollis. When Profumo left the meeting he apparently surmised (incorrectly) that MI5 must have discovered his relationship with Keeler and reported it to the Prime Minister. He therefore wrote a letter that afternoon to Keeler on War Office notepaper, ending their affair. Part of the rest of August he spent with his family on the Isle of Wight, by coincidence staying in Bembridge, the very village that the Deputy D-G, Graham Mitchell, visited at weekends.

Over the next few months there were signs that Ward was enjoying his role as an instrument for turning Ivanov and it became increasingly likely that MI5 might suffer some embarrassment as a result of his public activities. For example, during the Berlin crisis of September 1961 Ward persuaded Lord Astor to make representations on his and Ivanov's behalf to the Foreign Office. 'D' Branch realized that Ward was becoming increasingly indiscreet and had second thoughts about using him further as an agent. By coincidence Ward telephoned Woods for a meeting and this duly took place on 28 May 1962. MI5 were now so concerned about his eccentric behaviour that on 12 June 1962 a formal letter was sent to the Foreign Office warning them of Ward and Ivanov. During the Cuban missile crisis in October Ivanov again attempted to use Ward as an unofficial channel, this time to Sir Harold Caccia, the Permanent Under-Secretary at the Foreign Office, suggesting some back-door negotiations. The Foreign Office naturally flatly refused the idea and were so bemused by Ward's activities that they asked MI5 for further information about him. The request landed on Woods's desk and on 2 November 1962 he duly replied:

It is not easy to assess Ward's security reliability but we believe he is probably not a man who would be actively disloyal but that he is so under the influence of IVANOV that it would be most unwise to trust him.

In the months that followed the missile crisis several MI5 and Special Branch informants named Ward as a suspicious character and a possible security risk, but 'D' Branch saw no reason to interfere. In any case at this stage they simply had no idea that Profumo had been involved with Keeler. Contrary to Profumo's belief, neither MI5 nor the Prime Minister had any idea that such an affair had taken place.

In December 1962 the position dramatically altered with a shooting incident. A West Indian, called Edgecombe, tried to shoot his way into the Wimpole Mews house in an attempt to see Christine Keeler. The incident led to Edgecombe's arrest and his appearance in Court in January 1963 with Keeler appearing as a witness. This caused considerable press interest and offers for her 'life story'. When Ward learned that Keeler had entered into serious negotiations with Fleet Street, he warned Ivanov at a meeting on 18 January. The Assistant Naval Attaché immediately made arrangements to leave London on 29 January and these were discovered by MI5 through a telephone tap four days later. Profumo only got to hear of it on 28 January when Lord Astor called on him. Profumo's first reaction was to contact MI5 and in less than two hours Hollis was sitting before him.

Profumo's motive for seeing Hollis was to try to stop the Keeler story being published, or so Hollis thought. The Secretary of State recounted his meeting with Ward, Keeler and Ivanov at Cliveden in the summer of 1961 but neglected to mention that he had subsequently had an affair with Keeler. He thought Hollis already knew. When he turned to the subject of his interview of August 1961 with Sir Norman Brook, Hollis explained that MI5 had failed to recruit Ivanov as an agent. Then the meeting ended.

The following day Ivanov returned to Moscow and 'D' Branch received a report from a journalist alleging that the *Sunday Pictorial* had purchased Keeler's story plus two letters to her from Profumo. In fact the source had telephoned his story the previous day and told his case officer that, according to Fleet Street gossip, the War Minister had been having an affair with a call-girl. The case officer had demanded further details and these he supplied, but they arrived twenty-four hours after the Director-General's interview with Profumo.

This development was considered by the Directorate of the Security Service on Friday, 1 February 1963, and it was agreed that until further notice MI5 would proceed no further with the matter. The justification was straightforward: the Security Service could only be involved if Ivanov was still on the scene, but the watchers had monitored his exit from the country the previous day. Furthermore, there was absolutely no reason to think that any secrets had passed between Profumo, Keeler and the Russians. In effect, MI5 were dropping the case. As Hollis later stated, if Profumo had taken Keeler as his mistress, as now seemed probable, it was no concern of MI5's. A Minister's private life was of no concern to MI5 if it did not endanger the safety of the realm.

That situation was to last only a matter of hours. Soon after Hollis had left for the weekend Graham Mitchell, his Deputy D-G, received a telephone call from the Prime Minister's Principal Private Secretary, Sir Timothy Bligh, summoning him to 10 Downing Street. Bligh had previously been Secretary to the Three Advisers, the appeals board for the Positive Vetting system, so he was no stranger to MI5. Mitchell promptly drove round, followed by watchers who were trailing him night and day.* When he arrived Bligh explained that he had received a telephone call from a newspaper executive who had informed him that the *Daily Mirror* group had bought a story concerning a girl named 'Kolania', Profumo and the Russian Naval Attaché. The Prime Minister was abroad in Italy, did MI5 have any comments? Mitchell replied that the Security Service were indeed aware of the background and that Profumo had recently had a confidential interview with Hollis on the subject. Both men agreed that Profumo should be consulted again and Bligh agreed to undertake the task that evening. When he did, Profumo denied he had slept with Keeler and he was believed.

Over the weekend the *News of the World* published a picture of Keeler, linking her to the Edgecombe shooting case, and it was seen by Woods, Ward's case officer. When he reached the office on Monday morning he drafted an internal memo to the Director-General, Hollis, urging him to tell the Prime Minister of Profumo's relationship with Keeler and raising the possibility of another Radcliffe-style enquiry. It concluded:

If, in any subsequent enquiries, we were found to be in possession of this information about Profumo and to have taken no action on it, we would, I am sure, be subject to much criticism for failing to bring it to light.

The memo was discussed by Hollis and Mitchell and, in the end, Hollis decided that since Number 10 was aware of the Profumo story there was nothing left for the Security Service to do. He replied to Woods:

The allegations there referred to are known to Admiralty House. No enquiries on this subject should be made by us.

But again, the problem would not go away. Three days later Evan Jones, the Head of Special Branch, visited Leconfield House with dis-

---

* See Chapter 7 for details of the investigation of Mitchell, who at the time was under suspicion of being a Soviet agent himself.

turbing news. The police in Marylebone had taken a statement from Miss Keeler on 26 January and it had only now come into the possession of a Branch officer, Detective Inspector Morgan. In it she claimed to have had an affair with Profumo and insisted that Ward had asked her to find out the exact date that atomic weapons were to be delivered to West Germany. Little credence was given to the claim and 'D' Branch suggested no action should be taken. Mitchell then gave his approval and signed the file: 'No action on this at present. Please keep me informed of any developments.'

MI5 took no further action, but in the political arena events were moving fast. Rumours were rife and on 22 March Profumo made his statement to the House of Commons saying there had been 'no impropriety whatsoever' in his relationship with Christine Keeler.

Again the matter refused to die. The Home Secretary, Sir Henry Brooke, heard a rumour that MI5 had been sending anonymous letters to Mrs Profumo and summoned Hollis to see him on 27 March. Also present were the Commissioner of Police, Sir Joseph Simpson, and the Permanent Under-Secretary at the Home Office, Sir Charles Cunningham. Hollis assured them that the rumours were untrue and explained that because Ivanov had left the country the matter was no longer anything to do with MI5.

On the question of Stephen Ward, the Director-General described the situation to the Home Secretary for the first time: Keeler had made allegations to the police involving Ward in a possible breach of the Official Secrets Acts, but it would be difficult to prosecute because all the witnesses were so unreliable. He detailed Keeler's story about atomic weapons in Germany and this prompted Brooke to ask if the police thought there were grounds for prosecuting Ward. The Commissioner replied that he thought Ward might be convicted of living off immoral earnings but it seemed unlikely.

By the end of the meeting Hollis had agreed to re-examine the possibility of an Official Secrets prosecution. This he did, but a week later reported that it was unlikely to succeed.

The Commissioner, however, agreed that the Ward case should be passed to the police for further investigation and, on 4 April, they began taking statements from all concerned. When the investigation concluded that Ward had been living off immoral earnings, the decision was taken to prosecute. Meanwhile, two Labour Members of Parliament, George Wigg and Harold Wilson, who were in touch with Ward, were pressing the Conservative Prime Minister to re-examine the security aspects of the affair and, on 17 April, Macmillan so instructed the Director-General. Hollis replied on 25 April and broadly described Woods's contacts with Ward and the warning sent to Profumo via the Cabinet Secretary. He concluded:

We have no reason to suppose that Mr Profumo stands in need of further advice about security. There is no truth in the story that the Security Service was informed of the dates of, or anything else in connection with, Mr Profumo's alleged visits to Ward or to Miss Keeler.

The Prime Minister relayed this to Wilson, but he and Wigg were still not satisfied. Ward was becoming increasingly anxious about police investigations and tried to avoid prosecution by blackmailing the government. On 7 May he telephoned Timothy Bligh at Downing Street and made an appointment to see him later the same day. Bligh took the precaution of ringing MI5 and had an officer sitting in on the meeting, yet in spite of his presence Ward threatened to expose Profumo's lie unless the police dropped their case.

On 27 May Wilson said he would raise the matter in Parliament unless further action was taken over the links made by the Russian diplomat; reluctantly the Prime Minister again referred the case to Hollis. Two days later, for the first time, Hollis outlined the security angle to Macmillan. He explained that, although Ward had allegedly asked Keeler to obtain the date that atomic secrets would be given to the West Germans, Keeler denied ever asking Profumo, so in that respect there was no security threat. There was, he conceded, a possible case against Ward for asking Keeler, but the Security Service felt that such a prosecution would fail. In any case, Ivanov had left the country and Ward had made no attempt to contact any other Russians. 'The security risk that Ward now represents seems to me to be slight,' he said.

Macmillan accepted the Director-General's view, but arranged for Lord Dilhorne, the Lord Chancellor, to review the MI5 and police files of the case. By the time Dilhorne had completed his task, on 13 June, Profumo had resigned.

Profumo resigned from Parliament on 4 June and a public announcement was made the following day. The Opposition seized on the issue and demanded an enquiry, in spite of the Prime Minister's assurances that there were no security aspects involved. In the face of mounting pressure Macmillan consented to an enquiry and appointed Lord Denning to head it. He took evidence from 160 witnesses, including Hollis, Mitchell and several 'D' Branch personnel. On one occasion he even visited Leconfield House and observed a D1 surveillance operation on a Soviet diplomat in progress.

The final result was the *Denning Report*,* which, among other things, concluded that there had been no security lapse in Profumo's relationship with Christine Keeler. Fortunately for MI5 the entrapment planned for Ivanov was never disclosed. In the meantime Ward had been convicted on a charge of living off immoral earnings. At his well publicized trial

* HMSO, 1963.

Ward had been cross-examined by his Defence Counsel, James Burge, about his contacts with 'the secret service'. Much to MI5's embarrassment Ward named his case officer as 'Mr Woods of Room 393 at the War Office'. Luckily he had never discovered Woods's real name. Ward took an overdose of Nembutal on 3 August 1963.

It has been suggested that the Director-General's behaviour during this entire episode, from June 1961 to May 1963, was in some way unreasonable and supported the contention that he might have been a Soviet agent. This proposition is dealt with further in Chapter 10, but Lord Denning analysed every move made by Hollis during this period and he summed up MI5's role thus:

I find that they covered the security interest fully throughout and reported to those concerned. Their principal interest was in Captain Ivanov, the Russian Intelligence Officer: and secondarily in Stephen Ward, as a close friend of his. They took all reasonable steps to see that the interests of the country were defended. In particular they saw that Mr Profumo and another Minister were warned of Ward. They kept the Foreign Office fully informed. There is no reason to believe that there was any security leakage whatever.

7

BETRAYAL

'Any intelligence officer who assumes his service
is penetration-proof is ignorant of intelligence
history.'

WILLIAM HOOD, senior CIA counter-intelligence
officer before the sacking of Jim Angleton in
December 1974. Hood resigned at the same
time.

The Profumo affair was to have the gravest political consequences for
the Macmillan administration. At the general election held the following
year, 1964, the Opposition Labour Party were returned with the slimmest
of majorities ... just four seats. Macmillan himself was constantly
lampooned as 'the man who was never told anything'. The publication
of the *Denning Report* effectively cleared the Security Service of any
wrong-doing, although this was by no means the end of the matter for
MI5.

One of KAGO's most constant assertions had been the idea that his
defection would be viewed with such disquiet in Moscow that extreme
counter-measures would be taken to discredit him. At first his CIA
debriefers dismissed this claim as yet another example of his self-aggran-
dizement, but within six months KAGO's predictions began to take
place.

KAGO's principal message to the West related to the KGB's mastery
of disinformation. According to him, everything Moscow did or said
was carefully calculated and therefore all possible Soviet motives should
be examined with equal care before taking anything at face value.
KAGO predicted that his former employers would try and muddy the
already somewhat confused waters in the West by offering further 'defectors'. This is indeed exactly what happened.

Within weeks of KAGO arriving in the United States two Soviet sources had volunteered their services to the FBI in New York. Both worked under diplomatic cover at the UN and were code-named BOURBON and SCOTCH respectively by the CIA and FEDORA and TOP HAT by the FBI. One claimed to be a GRU officer, the other a KGB officer. Neither began undermining KAGO immediately, but instead supported the credentials of a third Soviet source, a KGB Lieutenant-Colonel named Yuri Ivanovich Nosenko, and cast a curious light on the Profumo affair.

BOURBON and SCOTCH both made claims concerning Ivanov's uncertain role in the affair. The principal allegation, from BOURBON, suggested that Ivanov had used Christine Keeler in a plot to extract atomic secrets from the War Minister and had wired her bedroom in Stephen Ward's flat for sound. The pillow talk had yielded valuable secrets which Ivanov had then boasted about to BOURBON. The Director of the FBI took the story so seriously that he had the details delivered by courier to the President, by-passing the usual channels. MI5 were able to establish that Ivanov could not possibly have done this.

When this news was received by the FBI in Washington it caused something of a stir. Had BOURBON lied? There were the usual two options available to the case officers: if BOURBON was a disinforma-tion agent, as KAGO had predicted, why had he given away so much good intelligence, such as the final clues to Vassall's identity more than a year earlier? Was this a case of the KGB deliberately discarding agents whom they believed to be beyond saving? Or had Ivanov become rather bumptious through drink and over-stated his part in the Profumo affair. BOURBON's other contention, that the French SDECE had played a sinister role in the matter, was mere speculation.

In the absence of any conclusive evidence the FBI continued to run BOURBON, living proof that intelligence bureaucrats are always reluc-tant to admit that their star agent may be a plant by the opposition. However, later information from this pair of UN double agents served to illuminate their possible motives.

On 3 June 1962 Lieutenant-Colonel Yuri Nosenko approached the CIA in Geneva, where he was attached as a security officer to the Soviet disarmament delegation, and offered to spy for them. The CIA case officer assigned to Nosenko was Peter Bagley, who was based at the CIA Station in Berne. He met Nosenko and, satisfied that he was not an *agent provocateur*, arranged a further secret meeting at which George Kisvalter (who had specially flown over from the United States) made the CIA's standard offer: if Nosenko returned to his job and acted as an agent in place, the CIA would extract him and his family when the right time came and give them a pension for life. Nosenko, now code-named AE/ FOXTROT, agreed to the deal and returned to Moscow. Meanwhile, he left his two American contacts two items of information as proof of

1 *Above left:* Sir David Petrie, the wartime Director-General of the Security Service. His evidence to Sir Findlater Stewart's committee in 1945 formed the basis of MI5's post-war structure.

2 *Above right:* Captain Guy Liddell MC. In 1952, exasperated by Sir Percy Sillitoe and embarrassed by the defections of Burgess and Maclean, he retired as Deputy D-G of the Security Service. He was then appointed the Atomic Energy Authority's Security Adviser.

3 Klaus Fuchs, the atom bomb spy. MI5 identified him from intercepted Soviet signals, but were obliged to play out an elaborate charade to protect their source. The ruse worked. The intercept programme, which had begun in Australia in 1944 (code-named U-TRAFFIC by MI5), continued to decrypt Soviet messages and eventually led MI5 to Donald Maclean.

4 Jim Skardon (left) and Henry Arnold during Klaus Fuchs's trial. A former Metropolitan Police detective, Skardon became MI5's resident interrogator and was then promoted head of the watcher service. Arnold had been appointed Security Officer at Harwell after wartime service in MI5. Both men persuaded Fuchs that he had volunteered a confession. In fact they had learned of Fuchs's guilt from Soviet signals decrypted by Government Communications Headquarters.

5 A unique newspaper story. The *Daily Express* (11 June 1951) catch the Director-General and Arthur Martin flying to Washington to explain why the Security Service failed to catch Burgess and Maclean. In Sillitoe's bag are the 'sanitized' files which had been altered to cover-up MI5's blunder. The FBI were not impressed.

6 The KGB in action. Karpinsky and Zharkov hustle Mrs Petrov aboard an aeroplane bound for the Soviet Union after the defection of her husband. The plane made a refuelling stop in Darwin and, with ASIO's help, she evaded her escorts and escaped.

7 Conon Molody, alias Gordon Lonsdale, the only Soviet 'illegal' caught by MI5. Evidence from an East German defector in June 1961 made 'D' Branch reassess their coup. According to him, Molody had been sacrificed to preserve a more important spy.

8 George Blake, the MI6 officer whose attempt to telephone his Soviet contact during a lunch-time break in his interrogation gave MI6 the ammunition needed to obtain a confession. After his conviction Blake was thoroughly debriefed, but once this had been completed the Home Office refused MI5's requests to transfer him from the Scrubs to a more secure prison.

9 John Vassall in his Dolphin Square flat. The MI5 watchers failed to find any evidence against Vassall even though they had established an observation post next door. Eventually the Director-General, Sir Roger Hollis, authorized a search. Rolls of film were discovered concealed in a specially constructed bookcase and Special Branch were alerted to make the arrest. Vassall surrendered his flat keys and was later astonished at the speed with which the police search uncovered his ingenious hiding-place.

10 Colonel Oleg Penkovsky (right), the senior GRU officer who spied for MI6 and the CIA, at his trial in Moscow with Greville Wynne. His identification of the Soviet Assistant Naval Attaché in London as a GRU colleague caused MI5 to launch a 'honey-trap' operation. The trap failed when the Secretary of State for War, John Profumo, became unwittingly involved.

11 Chief Technician Douglas Britten, the RAF Signals Intelligence expert who spied for Russia for six years from 1962. At the time of his arrest he was serving in a highly sensitive 'Sigint' post at RAF Digby in Lincolnshire.

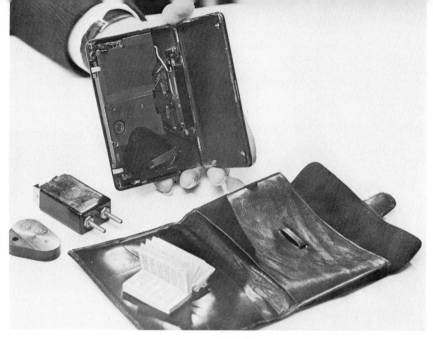

12 The Soviet spy camera disguised as a wallet that the KGB supplied to Chief Technician Douglas Britten. He used it to photograph secrets at RAF Digby. The edge of the 'wallet' was simply rolled against a document to expose the film.

13 and 14 Stephen Ward (left) and Captain Eugene Ivanov. Ward was recruited by 'D' Branch of MI5 to help blackmail the Soviet Assistant Naval Attaché. The 'honey-trap' failed and Ivanov returned to Moscow. When Ward was prosecuted for living off immoral earnings, he identified his MI5 case officer as 'Mr Woods of the War Office'. Fortunately for MI5, Ward had never learned 'Mr Woods' real name. Ward was convicted at the Old Bailey, but died of a drugs overdose before he could be sentenced.

15 *Above left:* Frank Bossard, the Ministry of Aviation official from the Guided Weapons Research and Development Division, who was caught red-handed photographing classified documents in his lunch-break. Over a period of four years he sold secrets to the Soviets for £5,000. Bossard's arrest caused a major review of Positive Vetting procedures, for he had been fully cleared for access to secrets even after he had been caught lying about his criminal background.

16 *Above right:* Joseph Frolik, the Czech intelligence officer who defected to the CIA in July 1969. When he arrived in America he named three British Labour MPs as spies and identified Nicholas Prager as the source of his V-Bomber information. He was flown to England to be debriefed by MI5's Soviet Satellites section. One of his first interviews with MI5 took place at a picnic near Marlborough in Wiltshire.

17 Sir Roger Hollis, Director-General of the Security Service from 1956 to 1965.

18 Oleg Lyalin, the Soviet trade official (and KGB officer) whose affair with his secretary caused him to spy for MI5. A drunk-driving incident in London in August 1971 led to his premature defection. He subsequently named several of his agents who were promptly arrested and prosecuted.

19 David Bingham, the Royal Navy officer who volunteered a confession to the Director of Naval Security soon after the defection of Oleg Lyalin in 1971. He was sentenced to twenty-one years' imprisonment in March 1972.

20 Sir Martin Furnival Jones, the Director-General of the Security Service from 1965–72. He inherited an organization paralysed by the fear of a Soviet mole. In October 1981 he and his former Deputy D-G, Anthony Simkins, wrote to *The Times* to state their belief in the innocence of his predecessor, Sir Roger Hollis.

his goodwill. The KGB, he claimed, had concealed dozens of micro-phones behind the central-heating radiators and in the walls of the US Embassy in Moscow. He also confirmed that there was a Soviet spy in the British Admiralty. He added the clue that the spy was a homosexual. It was this extra nudge that enabled MI5 to narrow the field of the investigation, initiated by KAGO, which led to Vassall.

AE/FOXTROT also stated that he was Deputy Chief of Department VII, the KGB section which undertook surveillance of foreigners in Moscow. One of his conditions of returning to Moscow was that he should not be contacted there by any of the local CIA Station's staff, or anyone else for that matter. He remarked that he knew only too well how efficient the KGB watchers were in the capital.

His relatively senior rank had apparently enabled him to learn of Vassall's recruitment and he threw some interesting new light on the continuing mystery of Popov's arrest. He stated that Popov had not been betrayed by either the FBI's heavy-handed operation in New York or by George Blake in Berlin. According to his version Popov had been caught after a CIA officer under routine surveillance had been spotted preparing a dead-letter drop. The KGB watchers had simply waited to see who turned up to empty the cache.

This explanation was studied carefully in Washington and appeared, on the face of it, to be genuine. Vassall was arrested in September and MI5 expressed their thanks for the second tip which had made their identification task easier. One person, however, had severe reservations about AE/FOXTROT.

Jim Angleton (who was KAGO's principal supporter in the CIA) analysed the AE/FOXTROT report and found it to be diametrically opposed to everything KAGO had reported. For example, KAGO had confirmed the existence of a well-placed mole in the CIA, code-named SASHA. Although he could not directly identify SASHA, he had offered several clues, one of which was the fact that this man's case officer, Viktor Kovshuk, had flown to Washington to meet him in 1957. Accord-ing to AE/FOXTROT, Kovshuk's mission had been to meet a low-grade military source code-named ANDREY. This reassuring news, combined with AE/FOXTROT's other 'discards', convinced Angleton that the so-called defector was merely one of the KGB plants that KAGO had predicted. After all, he argued, MI5 would have found Vassall sooner or later and the microphones in the Moscow Embassy had already been mentioned by KAGO and would have been spotted eventually by electronic counter-measures. His explanation of Popov's arrest was also suspicious because when his case officer, Russell Langrelle, had seen him at their last meeting Popov had indicated that he was operating under the KGB's control. Now it seemed that Popov had in fact been a free agent prior to his arrest. Could this be the KGB wishing to confirm the validity of Popov's controlled information?

When Angleton was sure AE/FOXTROT was a plant, he gave his KAGO file to Bagley to read. This was a daring step for Angleton to take because his prime concern was to isolate the elusive SASHA and he hesitated before letting any of his colleagues in on the secret. The case of his MI6 friend Philby had taught him the bitter lesson of trusting no one. At first Bagley defended his source, but he soon came to agree with the wily counter-intelligence chief. On 19 December Bagley issued a twelve-page summary which recommended that AE/FOXTROT in future be regarded as an opposition plant.

The case rested there until 20 January 1964 when AE/FOXTROT turned up again in Geneva with another disarmament delegation. He telephoned the emergency number that Bagley had originally given him and this summons promptly brought back Bagley and Kisvalter to Switzerland. All three met on 23 January and AE/FOXTROT began to impart details of Lee Harvey Oswald's KGB file.

This remarkable turn of events took the two CIA officers completely by surprise. AE/FOXTROT claimed that he had supervised Oswald's case when he had defected to Russia in October 1959 and had also reviewed the case after President Kennedy's assassination the previous November. Apparently the KGB had been concerned at a possible connection between the KGB and the suspected gunman and had ordered an enquiry. The conclusion, alleged AE/FOXTROT, was that Oswald was completely unreliable and had certainly not been recruited as an agent. No, he insisted, Oswald had never been debriefed on his Air Force work at a U-2 base in Japan and no, the KGB had absolutely no involvement with the President's death.

What made AE/FOXTROT's testimony so fascinating to the CIA was the obvious deduction that if he was a KGB plant, briefed to deny a KGB/Oswald connection, then there must indeed have been one. Bagley's orders to treat AE/FOXTROT as a hostile agent were quickly reversed and he was encouraged to defect, if only so that he could appear before the Warren Commission. This, it seemed, was AE/FOXTROT's intention too. He took up the CIA's offer of a $25,000 a year consultancy contract and a cash payment of $50,000, with an added bonus of $10,000 for having helped MI5 to identify Vassall. At a second meeting, held on 3 February 1964, he announced that he wished to start a new life without his family. He also claimed that he had come under suspicion. The previous day he had received a cable ordering him to return to Moscow.

Instead of catching the next day's Aeroflot flight to Moscow from Geneva, AE/FOXTROT donned an American Army uniform and was driven in a military vehicle to Camp King, the CIA's defector receiving station a few kilometres north of Frankfurt. He remained in this secure but inhospitable location (it had previously been used to isolate suspected war criminals) until 11 February when he was flown to the United States. He was to face more than three years of intensive debriefing. At first his memory of the KGB's Moscow surveillance files paid useful dividends. He confirmed KAGO's story that Ambassador John Watkins, a retired Canadian diplomat, had been blackmailed after a classic homosexual entrapment in Moscow.

The Royal Canadian Mounted Police's Security Service passed the allegation to their 'B Operations' section, then headed by Leslie (Jim) Bennett, a former Government Communications Headquarters' wireless operator who had emigrated to Canada after the war. Bennett duly confronted Watkins with the allegation and obtained a statement from Watkins in which he admitted having been in contact with the KGB. Nevertheless, he denied having acted as an agent; he died of a coronary before the interrogation could be intensified.

Another of AE/FOXTROT's leads resulted in the arrest in Nevada of Robert Johnson, a US Army sergeant who had tried to defect to East Berlin in 1953. The KGB had persuaded him to return to his post and nine years later their patience was rewarded. In March 1961 Johnson was transferred to the highly secret Armed Forces Courier Station at Orly Airport in France. This closely guarded bunker housed all American classified material in transit between NATO headquarters in Europe and the Pentagon. Johnson had managed to foil all the sophisticated security which surrounded the main vault and, by volunteering for an unpopular weekend guard duty, had obtained an impression of one of the keys to the top security area. His KGB case officer in Paris, Feliks Ivanov, then arranged for a technical team to be flown in from Moscow to deal with the one remaining combination lock. According to AE/FOXTROT the KGB team had specially developed a portable X-ray machine to learn the combination. The device had proved so powerful that all the members of the original research group had suffered a massive dose of radiation and had lost all their teeth. Whether this part was true or not, Johnson had successfully obtained access to the main safe seven times between December 1962 and March 1963 and photographed every document inside. In May 1964 he was transferred to the Pentagon to be near his wife, who was receiving psychiatric treatment in Washington. Six months later he was listed as a deserter after continued marital problems. He gave himself up and confessed on 24 November 1964 in Reno, Nevada, and was subsequently sentenced to twenty-five years' imprisonment.

When AE/FOXTROT's interrogation turned to the thorny subject of ANDREY, the results were less satisfactory. ANDREY was said to have been recruited in Moscow when working as a motor mechanic in the American Embassy. This was passed on to the FBI, who identified an Army sergeant, Roy Rhodes, as ANDREY. Sergeant Rhodes agreed he had met Kovshuk in 1957, but Angleton simply could not believe that such a high-grade KGB officer as Kovshuk would have travelled all the way to the States to meet someone who did not even have access to classified information. Angleton interpreted the meeting as a convenient cover for a rendezvous with SASHA and began a massive investigation to find his mole in the CIA.

At about this moment KAGO recalled some extra details of SASHA's case, which led the CIA to re-examine one of Bill Harvey's own agents in Berlin. The suspect was Igor Orlov, a Russian-born CIA agent whose real name was Alexander Kopazky. Everything about Orlov's background fitted into KAGO's profile of SASHA: the CIA had suffered losses whenever Orlov was posted to a new out-station in Germany; the FBI had photographed him visiting the Russian Embassy in Washington; incredibly, in his youth he had been nicknamed Sasha. One further parallel was also found in the original KAGO report: KAGO had mentioned that SASHA's true name began with the letter 'K'. On Orlov's CIA file was a request from his wife, Mrs Ellie Orlov, that her husband always be assigned a cover-name beginning with 'K' because they owned so many monogrammed wedding presents.

Orlov and his family had been brought to the United States in January 1961 after a disagreement over money with a senior CIA officer in Germany. They had enjoyed a brief stay at Ashford Farm and had then been told that there would be no further CIA employment. Instead Orlov had moved to Alexandria, Virginia, and opened a picture-framing business. Orlov was by far the best candidate for SASHA, so Bruce Solie of the CIA's Office of Security and Bert Turner of the FBI conducted a thorough investigation. However, Orlov refused to admit he was SASHA, in spite of six weeks' voluntary interrogation. In the spring of 1965 they pretended to abandon the case, but kept covert surveillance on him and his family in the hope that he might betray himself and possibly lead his watchers to another mole in the CIA.

AE/FOXTROT's role in the SASHA affair remained uncertain, but Angleton was convinced it was more evidence of his duplicity. His talk of the innocuous ANDREY had diverted attention away from SASHA. There were further flaws in his case. Under questioning he admitted that he had inflated his KGB rank and he was really only a Captain. When confronted with the fact that the NSA had analysed all the Geneva–Moscow cipher traffic for 3 February 1964 and had been unable to trace the recall cable, AE/FOXTROT confessed that he had made that up too, so as to impress Bagley and Kisvalter.

By December 1964, after several lie-detector failures, AE/FOXTROT's interrogation became extremely hostile and he was confined to a cell. Even his successes, which had initially won him some supporters in the CIA, were shown on examination to be rather less impressive and, in fact, possible discards. For example, John Watkins had left the Canadian Civil Service and had retired to Paris by the time the RCMP had caught up with him and it could be reasonably argued that the KGB had known KAGO had already identified him. In the case of Sergeant Johnson who had rifled the document bunker at Orly, there was evidence that the KGB believed Johnson had been discovered and 'turned'.

The KGB had good, but incorrect, reasons to suspect Johnson. On his seventh and last entry into the vault the routine had altered. Usually Johnson removed a handful of classified packets from the safe around midnight and handed them to his Soviet contact. The KGB officer then took them to his Embassy, had them photographed and returned them to Johnson at a prearranged rendezvous close to the bunker. On 21 April 1962 Johnson fell asleep after giving the papers to Ivanov and failed to turn up at the agreed meeting-place. As dawn approached Ivanov abandoned the rendezvous and drove straight to the bunker. There was still no sign of the American, so in desperation he threw the missing secrets into Johnson's car. When Johnson awoke he ran to his car in a panic, found the documents and managed to replace them in the safe just seconds before the relief guard appeared.

Ivanov naturally cross-examined his agent about the slip-up, but Johnson, reluctant to admit that he had fallen asleep, concocted an implausible tale about a surprise visit by an officer who had stayed in the vault until five in the morning. Ivanov knew that the story was a fabrication because of his close study of the procedures inside the bunker and concluded that Johnson had been 'turned'. Johnson's subsequent promotion and posting to Washington undoubtedly confirmed to the KGB that their source was blown. According to Angleton's theory the KGB had also decided to discard him through AE/FOXTROT and at least obtain some advantage from the situation.

Gradually a picture emerged of the ruling regime in the KGB dispatching a disinformation agent to the CIA with the dual aim of disowning Lee Harvey Oswald for the benefit of the Warren Commission and discrediting KAGO. AE/FOXTROT's timely arrival to give evidence about the suspected assassin was more than coincidental: it was ridiculous to believe that the KGB would ignore a defector who had recently been demobbed from the élite American Marine Corps. It was even more unthinkable when one considered the fact that Oswald had been trained as a radar technician and had served at an important U-2 base. Penkovsky had described how Gary Powers's U-2 had only been brought down in May 1960 after fourteen ground-to-air missiles had been fired. Having been made aware of their vulnerability to high altitude photo-reconnaissance, the Soviets were extremely anxious to learn more about the spy-plane which cruised at 70,000 feet.

By August 1966 AE/FOXTROT had become a severe embarrassment to the CIA's Soviet Russia Division. Two months after taking over the job of Director of Central Intelligence, Dick Helms gave the interrogators just sixty days to complete the case. To date the defector had been held in solitary confinement for nearly three and a half years and had experienced 292 days of increasingly hostile interrogation. Finally Bagley compiled a 900-page report itemizing AE/FOXTROT's contradictions. In all he pin-pointed twenty mistakes in his supposed KGB career and a further twenty areas where he had demonstrated ignorance of a subject he ought to have known about. For example, as the alleged second most senior KGB officer, with responsibility for watching and entrapping foreigners in Moscow, he had no idea of the floor-plan of the US Embassy or the secure offices which contained secret information. Such knowledge would have been basic training, if he was who he claimed he was. Indeed, he did not even appear to know where the staff canteen was located in the KGB's Dzerzinsky Square headquarters.

Bagley ended his report by repeating his belief that AE/FOXTROT was a complete fraud. Ironically, this conclusion was to place KAGO and a number of other defectors in an awkward position. KAGO had certainly denounced AE/FOXTROT as a disinformation agent, but he did concede, having listened to the tapes of his interrogation, that he was a genuine KGB officer. If AE/FOXTROT was a plant then what judgement should be made on the other Soviet sources, principally SCOTCH, who had all supported him and confirmed his bona fides? If SCOTCH was equally bogus, then the FBI had wasted more than six years of work and countless valuable man-hours. Worse still from MI5's point of view was the suspicion that Vassall had been a discard. Did this mean that AE/FOXTROT had decoyed 'D' Branch away from a more important Admiralty spy in the same way as he had drawn the SASHA investigators to ANDREY?

Incidentally, it is interesting to note that although initially SCOTCH (FEDORA to the FBI) went to considerable lengths to prevent his identity from becoming known, he is now believed to have been Viktor M. Lessiovski, the Personal Assistant to the Secretary-General of the United Nations, U Thant, between 1963 and 1966. He has now returned to Moscow and has ceased contact with the FBI. An FBI review of his case in 1980 concluded that he had been a KGB *agent provocateur*.

In the months before KAGO's arrival in England there had been several important new developments in the Philby case. Late in 1962 a former wartime MI5 officer discovered a significant new lead. He had been approached by a leading Zionist and senior Marks & Spencer executive,

Mrs Flora Solomon. Mrs Solomon had once employed Philby's second wife, Aileen, and it was she who had first introduced her to Philby. It seemed that before the war Philby had had occasion to confide in her and ask for her help. She had not come forward with the information because she had, of course, been unaware of the secret investigation and interrogation of her friend which had taken place in 1951. However, some of his recent pro-Nasser and anti-Zionist newspaper dispatches from Beirut had prompted her to denounce him as a KGB agent. The former MI5 officer immediately recognized the gravity of her evidence and introduced her to Dick White, the Chief of MI6. Mrs Solomon provided damning testimony against Philby and White decided that the evidence should be given to his former colleagues in MI5.

Accordingly Mrs Solomon was interviewed by Arthur Martin and he concluded that the case against Philby was now undeniable. The remaining problem was how to lure Philby back to London or extract a confession from him abroad. The matter was discussed by just a handful of officers: Hollis, Mitchell, the Director 'D' and two members of the D1 section. It was agreed that Martin should proceed to Beirut and offer Philby a formal immunity from prosecution in return for a complete confession. At the last moment White intervened and stated that it would be more appropriate if the case was handled by an SIS officer, and Nicholas Elliott, an old friend of Philby's, volunteered for the job. Elliott was duly dispatched to the Lebanon shortly before Christmas 1962.

Elliott's meeting with Philby appeared to go according to plan. Philby admitted espionage for the Russians and seemed to be anxious to take up the offer of immunity. He also begged Elliott to break the news to his American third wife, Eleanor. Elliott first went to the British Embassy and announced himself to Peter Lunn, who had succeeded him as the MI6 Head of Station in Beirut. Using Lunn's facilities he enciphered a telegram to London informing White of his success. He then returned as agreed to Philby's flat where Elliott found Philby dead drunk. Elliott then described to Eleanor his conversation earlier in the day with her husband. Elliott had one further meeting with Philby and then returned to London. On the evening of 23 January 1963 Philby vanished.

Philby's extraordinary volte-face served only to heighten MI5's suspicions of his somewhat limited 'confession' of the previous month. Indeed, Elliott was certain Philby was expecting him and had prepared his confession in advance. If his sudden departure from Beirut had been executed under KGB control, as seemed increasingly likely, then it followed that Philby's confession might also have been controlled. This view was reinforced when it was learned that Philby's Soviet case officer, Yuri Modin, had paid a surprise visit to Beirut shortly before Elliott's arrival. The inevitable conclusion was that there were others of the Soviet network left intact who had told the Russians of Philby's impending interrogation. No doubt Modin had tried to persuade the increasingly drunken Philby to defect, thus safeguarding other still unsuspected members of the ring.

The net result of this episode was a remarkable mole-hunt within MI5. The Philby confession fitted dramatically into a much larger jigsaw. The other pieces included all of MI5's post-war failures: the escape of Burgess and Maclean; the Cairncross trap; the Prybl trap; the escape of Vassall's case officer; the possibility that Lonsdale had been a decoy; the ineffective double agents run by 'D' Branch; the lack of defectors in London. All could be interpreted as clues to the existence of a Soviet source at a high level inside MI5. The fact that apparently only five MI5 officers had actually known that Philby would be confronted with new evidence seemed to be the best clue because it was then possible to identify and limit the field of suspects; they were: Roger Hollis (the Director-General), Graham Mitchell (the Deputy D-G), Malcolm Cumming (Director of 'D' Branch), Arthur Martin (D1) and his secretary. Martin calculated that he could narrow the field down further to Hollis and Mitchell. He discussed the matter privately with the Director 'C', Martin Furnival Jones, and then made an appointment to see Dick White, the MI6 Chief.

White took Martin's startling conclusion very seriously and, after twenty-four hours of deliberation, telephoned Martin to say that in his view Mitchell should be investigated. He also said that Hollis should be informed, although they ought to conceal the fact that Martin had consulted White. Martin agreed and immediately arranged to see Hollis later that same afternoon. Just before lunchtime KAGO, who was by now settled in London, telephoned Martin with some minor crisis. Martin was obliged to leave Leconfield House and cancel his meeting with the Director-General.

Martin returned to Curzon Street shortly before six in the evening, having dealt with KAGO's crisis. Although few staff were left in the building he found Hollis dictating to his secretary, Valerie Hammond. For almost half an hour Martin described his suspicion that the Security Service was penetrated. His central theme was that he could no longer be held responsible for KAGO's safety if there was indeed a Soviet spy inside MI5. The Director-General looked thoughtful, made no effort to defend the chief suspect, Graham Mitchell, and invited Martin to dinner at the Travellers' Club.

The dinner was taken up with inconsequential small-talk, at the end of which Hollis announced that he would think the matter over and then let Martin know his opinion.

Five days later Hollis held a secret council of war at his home in Campden Hill Square with Arthur Martin and Martin Furnival Jones. The three men went over the evidence again and decided to embark on a detailed D1 investigation of the Deputy D-G with Martin reporting his progress to Furnival Jones. The subject would be code-named PETERS. There was, however, one grave drawback to the operation: Mitchell had apparently grown weary of his job and had already sought permission to retire three years early. Hollis had agreed to him leaving on 6 September 1963 and Mitchell had accepted the consequent reduction in his pension. The overall effect of this early departure would be to give less than five months to prove a case against him, if indeed there was one.

The evidence pointing to Mitchell was entirely circumstantial, but it did have the appearance of giving a profile which did not exclude the possibility of him being a Soviet agent. He had been educated at Winchester and Magdalen College, Oxford, and played chess to an international standard. He had worked for a while for the *Illustrated London News*, had then joined the Security Service in 1939 aged thirty-four, having got married in 1934. He lived close to Chobham Common with his wife, son and daughter and commuted into the office each day by train. A former member of the Conservative Party's research department, his politics were generally Conservative although he had established something of a reputation at Blenheim during the war for being slightly 'pink'. All his wartime service in MI5 had been in 'F' Division, where he had taken responsibility for dealing with the political parties of the extreme Right. Apart from chess, his main recreation was yacht racing on the Solent. He was an active member of the Bembridge Sailing Club, a club which was once thought to be rather grander than that most élite of all clubs, the Royal Yacht Squadron in Cowes.

During the Burgess and Maclean crisis of 1951, Mitchell had defended Philby (as had several others) and actually prepared the Prime Minister's brief on the case before his reply to Marcus Lipton in the House of Commons in October 1955. His office relations were not entirely without blemish. A former wartime 'F' Division colleague denounced him bitterly when approached on the subject and his former secretary had resigned without giving a reason. She was traced without difficulty (she still visited the office on Armistice Day to sell poppies). Reluctantly she gave her reason for leaving: Bruno Pontecorvo's personal file had passed over Mitchell's desk and he had made an entry that a certain action had been taken. His secretary knew he could not have done this without her knowing and decided to leave the office rather than cause a row. Pontecorvo had been a colleague of Fuchs at Harwell and had defected to Russia in October 1950. He was a naturalized British subject and had in fact arranged to leave Harwell and take up an academic post in Liverpool. Virtually every member of his family in England and in Italy had Communist Party connections and Wing-Commander Arnold had already tackled Pontecorvo over his apparent omission of this detail on the standard Atomic Energy questionnaire he had completed when he first joined the Harwell staff in January 1949.

In 1957 a F1(a) officer had quarrelled with Mitchell on some unknown subject and had resigned from the office. Whilst none of these items added up to anything approaching espionage, they provided the investigation with plenty to work on. After a month of discreet background enquiries the D1 reported to Furnival Jones that there was some evidence of suspicious behaviour and Hollis authorized the indoctrination of a second officer from F1(a). He was joined by a small team of specially recruited 'amateur' watchers. Each day Mitchell was trailed to and from Waterloo Station and his every move recorded.

By the middle of June 1963 the investigation had hardly progressed and Martin asked Furnival Jones for a telephone tap on Mitchell's home line. The request was passed on to Hollis, who was in the midst of the Profumo affair. He turned the idea down flat with the comment that he was in no position to tell the Secretary of State that his own Deputy D-G might be a Soviet agent. This refusal came as a severe blow to the PETERS investigators and they turned to the MI6 Chief for help. White agreed to remonstrate with Hollis and, in due course, the Prime Minister authorized what are described as 'technical facilities'. In practice this involved Peter W., MI5's scientific adviser from 'A' Branch, rigging up a closed-circuit camera over the door of Mitchell's office. Nearby the investigators took turns to monitor the television screen. (At that time MI5 did not possess any videotape recorders.) In the same month the Director-General allowed one further officer to be let in on the PETERS secret. He was Malcolm Cumming, the Director 'D', who was understandably astonished to learn of the operation being carried out under his very nose. At his request a further case officer was indoctrinated for liaison purposes.

In mid-August there was a review of the progress to date. Mitchell was evidently deeply troubled about something because when alone he looked utterly miserable and frequently had his face completely hidden in his hands. On one occasion there was a dramatic example of his terrible desperation. He looked up at the communicating door into the Director-General's office with a deathly look on his face and was heard to groan, 'Why are you doing this to me?'

There were two specific incidents which helped convince the watchers of the gravity of the situation. The first was the discovery of a hand-drawn sketch-map made and discarded by Mitchell shortly before he went to catch his train at Waterloo. The remains of the map were recovered from his waste-paper basket and reconstructed. It was marked 'RV', possibly indicating a rendezvous, and was found to be a reproduction of all the various paths criss-crossing Chobham Common, close to Mitchell's home. The KGB frequently give their agents such maps to

guide them to meetings with their case officers. The watchers staked out
the area, but no covert meeting was ever spotted. Although the map
itself was perhaps not vital, the D1 staff felt that Mitchell had chosen a
strange time to prepare it, within minutes of leaving the office.

The second incident, or series of incidents, concerned Mitchell's behaviour to and from work. He sometimes took his car out having only
just arrived home and appeared to drive around aimlessly. Sometimes he
would simply sit staring straight ahead of him. He also aroused suspicion
by taking evading action on his way to the train in the evenings. His
actions were designed to detect the presence of watchers.

There was also a second, rather more subtle part to the PETERS
operation. It depended on a number of identifiable pieces of bogus
intelligence, notionally from KAGO, being fed to Mitchell with the
object of seeing whether they reached the Soviets. Government Communications Headquarters were monitoring all the wireless traffic from
the Russian Embassy and were instructed to keep a special eye on
material that related to the defector. The information given to Mitchell
was monitored in much the same way that physicians follow the progress
of barium meals. No positive result was achieved with the scheme
although some thought it strange that Mitchell had not used the material
as an argument against KAGO, given his recognized opposition to
him.

All involved in the PETERS operation finally agreed in August
that there was insufficient evidence to justify an interrogation, but the
overall handling of the operation had caused great disquiet.
The Director-General, therefore, ordered a full written report on the
PETERS affair and the chosen author was the D1. He concluded that
Hollis and Mitchell were really the only two people with the right
access.

The D1's report was submitted to the Director-General of MI5 and to
the Chief of MI6 for approval and both initialled the document.

Eventually the day came when Mitchell left Curzon Street for the last
time. He left a deeply divided office. Some of the Directors were angry at
having been misled about the PETERS affair (a degree of deception had
been inevitable with such a highly placed suspect), whilst others concluded that if Mitchell was clean, then Hollis remained the only likely
suspect. In any event Hollis flew to Washington in September 1963 to
tell McCone and Hoover of the affair and to warn them of the American
agents that might have been compromised. The implications were considerable for all the CIA sources known to MI5 had continued to
function without apparent interruption. Should they all be regarded as
hostile double agents?

The prospect of re-evaluating each and every CIA source that had been known to MI5 during the period before the PETERS enquiry was a difficult pill for the Americans to swallow, but they had to accept it. Events during 1963 had convinced most of the remaining doubters that the British intelligence structure was riddled with KGB informers. The CIA's counter-intelligence staff were among the foremost in this opinion and they had good reason for holding it. In any event KAGO was sure, and he thought he had first-hand knowledge. In the middle of July KAGO suddenly returned to the United States.

On 11 July 1963 the Legal Adviser, Bernard Hill, had received a disturbing telephone call from Colonel Sammy Lohan. Lohan was Admiral Thomson's successor as Secretary of the 'D' Notice Committee and, as such, acted as the official link between MI5 and Fleet Street. He had informed Hill that the *Daily Telegraph* was proposing to publish a story concerning a recent defector from the KGB whom they believed to be in the country. The story was all the more remarkable because only a tiny number of people knew of KAGO's arrival in England. Inside MI5 a body of opinion suggested the source was the *Telegraph*'s editor, Colin Coote, who happened to be a golfing friend of the Director-General's. MI5's first priority was KAGO's safety and opinions divided about the advisability of issuing a 'D' Notice. The problem was made more awkward by the absence of Hollis, who was attending a regular meeting with Sir Bernard Burrows, the Chairman of the Joint Intelligence Committee, and was therefore unavailable. If a 'D' Notice was to be issued it had to reach all the newspaper editors by midday, so Graham Mitchell called all the indoctrinated KAGO officers together to discuss the matter. After a short debate it was decided that MI5 had little to lose by issuing a Notice and the D1 was told to prepare a draft for the Legal Adviser.

MI5 had no way of knowing the quality of the newspaper's information and so bureaucratically followed the rules and included KAGO's real name. However, entirely by mistake, Arthur Martin got KAGO's name wrong in the draft. Like all the indoctrinated staff Martin had always referred to him by his MI5 code-name KAGO or his CIA acronym, AE/LADLE. He had, of course, met Golytsin several times by this date, which probably lulled him into thinking he did not have to look up KAGO's name in the relevant 'Held' personal file. In any event, when he presented the draft to Hill, Golytsin's name had been corrupted to Dolnytsin. Hill duly completed the draft and failed to correct Martin's error because he had never heard of the case anyway. Hill then sent the final 'D' Notice version to Lohan who distributed it around the Fleet Street editors ... over the Press Association's newsprinter. This in effect 'blew' an exclusive *Telegraph* scoop to every other journalist in Fleet Street. The *Telegraph* were understandably furious.

They were so angry that they decided to print their story regardless and told Lohan of their determination. MI5 were appalled, and when Hollis returned to the office he flew into a rage. This rage was not helped by the D1's announcement that he could no longer be held responsible for KAGO's safety in the UK. Hollis therefore authorized him to warn KAGO. This proved to be rather easier said than done for KAGO and his family were still moving around the countryside from hotel to hotel. Fortunately, Martin recalled that in a rare slip KAGO had mentioned the previous day that he was calling from Winchester, so the D1 promptly drove down and began checking every hotel and guest house in the town. When he eventually found the defector, KAGO took the news quite calmly but assumed that the story had been planted by the KGB in an attempt to identify him. The D1 could not deny the possibility in the absence of any other explanation and he was therefore obliged to stand and watch while KAGO, his wife and two daughters packed up and reserved four seats on a flight to New York that very night.

The following day, 12 June, with KAGO safely back in America, the story appeared on page one under the by-line of John Bulloch, the *Telegraph*'s Diplomatic Correspondent. Headlined 'SOVIET SPY GETS BRITISH ASYLUM', the article described how 'the Russian was sent to Britain in an ordinary commercial flight, escorted by CIA officers'. This, of course, was far from the truth and Bulloch avoided actually naming the defector. Nevertheless, his ultimate paragraph made it clear to those in the know in MI5 that he was talking about KAGO. He finally commented: 'Not since Gouzenko, the Russian cipher clerk, walked out of his embassy in Canada with details of the Russian organization there, has the West received such a windfall.'

Martin was summoned to an interview with the Director-General. By this time both had discovered that Golytsin's name on the 'D' Notice was mis-spelled. The D1 expected to be carpeted, but instead Hollis warmly congratulated him. The Security Service had gained a small advantage and in future journalists would be misled into relying on the official, erroneous version of Dolnytsin. This indeed is exactly what was to happen. Hollis was hugely amused and several writers were later completely duped, albeit unintentionally.

The question remaining was: who tipped off the *Telegraph*? As usual the 'No Contact' rule on journalists applied and no enquiries were made. Bulloch himself was well known to MI5 because of his account of Lonsdale's Portland network in *Spy Ring** and an experience he had had the previous year. Lady Kell, the widow of the first Director-General, had collaborated with Bulloch to produce a book about MI5. In fact she had written her own account of her husband's life, entitled *A Well Kept Secret*, and her son John had tried unsuccessfully to find a publisher. She believed, with some justification, that her late husband had been shabbily

* Secker & Warburg, 1961.

treated by Churchill and wished to set on record his achievements. When Bulloch approached her for help with his own book, she willingly gave it. The Security Service only learned of Bulloch's book whilst it was at his publishers. A copy of the typescript was demanded (through the 'D' Notice office) and numerous deletions requested. The alterations centred on the early months of the war years and were based on Lady Kell's recollection of the office at that time. The publishers, Arthur Barker, refused to make the changes. Finally Bulloch had been summoned to a meeting with Henry Brooke, the Home Secretary, who successfully appealed to the author's patriotism. Nine pages of the first edition were reprinted and rebound with the extra costs being born by MI5.*

In fact the CIA had been responsible for leaking Golytsin's existence in an effort to coerce their defector to return home. They certainly appeared the likeliest suspects to MI5 because the details of the story were so distorted. For example, KAGO always insisted on organizing his own travel arrangements. No one who knew him would credit the idea of him travelling with CIA bodyguards. These inaccuracies were deliberately fed by the CIA to the *Telegraph*'s Washington correspondent to avert accusations of double-dealing. The entire incident caused much discomfort to the Security Service because once again the FBI (who even issued a press statement on the subject) thought (erroneously) that they had proof of MI5's inability to keep secrets. Meanwhile the debate on Dolnytsin's real identity continued in the press with the Russian Embassy issuing a statement on 15 July describing the business as a 'ludicrous fabrication'. Some enterprising journalists had discovered that, by coincidence, before September 1961, there had been a protocol clerk named Anatoly Alexander Dolnytsin listed at the Soviet Embassy in London. Was he the subject of the 'D' Notice? The speculation was endless. The fact that the Russian who had distributed the release, Mr Stepanov, was due to return to Moscow shortly caused even further comment.

KAGO had left England by the time MI5 had to suffer a humiliating defeat from a disinformation agent. Like all the best deception plans it appeared on the surface to be extremely attractive. The source was the FBI's FEDORA, known to the CIA as SCOTCH, and the information related to another leak from within the Atomic Energy Authority.

By 1963 security at all the Atomic Energy Authority's establishments had been dramatically tightened since the days of Fuchs, Nunn May and Pontecorvo, but according to SCOTCH, the Soviets had yet another 'foreign' ideological source inside a research establishment. The story could not be checked with KAGO because the source had only come on stream since KAGO's defection in December 1961. This narrowed the field considerably and all the personal files which might fit the profile

* *MI5* (Arthur Barker, 1963).

were examined. None appeared to fit the description. It was then suggested that the spy might have become active after KAGO had left Moscow but before he had actually defected, and this proved to be the case.

Under those conditions the investigation quickly centred on a thirty-nine-year-old Italian physicist, Dr Giuseppe Martelli, who had joined the Atomic Energy Authority's Culham Laboratories in September 1962 from the Euratom organization. According to his file he was a married man with an impeccable academic background. He had been a lecturer in physics at Pisa University and had then taken up a research post at Birmingham University. Although he was apparently married in Italy, he was living with a fellow scientist, Pamela Rothwell, in Abingdon, who had borne him a baby daughter and changed her name by deed-poll to Martelli. To complicate the matter further Pamela was the daughter of a retired senior scientific civil servant, Percy Rothwell. She had also worked closely with Bruno Pontecorvo at Harwell.

The most obvious drawback to the case was that Martelli had not been cleared for access to secret material and was therefore not in a position to fill SCOTCH's profile of the spy. Furthermore, Culham Laboratories were not generally engaged on secret work. However, it was known that Martelli sometimes visited colleagues at Harwell. In Italy it was revealed that Martelli's wife, Maria (an Italian citizen, born in Central Asia and educated in the Soviet Union), was a member of a left-wing organization, the Union of Italian Women, and that several members of his family were communists. His sister, Adriana, worked for the Committee for Spanish Political Refugees, a cultural organization which was sponsored by, among others, the Communist Party, and was married to the political secretary of two branches of the Italian Communist Party. According to the Italian Security Service, Martelli had once worked at a cosmic ray laboratory at the Testa Grigia in Italy at the same time as members of a communist cell led by Professor Cortini. He was also known to have once met Mikhail Rogov, a Press Attaché at the Russian Embassy in Rome and a suspected Soviet intelligence officer. 'D' Branch decided to carry the case a stage further.

An illicit search was made of Martelli's office desk in Room 103 at Culham and a surprising discovery was made. In a locked drawer the Security Officer found a file marked 'Private and Confidential', which contained records of Dr Martelli's meetings with Soviet agents. The watchers were quickly alerted and Martelli became the focus of a full-scale operation.

As is usual in these cases the evidence necessary for a prosecution proved extremely difficult to acquire. On one occasion Martelli's contact with a Soviet led watchers to suspect that a spy was delivering secrets to his case officer. An attempt was made to intercept the Russian contact, but he simply refused to stop and drove quickly away. The 'D' Branch investigators were convinced by this incident that Martelli was their man and, on 22 April, gave the case to Special Branch. Martelli was at that moment on holiday in Greece and Yugoslavia with his mother and his two Italian children. Upon his return to the UK he was detained at Southend Airport, where he had arrived from Ostend, by Detective Sergeant Taylor of the Essex police. A call was then made to Scotland Yard and Chief Inspector David Stratton drove down to the airport, arriving shortly after lunch.

Martelli was searched at the airport as was his car, which was parked outside. He recognized the photograph of a man who was subsequently identified by 'D' Branch's Soviet order of battle section as Nicolai Karpekov, Vassall's former Soviet case officer. When the case came to Court, formal identification was provided by Detective Sergeant William Little of Special Branch who had kept a watch on Karpekov in December 1961.

Martelli also had in his luggage a map showing an intersection between King's Road, Wimbledon, and Dudley Road, which may have indicated a rendezvous. In a diary two sentences were found which could be construed to be a reminder of a recognition signal: 'Where is Charles Place?'; and the answer: 'Do you mean the art gallery?' A shoe found in the boot of his car had hollow heels (quite common in Italian summer shoes), possibly another secret hiding-place. The other shoe was found at his home in Abingdon. His diary showed an entry indicating the name Agrefenni, remarkably similar to that of the Third Secretary at the Russian Embassy in Brussels, Agrafenine.

While all these items were being catalogued, Martelli's home in Fitzharry's Road, Abingdon, was undergoing a thorough examination. A brown-leather cigarette-case was found which had been converted into an ingenious container for secret messages. Although seven of the cigarette tips inside were real, the stems of the remaining six had been cut away leaving a small space in which were concealed two sets of one-time pads. The pads were made of a cellulose film coated with highly inflammable nitrous-oxide. One was printed in red, the other in black, so as to distinguish the correct tables for sending and receiving. Each page consisted of forty lines of ten five-figure groups. They were promptly sent to Cheltenham for examination by Government Communications Headquarters and one page was found to have only thirty-seven lines left, suggesting that at least one message had already been sent using that particular pad. Later, at his trial, he explained that he had burnt part of a pad to 'see how fast it caught fire'. A diary was found which contained what appeared to be part of a classic Soviet conversion table, the mononome dinome grid. The system looked like a number of boxes within a larger box and was used in conjunction with the one-time pads to encipher messages. The diaries also contained photographic instructions, related to the correct exposure required for taking close-up pictures, and could have applied to the photographing of documents.

Martelli was charged with Official Secrets Acts breaches 'between 23 September 1960 and 4 April 1963'. He pleaded not guilty and the case went to trial at the Old Bailey on 2 July 1963, before Mr Justice Phillimore.

The defence, led by Jeremy Hutchinson QC, centred on two points. The first was that Martelli had never had access to secret information and therefore could not have broken the law. The second was that he had been blackmailed by Soviet agents since, when they had first contacted him, they told Martelli that his wife was applying to return to the Soviet Union with his children, but that they would refuse a visa for his children as long as he collaborated with them; if he did not, he might not be able to see his children again. The defence argued that they would prove Martelli was planning to 'turn the tables' on the blackmailing Soviet agents once he had discovered some information which could be used against them – hence the file he kept in his office. Possession of spying paraphernalia was admitted, but this is not in itself a crime, and during the trial most of the other circumstantial evidence was proved to be perfectly innocent.

The case was to become a watershed for MI5. They believed that they had presented a copper-bottomed case. The defence insisted there was no evidence or intention of espionage. Martelli admitted various contacts with Soviet intelligence officers abroad and volunteered further information about his meetings. He stressed, however, again and again, that he had been put under pressure because of his wife's intention to return to the Soviet Union with their two children. Furthermore, Martelli claimed that he had told Stratton at Southend that he must contact 'Colonel Young of British Intelligence'. This was construed as meaning that he was in contact with MI6. This extraordinary development certainly muddied the waters. He was thought to be referring to George Young, Dick White's Vice Chief who in fact had retired in 1961 to join Kleinwort Benson, the City firm of merchant bankers. He had been replaced by the MI6 Head of Station in Washington (and future Chief of MI6), Maurice Oldfield, but according to Martelli he was a close friend of Mr Rothwell's. Hutchinson also cross-examined extremely uncomfortable witnesses on the subject of Karpekov's departure from England six days before Vassall's arrest the previous September. 'D' Branch could not understand where the barrister had learned such information.

Nevertheless, the Security Service fielded an impressive array of expert witnesses. 'Mr A' was introduced by the Prosecuting Counsel, Edward Cussen, during the commital proceedings at Southend. He was MI5's photographic expert and he testified that the photographic instructions in Martelli's diaries were designed to help someone choose the correct lighting, apertures and exposure times for photographing documents. He assured the Court that there was no other possible use for them. In fact it was shown that the camera thought to be involved had been used as part of an experiment at the Physics Department at the University of Birmingham where Martelli had been working for several years and that the experiment performed there required the same settings. 'Mr A' was followed by 'Mr B', the MI5 chemist, who said that he had examined the one-time pads and they corresponded exactly in composition to other pads manufactured by the Russians. 'Mr C' from Government Communications Headquarters described in detail how the coding grids and one-time pads were to be used. A suspicious series of numbers preceded by the letter 'K', the initial of Karpekov, found in a diary, turned out to be a list of six quartets which Mozart had dedicated to Haydn and which Martelli intended to buy. ('K' is the initial of *Köchelverzeichniss*, the catalogue reference of Mozart's compositions.) 'Mr D' explained how he had photographed Martelli's diaries to clarify entries which had been obscured by cancellations. Finally, 'Mr E' was introduced. He testified that he had been a Security Officer for sixteen years, the last five of which had been spent in studying Soviet personnel at the Russian Embassy. He confirmed that Nikolai Karpekov was indeed an intelligence officer and not a bona-fide diplomat.

Martelli's defence was heard in full in July at the Old Bailey. He admitted having first met Karpekov, who acted as an interpreter, at an international conference on elementary particles in Pisa in 1955. During the next four years he had several further meetings with him, and at one, held in Harrow in March 1961, Karpekov had produced what appeared to be a list of numbers and had begun checking the index numbers of cars parked around the pub where they were to lunch together. When asked what he was doing Karpekov had boasted that he had a record of all 'the special cars used by MI5', where the Soviets 'had very highly placed friends'. For this reason, Martelli argued, he did not trust the police and had therefore not approached them earlier.

Martelli agreed that Karpekov and one of his colleagues had pressed him to take a job dealing with classified information in California, but he had resisted them. He stated, and was supported by defence witnesses, that he never handled secret or restricted documents, and actually shunned any classified work or information. He was described as 'non-political' by a senior Atomic Energy Authority scientist, Dr William Thompson, who headed the Theoretical Physics Department at Culham. He was also aided by an unlikely witness, ex-Detective Superintendent George Smith, the recently retired Special Branch officer who had arrested Vassall. He testified that Martelli did not fit the usual mould of

Soviet agents. On 15 July, after retiring for nearly ten hours, the jury agreed and Martelli was acquitted on all nine charges.

The case had turned into a total humiliation for MI5. So much so, in fact, that they told the FBI that the case reflected badly on the original source, SCOTCH. Might it have been possible for the Soviets actually to have wanted a prosecution? Were they so familiar with the provisions of the Official Secrets Acts that they had engineered the entire case? To some it looked as though the Russians were determined to undermine the law. It was now apparently perfectly legal to own spy equipment and be in contact with the KGB provided one was not caught red-handed with the actual information.

8

PENETRATION

When KAGO returned to the United States in July 1963 he went with the promise of an honorary CBE. He was, perhaps, even more determined than ever to continue his crusade against Moscow's apparently unstoppable campaign of disinformation. He saw his first task as isolating the KGB 'assets' within the West's security organizations and planned a world-wide tour of the Allied counter-intelligence staffs to root out the traitors.

This second stage of KAGO's career is his most controversial. Before his short visit to England his clues had all proved true and he had received the praise of such men as Sir Charles Spry of ASIO and Arpjorn Bryhn of the Norwegian Security Service. He had helped uncover KGB networks in every part of the globe although not all had resulted in prosecutions.

By the time Hollis visited Washington in late September 1963 the CIA had developed some understandable suspicions about MI5. During the past twelve months alone they had apparently let Philby off scot-free and had bungled an important prosecution. Now it seemed the recently retired Deputy D-G was also a suspected traitor. None of these items inspired confidence.

The most serious problem confronting the Americans was the matter of sources. Which were genuine and which were KGB plants? If, for example, the PETERS operation was justified, then the Petrov case must be tainted. Mitchell had been indoctrinated at an early stage and, if he had been a spy, he would surely have told his Soviet case officer instantly. If he had, why did the defection go so smoothly?

It was doubts like this which forced 'D' Branch to reopen the PETERS case. The D1 was asked to review all the files again and in January 1964 concluded that he could not be completely certain that the Service currently had a spy, or that there had been a recent penetration. However, he recommended that further enquiries should be made without delay.

This conclusion was accepted by the Director-General and his new

Deputy D-G, Martin Furnival Jones. (His replacement as Director 'D' was Malcolm Cumming from 'A' Branch. In his place Hollis had promoted a Scot and former wartime Deputy Chief of Security Intelligence Middle East.)

That Hollis agreed with the D1's conclusion is important. He knew that the original PETERS enquiry had suggested that the only candidates with sufficient access were Hollis and Mitchell. By agreeing to look elsewhere Hollis was authorizing an investigation of himself.

As it happened 'D' Branch began their search elsewhere. There were several possible suspects for the internal mole-hunt and a larger number outside the Service. One of the first candidates had been Jim Hale, brother of Lionel, the theatrical producer. Jim Hale, an Oxford-educated barrister, had done wartime service in MI5's legal department and after the war had become a chronic alcoholic. His marriage had been annulled on the grounds of non-consummation and his irrational behaviour was interpreted at one stage as being symptomatic of a Soviet agent's double life. He had, however, died of a brain tumour long before he could have been interviewed. The external category included two former MI6 officers who had served in New York during the war. One had been a prominent member of the Communist Party of Great Britain, the other had been interviewed after a routine telephone tap on the Soviet Embassy in London had revealed that his publishing company had received substantial financial support from Moscow.

In his original report, the D1 had also indicated that top of the internal suspects was Sir Anthony Blunt. Once again there was a lack of evidence which could be presented in Court. As well as having been interviewed formally no less than eleven times since the defection of Burgess and Maclean (chiefly by Courtney Young), he had met socially with his old friends Guy Liddell and Dick White. He persisted in his denials, so 'D' Branch retraced their steps and arranged an interview with John Cairncross who was then lecturing at the University of the North-West in Cleveland, Ohio.

Late in March 1964 Arthur Martin flew to Cleveland to talk over the situation with Cairncross. The years abroad had mellowed him and he appeared ready to admit his espionage for the Russians. He described his recruitment at Cambridge by Guy Burgess in 1935 and recalled the day when he was supposed to meet his Soviet case officer to discuss the defection of Burgess and Maclean. The Russian had failed to turn up at the agreed time and Cairncross felt he had been left in the lurch. This confirmed the D1's recollection of the B2(a) abortive trap in 1951. Although Cairncross detailed his own experiences, he denied knowledge of any other Soviet agents. No, he knew of no Ring-of-Five.

Martin was satisfied with his interview with Cairncross and prepared to return to London. On the way he stopped overnight in Washington where he met his opposite number in the FBI, William C. Sullivan. Sullivan had been in the FBI since 1942 and in 1961 had been appointed Assistant Director of the Intelligence Division in charge of all the Bureau's counter-espionage operations. While reviewing the Cairncross case Sullivan, who loathed his Director, revealed that Hoover knew all about the communist cells at Cambridge because the FBI had its own special source on the subject. Martin was astonished and demanded further information. Apparently the FBI informant was an American who had been an undergraduate at Trinity during the 1930s and had been recruited into a covert CPGB cell. Sullivan had passed the normal FBI retiring age of fifty the previous year and reckoned he had little to lose. He offered to introduce the source the following day and Martin jumped at the chance.

The former communist was Michael Straight, a magazine editor living in Washington. The White House had offered him a Federal arts post and Straight had volunteered a statement to the FBI to declare, quite properly, such skeletons as existed in his cupboard. Without hesitation he told Martin that he had been recruited into the CPGB by Sir Anthony Blunt. He also said he was perfectly willing to confront Blunt face to face with MI5 officers present. This was the break MI5 had been waiting for. Evidently Hoover had not trusted MI5 with it.

The D1 returned to London and informed the Director 'D' of this startling development. It now seemed likely that the Security Service was about to learn the extent to which it had been penetrated by the Soviets. Blunt himself had served in 'D' Division, had been appointed Guy Liddell's personal assistant and had then moved to B1(b). Was he one of KAGO's Ring-of-Five?

The importance of obtaining Blunt's co-operation was well understood in Curzon Street but the question of how to achieve this remained. The problem was finally solved by the Attorney-General, Sir John Hobson, who gave his approval to a plan which involved Blunt being granted complete immunity from prosecution in exchange for a frank confession. When Martin dangled this carrot before Blunt on 22 April 1964, Blunt took only seconds to consider the offer and accept. He confirmed that he had been recruited as a Russian spy by Guy Burgess in 1936.

At Blunt's subsequent debriefing he described talent-spotting for Burgess and named Cairncross as one such recruit. Another, he said, was Leo Long, a former MI3 officer who had been appointed Deputy Director of Military Intelligence in Germany after the war. When confronted with this evidence and offered the 'inducement' of not being prosecuted, Long too admitted his espionage for the Russians.

Blunt appeared to co-operate fully with Martin and they would meet two or three times a week, during which time he identified all his Soviet case officers from copies of their photographs taken from their diplomatic passports. On one unfortunate occasion Blunt asked who had succeeded Graham Mitchell as Deputy D-G. When told the job had gone to Martin Furnival Jones he let out a huge guffaw. This was recorded on the tape recording of the meeting and caused some embarrassment and amusement at Leconfield House.

The next hurdle facing the Security Service was the extent of the internal rot. Blunt denied knowing any traitors within the organization, but agreed that the Russians had allowed him to leave MI5 in 1945 which indicated that they had other sources in place. He also indicated that Philby's 'confession' to Nicholas Elliott was a good deal less than the truth.

After some two weeks of debriefing Blunt, the D1 was informed by the Director 'B', John Marriott, that he would be losing one of his investigators. Martin exploded with all the pent-up tension of his conversations with Blunt and sought the support of his own Director 'D', Malcolm Cumming. In fact Cumming was less than sympathetic to Martin's case. Cumming had been manipulated to feed Mitchell barium meals during the first stages of the PETERS operation and he was aware that Martin resented someone who had spent virtually his entire career in 'A' Branch being appointed Director 'D'. Two days later, on a Friday morning, Martin was informed by Cumming that he had mentioned their meeting to the Director-General, who had then asked him to prepare a summary of it in writing. Martin felt the text of Cumming's summary was an inaccurate account of the exchange that had taken place and insisted on seeing Hollis. The following Monday afternoon Hollis summoned the D1, accused him of causing dissension in the office and suspended him for two weeks. In his absence Peter W. took over Blunt's debriefing.

It has been suggested elsewhere that Blunt's debriefer was suspended for other reasons. For example, Chapman Pincher alleged:

The case officer wanted to interrogate Blunt without delay but Hollis took the view that there was no need to hurry and the right course was to treat Blunt very gently. An argument ensued and Hollis made it an excuse for suspending the case officer from duty for two weeks.*

As has been demonstrated, this version is wrong. Equally inaccurate is Chapman Pincher's description of Martin's departure from MI5. The decision to remove Martin was a collective one made by the Directorate of the Security Service, that is, all six Directors together with the Deputy D-G and the Director-General. On the date that this decision was taken only the Director 'E' was absent. It is therefore absurd to suggest, as it has been, that Hollis fired Martin and Dick White promptly hired him.

Martin was summoned to the Director-General's office and informed

* *Their Trade is Treachery* (Sidgwick & Jackson, 1981).

that he was a disruptive influence within the office. Several other officers found him hard to work with and a two-year secondment to MI6 had been suggested by Sir Dick White. In exchange MI5 would have the services of Terence Lecky. If Martin declined the offer, he would be dismissed without a pension. Before he left, the Deputy D-G, Furnival Jones, confirmed that Martin would be welcome back two years hence. A week later Martin moved into an office in the Counter-Intelligence Division of MI6.

Martin's departure from MI5 closed a chapter in the pursuit of the moles, but there was still more work to be done. For example, only four of the Ring-of-Five had been identified. Burgess, Maclean, Philby and Cairncross were members, but Blunt did not fit the profile of the fifth. There was another distasteful consideration. Was it likely, knowing the KGB's penchant for disinformation and cover-plans, that there were only five members of the Ring-of-Five?

While MI5 prepared to embark on a second mole-hunt in London, KAGO was involved in a new campaign to clean up the CIA.

KAGO's return to America in July 1963 was welcomed by the CIA's counter-intelligence staff as an opportunity to start afresh with him. The defector's experience in England had served to bring home to him the power of his former employers, the KGB. It had not escaped him that the Security Service had been paralysed by an internal investigation (which had remained secret from even some of the organization's most senior officers) and the newspapers reported daily on the Martelli atomic spy trial at the Old Bailey.

In 1963 the D1(a) spotted a deliberate KGB disinformation plan. A homosexual Soviet film-maker named Yuri Krotkov arrived in London on a cultural visit and identified himself to a watcher as a KGB officer with vast knowledge of homosexual entrapment schemes in Moscow. MI5 were particularly anxious to learn the names of other Britons who had suffered Vassall's misfortune and agreed to receive him. Arrangements were therefore made for Krotkov to leave his hotel in the Bayswater Road and walk across Hyde Park, thus preventing his KGB guardians from following by car. At the appointed time Krotkov took his walk and then jumped into MI5's car waiting near Hyde Park Corner.

During his debriefing Krotkov detailed the entrapment of John Watkins, a former Canadian Ambassador to Moscow who had retired to live in Paris. The information was passed on to Jim Bennett of the Royal Canadian Mounted Police's Security Service. Bennett confronted Watkins with the allegations (which, incidentally, had previously been made by KAGO and AE/FOXTROT), who promptly died of a heart attack. The central theme of Krotkov's account was the existence of a large network of blackmailed homosexual agents operating from Paris. The

DI(a) put Krotkov through an 'integrity test' and concluded that he was a plant. His entire story was an elaborate cover to distract the French authorities away from the rings KAGO had given clues about eighteen months earlier. The inclusion of Watkins in the scheme had been a discard to increase Krotkov's authenticity. MI5 narrowly escaped being embroiled in an operation designed to undermine Anglo–French co-operation on KAGO's leads.

KAGO found the situation in the CIA little changed. Angleton had made no progress with the SASHA case; instead he had become cap-tivated with KAGO's theory that SASHA had been under the protection of a senior CIA officer. To assist the search Angleton gave KAGO access to some of the CIA's personnel files. KAGO's first candidate was a Russian-speaking CIA officer named Richard Kovich. KAGO claimed that Kovich had been run by the KGB via a Norwegian double agent, Ingeborg Lygren, a former secretary to the Norwegian Ambassador in Moscow. Miss Lygren had by now returned to Oslo and had become secretary to the Norwegian Director of Military Intelligence, Colonel Wilhelm Evang. She was arrested, accused of espionage and later acquitted and reinstated. The real Soviet agent remained at liberty for some further time. The incident did little good for KAGO's credibility and less for Kovich's career. Kovich was transferred to a South American CIA Station and then retired in disgust.

Gradually everyone connected with Igor Orlov's work in Germany came under suspicion. David Murphy, the CIA's Soviet Russia Division Chief, had dealt with him in Berlin and so he was transferred to the CIA Station in Paris. An element of paranoia pervaded Langley as the counter-intelligence staff initiated investigations and probed officers' Russian connections. Despite his name Murphy was Polish in origin and was married to a Russian. The irony was that Murphy had been a keen supporter of KAGO.

There were others. KAGO recalled that the details of Deriabin's debriefing were known in Moscow and Peter Bagley, the CIA case officer concerned, was investigated. Bagley had since become Deputy Chief of the CIA's Soviet Russia Division, an indication of how few people failed to come under suspicion at one time or another. At first most of the CIA's staff had no idea that a purge was being conducted, but when word spread that a Russian defector had been examining individual personnel files there was a strong reaction. The counter-intelligence officers were accused of being manipulated themselves by the KGB and KAGO promptly denounced his detractors.

Opinions of KAGO in the Agency divided. Some believed he had been the centre of attention so continuously that he was now trying to create a long-term role for himself. Others implied that he had run out of relevant information and was therefore making up plausible leads. The immediate CIA solution was to encourage his travel plans. KAGO's clues had been very well received by the various Western or Allied security services and each had extended an invitation to him. Now the CIA encouraged him to take up the offers and embark on a world tour, lecturing to counter-intelligence staffs. One particular fan of his was Sir Charles Spry from ASIO and KAGO was soon to become a regular visitor to Australia.

In England MI5 began to recover from the PETERS operation and the reports of various Security Committees. The first such report had been commissioned in May 1961 to review the Portland case and then the Blake case,* and was published on 5 April 1962. The second Radcliffe Inquiry initiated on 15 November 1962 reported its findings on the Vassall case on 25 April 1963.** These 'stable-door' operations identified a common strand running through all the cases that came within their brief: none of the spies concerned would have stood up to the skimpiest of security examinations. Blake had enjoyed numerous communist connections, quite apart from his period of captivity in North Korea, and Harry Houghton had survived because several warnings had been ignored. In the Vassall case, the Positive Vetting system had completely failed. Vassall's name had been submitted for clearance in August 1956 when Vassall had been due to take up his new post in the Naval Intelligence Department, and a former Deputy Commissioner in the Nigerian police, Mr E.S. Sherwood, had been assigned his case. Sherwood interviewed Vassall, checked his passport and was apparently impressed by the fact that Vassall was a member of the Bath Club. Vassall's two original referees had not seen him for years yet the Admiralty Positive Vetting unit failed to draw the right conclusions. His alternative referees turned out to be two elderly ladies. One of them, a retired civil servant, Miss Elizabeth Roberts, told Sherwood that Vassall 'took very little interest in the opposite sex', but again the comment was overlooked. Vassall was cleared 'for access to classified atomic energy information and for regular and constant access to Top Secret defence information' on 10 December 1956.

Both Burgess and Philby should have been excluded from secret work because of their pre-war connections with the Communist Party of Great Britain, but no one had bothered to challenge them. The same could also be said of Leo Long, who had risen after the war to become the British Deputy Director of Military Intelligence in Germany. Even the most superficial of checks on their backgrounds would have revealed their unsuitability.

---

* *Security Procedures in the Public Service* (HMSO).
** *Report of the Tribunal appointed to Inquire into the Vassall Case and Related Matters* (HMSO).

The Reports illustrated how ineffective the 1952 Positive Vetting system had been. Initially, as we have seen, it was designed to spot personnel with communist links and consisted of a security questionnaire, the nomination of referees and a check against MI5's Registry. Individual government departments only instructed their tiny security staffs to double-check in the field if the first stage had proved unsatisfactory. It was more than two years before field enquiries became common practice, whether or not the initial view was favourable. The beefed-up system introduced on 31 March 1954 also went beyond the search for communist connections. Homosexuality, drunken behaviour, indebtedness and other potential sources of blackmail were taken into account, including relatives behind the Iron Curtain. The number of Civil Service posts requiring Positive Vetting was also greatly expanded. New vetting procedures also formalized the recruitment methods of both MI5 and MI6 which had previously relied on the 'I knew your father' system. Hollis himself was particularly sensitive about this issue having served as the post-war Director of 'C' Division. In this post he had spent much time explaining the rudimentary principles of physical security procedures to civil servants and government contractors. Hollis must have been pleased when he read Lord Radcliffe's comment that 'All the evidence which we heard showed that contracting firms respect and welcome the advice and prompt assistance which they receive from the ['C' Branch] Security Advisers, both in the course of their regular visits and ad hoc when special problems arise.' Lord Radcliffe's Committee concluded by recommending that 'the team of Security Advisers should be strengthened', which meant an increase in the size of 'C' Branch.

A further consequence of the apparent spate of spy cases was the creation of a Standing Security Commission. This new, permanent 'watchdog' body was headed by a distinguished judge and former Naval Intelligence officer, Sir Rodger Winn. His two fellow Commissioners were Lord Normanbrook, the retired Secretary to the Cabinet, and Admiral Sir Caspar John, a former First Sea Lord.

Hollis himself had entirely escaped criticism from the various enquiries and remained as Director-General until late in 1965. During his last twelve months in office he saw two 'loose end' cases come to fruition. Neither concerned penetration of MI5.

The first was that of an Air Ministry official, Frank Bossard, who had been supplying the Russians with photographs of secret documents since 1961. He worked in the Guided Weapons Research and Development Division and was arrested on 15 March 1965 by Superintendent Wise of Special Branch as he was leaving Room 229 of the Ivanhoe Hotel in Bloomsbury. During his lunch-hour he had led his MI5 watchers to the Left Luggage office at Waterloo Station, where he kept his espionage paraphernalia in a blue suitcase. He then checked into the hotel as 'John

Hathaway' and photographed the contents of four files which had passed over his desk earlier in the morning.

The Soviets had run Bossard with only the minimal personal contact. He exchanged his films for money at dead-letter drops and was therefore never spotted in the company of a known Russian intelligence officer, although he did later confess to one covert rendezvous with a Soviet at Cobham station.

He had originally been recruited by a man known to him as GORDON whom he had met casually in a pub, The Red Lion in Duke Street. Bossard collected coins and the Russian claimed to share his interest. After a further meeting in a restaurant at which Bossard described his financial troubles, £200 passed hands for some relatively innocuous information. Thereafter Bossard tuned in to Radio Moscow between 7.45 and 8.30pm on the first Tuesday and Wednesday of every month and listened for particular records, such as *The Sabre Dance* and *Moscow Nights*. He would then visit the appointed dead-letter drop near his home at Stoke D'Abernon in Surrey. Each tune had a particular message – *The Volga Boat Song*, for example, meant 'cease operations immediately' – or indicated the next dead-letter drops to be used. One was a silver-birch tree in Woking, another a broken drain-pipe on a housing estate in Weybridge. When he was arrested Bossard was carrying a list of nine regular hide-outs lettered 'A' to 'K', with one reserve drop lettered 'P'. Radio Moscow's broadcast frequencies on short wave were found noted in the back of his diary.

The post mortem on the case revealed that Bossard had a criminal record dating back to March 1934 when he had been convicted at King's Lynn for buying a watch with a dud cheque. He was sentenced to six months' hard labour and asked for nine similar offences to be taken into account. He had forged one of the references he produced when he joined the RAF in December 1940; once again someone had slipped through the net who should have been spotted much earlier. After the war, in which he served in the radar branch in the Middle East, Bossard had been demobbed with the rank of Flight-Lieutenant. He had briefly joined the College of Air Services at Hamble before being seconded in December 1951 to the Scientific and Technical Intelligence Branch in Germany. For the next four years his responsibilities included interviewing refugees from the East who had some useful technical knowledge or training. He was later promoted and attached to the British Embassy in Bonn with Second Secretary rank. In March 1954 he became eligible for Positive Vetting, but he was not given the Stage I questionnaire until August the following year. He duly completed the form (omitting any mention of his criminal convictions) and returned it. Six months later, when his form was being processed, Bossard was asked to supply the name of another referee, as one of the ones nominated by him had only known him for a year. Bossard, who was in Germany at the time, complied, but his 1934 convictions were discovered when his name went through the routine Stage I check with the Criminal Records Office. Instead of confronting Bossard (even if he was in Germany), the Ministry of Defence Positive Vetting unit wrote to him for an explanation. Bossard simply apologized for a 'lapse of memory' and, when his third referee provided a satisfactory answer, was granted his clearance.

On 10 May 1965 Bossard was gaoled for twenty-one years by the Lord Chief Justice, Lord Parker, at the Old Bailey. The following month the Security Commission were critical of the apparent lack of safeguards highlighted by the case,* but prefaced their remarks with the statement: 'First, there was no failure or inefficiency in either case on the part of the Security Service.'

Bossard's case was linked with that of Staff Sergeant Percy Allen, who was arrested by Special Branch on 16 March 1965 in the act of handing a bundle of classified documents to Major Abdul Al-Abbasi, the Iraqi Military Attaché, underneath Charing Cross Arches. Allen had got into financial difficulties and had decided to capitalize on his War Office job in the Land/Air Warfare Directorate. He had access to Western intelligence estimates of the Egyptian armed forces and simply offered them for sale to the Iraqis – from the public telephone directly outside his office. On the day of his arrest the MI5 watchers had kept him under observation from the moment he had left his office in Northumberland Avenue.

Allen's initial contact with the Iraqis had proved unrewarding, so on 22 February he had approached the Egyptian Military Attaché, Major Kamel. A routine intercept on the Egyptian Embassy revealed the plot. In one of the most straightforward cases of its kind MI5 passed the case to Special Branch and an arrest was made. Allen had been paid a mere £75 for his one month's work, for which he was sentenced to ten years' imprisonment. In total Allen had removed secret documents from his office on no less than seven occasions and had replaced them. Once again the system had broken down. Allen had undergone vetting in 1957, but there had been no Stage 4 field investigation. In spite of this, and in clear breach of the regulations, Allen had access to more than a hundred of the very highest classifications of secrets. Fortunately, he was circumspect in what he offered his Iraqi and Egyptian contacts. After his arrest the Security Service checked with the police at Llanbradoch, where he was born and brought up, and discovered that he had been convicted twice in 1947 as a juvenile, once for damage, another time for theft. Because these cases had been heard by a Juvenile Court, the details had not been sent to the Criminal Records Office. Furthermore, the security

* Report of the Standing Security Commission, June 1965.

questionnaire used by the Army during Allen's Positive Vetting, did not require a declaration of juvenile convictions. Unbelievably, Allen's security status had been reviewed in 1962, after the usual five years, and cleared.

In strategic terms Allen might almost have been said to have acted in the West's interests. Some of the documents he sold were subsequently published in *Al-Ahram*, the semi-official Cairo daily newspaper. The assessments were on the whole accurate, especially in respect of the Egyptian Air Force, and it appeared from the stolen papers that the British government had not ruled out further direct intervention in the Middle East. This interpretation was thought by some to have had a salutary effect on President Nasser.

Hollis's last case was the disastrous prosecution in February 1965 of Alfred Roberts and Godfrey Conway, the culmination of AIR BUBBLE.

AIR BUBBLE had originated when the Belgian Sureté d'Etat informed MI5 in January 1964 that one of their double agents was receiving details of certain manufacturing processes from a member of the Communist Party of Great Britain who worked for Kodak Limited at their Wealdstone factory. The information related to anti-static coatings and other film processes. None could be classed as secret in the military sense but, according to the Belgians, their agent had made no less than eleven visits to England and had purchased what were termed 'secrets of a commercial nature' for an East German firm, Diachemie. The double agent was a sixty-nine-year-old retired industrial chemist, Dr Jean-Paul Soupert, who had recently 'blown' Herbert Steinbrecher, an East German 'illegal' who had been organizing agents inside various Concorde assembly plants before being caught by the French Security Service, the DST. Soupert, who had been first recruited by Steinbrecher (whom he knew as Hans Olaf Deitrich) in Brussels, willingly volunteered details of his contacts with the two Kodak employees. He had apparently met Alfred Roberts first, in November 1961, but Roberts had been unable to provide enough information for Soupert, so some ten months later Roberts had introduced his colleague, Godfrey Conway, at a rendezvous in Ostend.

Soupert had been 'turned' by Belgian intelligence in November 1963 and from that moment onwards all his meetings with the Kodak employees were monitored. On 11 January 1964 Soupert, code-named AIR BUBBLE, was kept under surveillance by MI5 as he met Roberts and Conway at a café in Northumberland Avenue. They then had a further meeting at the Regent Palace Hotel where Soupert received various Kodak documents.

In March later the same year Roberts made another trip to Ostend to meet HERBERT, who was apparently to replace Soupert as his case officer. Roberts, however, had become increasingly nervous about his relationship with the foreigners, a feeling that was justified on 29 November when his home in Barchester Road, Harrow, was raided by Special Branch.

Since no military secrets were at stake, Roberts and Conway were charged under the Prevention of Corruption Act in that they had received 2,000DM corruptly from Soupert. Both men were defended by Jeremy Hutchinson QC, who had so successfully demolished the Martelli case. On this occasion the prosecution, with support from 'Mr A' and 'Mr B', both Security Service watchers, was handled by Edward Cussen, a former wartime MI5 officer, but it fared little better. Hutchinson was able to show that Kodak had agreed to pay Soupert £5,000 for his evidence, which severely undermined his credibility as a witness for the prosecution. Soupert was also forced to admit that, on at least one occasion, his passport had been doctored to show he had been in England when in fact he had never left Belgium. The judge, Mr Justice Melford Stephenson, made some characteristically apposite comments about Soupert's reliability. The two defendants were acquitted.

This second embarrassment led to an investigation into Jeremy Hutchinson QC. However, the subsequent 'D' Branch enquiry recorded only three items of interest: that he was acknowledged to be a brilliant barrister; that he was married to the actress Dame Peggy Ashcroft who was a well-known political left-winger; and that he had been a member of the Haldane Society.

The Roberts–Conway case acted further to limit MI5's operations. Roberts had been of interest to 'F' Branch for years and Soupert's evidence (though discredited) clearly showed a long-term interest by the East Germans in the acquisition of Western industrial secrets. MI5 had participated in the prosecution because of the allegation of subversion: a CPGB member selling a trade secret. The dismissal of the case was a sharp rebuke and served to remind 'F' Branch and D2 that their overt involvement in a trial could be skilfully turned to the advantage of the defence.

The Martelli and Roberts–Conway cases had their impact, yet it was widely believed within MI5 that other, better publicized, cases, such as the Profumo affair, had been more damaging. In the latter Hollis had been working at a distinct disadvantage. He had not learned the full implications of Profumo's apparently marginal involvement with MI5's target, Ivanov, until too late. Certainly 'D' Branch had regarded the operation as being of only minor importance and had therefore handled it at a relatively low level. That the Director-General did not disclose to the Prime Minister the War Minister's lie is entirely to his credit if one takes account of MI5's strict Defence of the Realm guidelines. As Hollis successfully argued with Lord Denning, it was none of his business if a Minister chose to take a mistress or lie to the House of Commons, provided, of course, there was no security risk involved, which there was not.

It is equally possible to suggest that Hollis might have been well advised to confide the full details to the Prime Minister as soon as he learned the full facts of the Keeler–Profumo relationship, but such speculation ignores two relevant factors. The first is the Director-General's underlying lack of strength in respect of his own organization. His own Deputy D–G was under investigation as the likeliest suspect for the Soviet mole inside MI5. Hollis knew that there was a strong possibility that before September 1963 he would have no alternative but to tell Macmillan about the PETERS investigation. Had the operation led to a confession it would have compromised the entire organization and the Cabinet would probably have been obliged to disband MI5, if only to restore the confidence of the Americans.

A second factor was the Prime Minister's abhorrence of all matters relating to sex. Profumo himself was unable to discuss the matter directly with Macmillan and had to deal with such intermediaries as the Cabinet Secretary and the Chief Whip, Martin Redmayne. If Hollis had approached him with the allegation that his Secretary of State for War had been involved with a call-girl, he would not have received any thanks. Furthermore, Hollis was never in a position to provide solid evidence of such an allegation and it was unquestionably against his nature to volunteer such sensitive intelligence without a solid foundation.

When Hollis retired to his home in Wells in December 1965, he could reflect on some nine years in the post of Director-General, a longer period than any previous Director-General apart from the Security Service's founder, Sir Vernon Kell. He had broken with tradition in that he had never served in the counter-espionage branch and he had also survived more inquisitions than all his predecessors. As successes Hollis would have pointed to the Portland five, the capture of Vassall and MI5's generous treatment by Lord Denning. However, there were other opinions held about the value of the Portland case and indeed Vassall. Supporters of KAGO argued these 'successes' were nothing more than decoys. The only major public failure that occurred during his term of office was the Martelli case, which had been interpreted so badly by 'D' Branch. Martelli had offered comprehensive explanations for every item of apparently incriminating pieces of evidence. Fortunately for MI5, the case was not a total write-off in intelligence terms for Martelli had agreed, after his acquittal, to co-operate with MI5 and had been de-briefed by them in the presence of his solicitor.

The Security Service that Hollis handed on to his successor, Martin Furnival Jones, was an organization almost paralysed by self-doubt. Relations with the Americans had been thoroughly undermined by the destructive mole-hunts and, worst of all, there had not been any satisfactory conclusions reached. 'D' Branch were certain that they had been penetrated, but they were still no closer to identifying the culprits. At first PETERS had been the prime suspect, but after a lengthy investigation the D1's report had, on balance, concluded in his favour. The problem facing the mole-hunters was twofold: who was the alternative suspect, and were the internal enquiries not counter-productive in terms of morale and relations with the Americans?

Opinion on the subject divided into two camps. One group favoured an all-out mole-hunt to clear the air and establish the truth, whatever the cost. All the so-called unexploded bombs would be dragged out for examination. The other view saw the entire exercise as destructive and unlikely to achieve anything except the continued paralysis of the Service. Some officers asked the embarrassingly pertinent question: what would the Soviets prefer us to do?

9

SIR MARTIN FURNIVAL JONES

Furnival Jones, known to most as 'F-J', had joined the office after the war had begun and had worked for Brigadier Harry Allen in 'D' Division liaising with the Services. After D-Day he had joined SHAEF as one of MI5's representatives and had then returned to 'C' Division. His transfer to Director 'D' in 1956 had taken many in the office by surprise because of his relative lack of experience in the field of counter-espionage, but the following six years more than made up for it. As Director 'D' he had supervised all of 'D' Branch's apparent successes and had been one of the first to be indoctrinated into the PETERS investigation. He had been appointed Deputy D-G in 1963 on Mitchell's retirement.

Martin Furnival Jones took over the Director-General's chair in December 1965 and appointed Anthony Simkins as his Deputy D-G. Michael Hanley was promoted to his place as Director of 'C' Branch from D2. Malcolm Cumming took early retirement and was replaced as Director 'D' by the D1.

Furnival Jones and his Deputy D-G had come from similar backgrounds and they had been born within two months of each other: F-J had gone to Cambridge (Gonville and Caius), Simkins to Oxford (New College); F-J had read law (Exhibitioner), Simkins had read Modern History (First Class Honours); F-J had joined Slaughter & May as a solicitor, Simkins had been called to the Bar at Lincoln's Inn. F-J's seniority in MI5 stemmed from his joining the office in late 1940; Simkins had spent the war as a prisoner in Germany.

The PETERS investigation had been traumatic for all involved if only because of the deception colleagues practised on each other. Such conduct is hardly conducive to good working relations but there is something worse: the suspicion that there is an undetected traitor at hand. Graham Mitchell had retired to his chess and nothing had ever been proved against him. In fact the weight of opinion was in his favour. The logical conclusion therefore was then someone else had escaped suspicion. But who was it? At this stage it is worth re-examining the evidence.

Before the spring of 1963 there had merely been a suspicion that the office had been infiltrated. There was no direct evidence although three factors seemed to tip the balance: the lack of defectors, the failure of the double agents and the apparent warnings given to important suspects. KAGO's assumption of wholesale KGB penetration everywhere crystallized fears and made them appear a certainty. His information, however, had been characteristically sketchy. He firmly believed MI5 had been targeted by his former employers and in his experience such intentions were usually transformed into operational facts sooner or later. He could provide no clues or names, but he did make one categoric statement. It involved a special file of documents kept at KGB headquarters in Moscow which were supposed to be MI5 originals. Although he had never had access to them KAGO had once seen their index, a book listing each one. He believed the entries dated into the late 1950s, which ruled out the only known Soviet source to date, Anthony Blunt.

If Philby had indeed been warned by this source then, according to Arthur Martin's calculation, he had to be one of just five people: himself, his secretary, Cumming, Mitchell or Hollis. By the end of 1965 all had left MI5: Martin had transferred to MI6; all the others had retired. Mitchell, as we have seen, was the first to go; he had been followed by Cumming who had spent more than thirty years in the office, pre-dating everyone else. He could safely be ruled out, as could Martin's secretary and presumably Martin himself. After all, he had been the most tenacious MI5 officer in pursuing the moles. That left only Hollis.

Here was the classic unexploded bomb waiting to do terrible damage at the worst possible moment. If Mitchell was innocent then who else was left? The only plausible candidate was Roger Hollis himself. Whatever the truth Furnival Jones was determined to root it out rather than leave the matter where it stood or risk a scandal later. In the meantime, he proposed a reorganization of 'D' Branch, or rather its abolition. Henceforth it would be known as 'K' Branch and would include a permanent section, K7, to counter Soviet penetration. Several indoctrinated officers were assigned to investigate further. They included John Day from the old 'D' Branch and Ian Carrel from Registry. Carrel, a former Balliol Scholar and Security Liaison Officer, Hong Kong, had succeeded Harold Potter as Head of Registry on the latter's retirement.

The first task was to conduct an interrogation of Mitchell and this was undertaken by John Day, a former Royal Marines Colonel. Mitchell was confronted with the evidence of his apparently eccentric behaviour and he provided an explanation for every incident itemized by the watchers. Yes, he did carry out routine tests to see if he was being followed to and from Curzon Street. That, he said, was his well-established practice. Yes, he had drawn a map of Chobham Common, but he had used it to plan a charity paper-chase that his daughter had participated in.

Some things, he protested, he simply did not know about. For example, one of the chief functions of the Deputy D-G was to assign particular cases to the watchers. The individual section heads of 'D' Branch, and occasionally 'F' Branch, would meet in the briefing room on Friday mornings and 'bid' for teams of watchers. If, say, the Soviet Satellite section (D2) wanted to trail a Hungarian diplomat from his Embassy in Eaton Place to a suspected dead-letter drop, the D2 would ask for the watchers' service for the appropriate length of time the operation would require. In the event of there being more bids than watchers the Deputy D-G would adjudicate and determine which operation had priority. This system was democratic in the sense that everyone had the opportunity to apply for a watcher service, but it also involved a serious risk to internal security. If the D4 was mounting a major operation, all the other officers attending the meeting were bound to learn of its existence. Probably more matters of a current operational nature were discussed at those regular meetings than virtually anywhere else in the building. At the meeting's conclusion the Deputy D-G would summon the chief watcher, Harry Hunter (latterly Jim Skardon), and draw up a plan of campaign for the following week. Hunter would then return to his office at 72 Grosvenor Street and distribute the cases to the teams of watchers.

Mitchell was now questioned about the suspicion that these bids meetings had been tape-recorded. The PETERS investigators had opened the small, unused drawer in the board-room table in the centre of the briefing room and noticed what appeared to be four marks in the dust. Were they evidence that a tape-recorder had been running during the proceedings? Mitchell denied this. If he was telling the truth and there had indeed been a listening device inside the table, then suspicion now fell on Hollis.

In due course Hollis was asked to return to the office, where he was interrogated by Furnival Jones and Simkins. He too categorically denied taping the bids sessions. The investigators decided to look further afield and, with Ian Carrel's specialized Registry knowledge, began sifting through the old files. At this stage they widened the scope of the enquiry to take in MI6 suspects. Their reason was twofold. Hollis had, after all, informed MI6 that he intended to question Philby further (at which point Dick White had taken over the case and passed it to Nicholas Elliott). This meant an automatic increase in the D1's original limited set of suspects. The second motive was a suggestion made by KAGO. One of his key arguments related to finding clues to current KGB penetration in the 1920s and 1930s and he advised an examination of all the old personal files of the period.

This was a mammoth task, especially for MI6. After the First World War they had recruited dozens of intelligence officers with Russian backgrounds, people who had either been born or educated in Russia, who spoke English badly in spite of their English names. Others had been the sons of British merchant families who had lost all their possessions during the Revolution. They had joined MI6 as a crusade against the Bolsheviks and some had remained in the Service long after the Second World War had ended. For example, the Gibson brothers, Harold and Archie, had spent most of their lives running agents behind the Iron Curtain. Harold Gibson, who had twice married White Russians, had been Head of Station in Prague until 1939 and had then transferred his base to neutral Istanbul. His brother had also operated in Eastern Europe and then switched to the Middle East in the face of the German advance in 1940. Attention had been focused on Harold Gibson before, because he had shot himself in Rome late in August 1960. MI5 had investigated the incident at the time but had come to no conclusions.

A senior MI6 officer with strong Russian connections, whose personal file was examined with particular care, was Dick Ellis. One curious, dismissive entry on his file had been made by another MI6 colleague concerning the post-war interrogation of an Abwehr officer. The German had claimed to have had a pre-war MI6 source in Paris called 'Captain Ellis'. The name had initially been corrupted during translation, so it was not until the war had been over some years that a link had been made between the pre-war source and Dick Ellis. The officer who had been responsible for making the entry in the file had been Kim Philby. Dick Ellis had by then retired and written *The Expansion of Russia*. However, he had since returned to the MI6 Registry to help 'weed' defunct files. He had left MI6's Far East Division in 1953 and had spent a brief attachment to the Australian Secret Intelligence Service during the Petrov defections. Further digging by MI5 revealed that shortly before the war a successful telephone tap on the German Embassy in London had apparently been discovered by the Germans, who had promptly abandoned its use. As a German linguist, Ellis had been one of the MI6 officers assigned to translating the transcriptions. Might he have betrayed it to the Russians, who in turn had told their ally, Nazi Germany?

Ellis was invited back to the office and confronted with the allegation made by the Abwehr officer. He was told that the German had been traced and was willing to fly to London to identify him formally. Ellis denied the charge, but the following day, when he returned for a further session, he agreed that he had been a source for the Abwehr. He claimed he had been desperately short of money in Paris and had made ends meet by passing on MI6's complete order of battle in London. Nevertheless, he insisted that he had never given information to the Soviets. Was the Ellis confession incomplete? Why should Philby have acted to protect him? Ellis continued with his denials leaving his interrogators baffled. Two other MI6 officers had been strongly suspected of having worked for the Russians whilst attached to the wartime British Security Co-ordination (BSC) in New York. Ellis had been Sir William Stephenson's deputy at BSC at the time and claimed he was unable to throw any light on the other two suspects even though one, Cedric Belfrage, had been denounced during the McCarthy hearings in Washington.*

The Ellis confession hardly took the mole-hunt any further forward. If the Soviets had known he had been a German source, surely they would have blackmailed him later in the war and possibly afterwards? If that was the case, had he compromised the Petrov defections? Vladimir had made his escape without difficulty, but the unscheduled arrival of Karpinsky and Zharkov, the two 'diplomatic couriers', had almost prevented his wife's defection. Had they been tipped off in advance, and should the incident be interpreted as a close-run thing? Ellis, Hollis and Mitchell had known in advance of the ASIO operation. Alternatively, would the KGB risk exposing such a well-placed agent, in circumstances that would throw suspicion on him, if their plan to detain the Petrovs had succeeded? In any event Ellis showed no signs of implicating anyone in MI5 and he had not been in any position in the late 1950s to give the KGB the documents described by KAGO.

The conundrum continued, but events in America were to help illuminate the Soviets' technique of providing disinformation cover-plans to protect their moles. It should also be borne in mind that at this stage much of the intelligence evidence was pointing to Hollis. This evidence was naturally highly circumstantial and spanned Hollis's entire career. None of it, however, tied in with KAGO's suggestion that the mole had strong Russian connections during the late 1920s or 1930s. Unlike the cases of Burgess, Maclean, Cairncross, Philby, Blunt and Long, there were no direct overt communist connections in his early career.

Roger Hollis was born in December 1905, the third son of the Bishop of Taunton. He was educated at Clifton College and Worcester College, Oxford. His elder brother Michael had gone to Leeds Grammar School and then become an Anglican priest, whilst his brother Christopher had gone to Eton and then become Tory Member of Parliament for Devizes in Wiltshire. His younger brother Marcus had been a wartime MI6 officer.

Roger Hollis only spent two years at Oxford, then, in 1927, he travelled to the Far East by boat and obtained a post with the British American Tobacco Company in Shanghai. There he remained until seven years later, in December 1934, he suffered a recurrence of tuberculosis which he had first contracted in his youth in England.

The MI5 mole-hunters concentrated their attention on his time at Oxford and in China, in so far as it was practicable to do so. New MI5

---

* The other had been identified through a routine telephone tap on the Russian Embassy in London. See page 121.

recruits spend much time in 'F' Branch (or Division as it was then) reading up case histories; they are then obliged to declare their knowledge of any left-wing individual or person considered potentially subversive by MI5, in their personal files. Understandably, new arrivals are reluctant (as they might see it) to jeopardize their future by naming unsavoury characters, so that this rule has been frequently ignored. Hollis was certainly at fault in this respect, for he failed to enter on his file the fact that he had known Claud Cockburn who had been at Keble at the same time as he was at Worcester. However, a number of his contemporaries had been equally remiss in naming names, as the authorities well knew because the Oxford-based communists had been kept under close watch by the Security Service during the early 1920s. One of MI5's veteran officers, Max Knight, had recruited several informants in Oxford, including Dennis Wheatley's stepson, William Younger, and Tom Driberg, a covert member of the Communist Party of Great Britain.

The China episode was open to rather more sinister interpretation. It coincided with Dr Richard Sorge's most active two-year period of recruitment for his Shanghai-based spy network. Sorge was the Russian-born son of a German oil engineer stationed in Baku. His grandfather, Adolf Sorge, had been Karl Marx's secretary and in October 1919, aged twenty-three, he had joined the Hamburg branch of the German Communist Party. Five years later, having graduated with a doctorate in Political Science, he travelled to Moscow to become a full-time agent for the Comintern. In January 1930 he appeared in Shanghai, apparently working as a journalist for an obscure German journal, the *Soziologische Magazin*. In reality Sorge's job was to take over the leadership of a ring of covert communists which was gathering intelligence about the Japanese military. During his time in China, Sorge was responsible for the recruitment of around twenty Soviet agents. They included his radio operator, a German Signals Corps veteran named Max Klausen; Agnes Smedley, a well-known leftist American journalist; and a number of Japanese newspaper correspondents.

Sorge left Shanghai for Moscow in December 1932 and the following September was reassigned to Tokyo. By the time he arrived there, he was a member of the German Nazi Party and was the accredited correspondent of the *Frankfurter Zeitung*. When the war started in Europe in September 1939 the German Ambassador in Tokyo, Colonel Eugen Ott, appointed Sorge his Press Attaché. Sorge remained in that post, secretly working for the Soviets until his betrayal and arrest on 18 October 1941. He then made a long statement to the Japanese police in which he detailed his pre-war activities in China and implicated nearly fifty of his recruits. He was hanged on 7 November 1944.

Did Hollis become entangled with all this Soviet espionage? A possible source for the answer, apart from Hollis himself, was the Special Branch

in Shanghai. When Hollis was in China, the Shanghai Municipal Police
was run jointly by the French and the British, and in particular the local
British Consul-General, Mr Harry Steptoe, and the British Commissioner of Police, Mr T.P. Givens. Steptoe was also the MI6 representative
and a fierce anti-communist. During the first part of the war, he was
interned in Japan with a number of other British diplomats, but he was
repatriated to become one of the first officers in Section IX of MI6, the
anti-Soviet unit. Under Steptoe's guidance the Shanghai Special Branch
had penetrated several Soviet networks, but had found only one Briton
among them. He was Gunther Stein, a German Jew who had travelled
to Hong Kong for Sorge in 1938 and had become a naturalized British
subject in 1941. He was later the *British Financial News* correspondent
in Japan. MI5 found no record of anyone bearing Hollis's description in
any of the police dossiers.

The Japanese had launched the most thorough investigation into
Sorge's spy-rings in the Far East, but again there was no mention of
Hollis in their files. After the Japanese surrender well-documented records of the cases were inherited by the American occupation forces and
passed to Colonel T.P. Davis, the American Military Intelligence representative. The Americans double-checked all the available Japanese files
in the hope of identifying any surviving Soviet agents in America. In
addition the files were cross-referred with Soviet signals intercepted by
the Japanese, the Shanghai International Settlement Police records,
Sorge's own statements and documents recovered from his home. The
Americans also interviewed several survivors of Sorge's ring whom they
had liberated. Some made statements; others, such as Max Klausen,
were hastily repatriated to Russia after the intervention of the newly
opened Soviet Embassy in Tokyo. Whilst it is entirely possible that a
British recruit such as Hollis might have escaped detection, it is improb-
able. What is certain is that no evidence exists of any contact between
Hollis and any member of the Sorge networks.

Hollis returned to England on leave in 1934 and left Shanghai for good
in June 1936. On that occasion he avoided the overland route via
Moscow and instead travelled through Canada. Once back in England
he was invalided out of British American Tobacco and, in July 1937, he
married Evelyn Swayle, the daughter of a wealthy Glastonbury solicitor. The following year, after a spell in a tuberculosis sanatorium at
Davos in the extreme east of Switzerland, Hollis met Jane Sissmore, a
senior MI5 officer. She recommended that in view of his overseas experience he should apply to join MI6. The Secret Intelligence Service
turned him down on health grounds so, in 1938, he went to work at
MI5's Horseferry Road headquarters as Miss Sissmore's assistant. There
was no Registry record of any communist connections against his name.

An illustration of MI5's thoroughness in analysing Hollis's pre-war career is provided by their determination to learn all they could about the few months Hollis spent in the TB sanatorium. As Alexander Foote had then revealed in 1946 there had indeed been a Swiss link to Soviet espionage operations in England. Ruth Kuczynski, code-named SONIA, had been living near Montreux, and it was known that she had been active as a Soviet agent in China before joining the LUCY ring. Was it a coincidence that she should have been in three different countries at the same time as Hollis? When challenged by the mole-hunters Hollis denied ever having come into contact with SONIA. He did, however, agree that he had met Agnes Smedley, the journalist, and one of Sorge's senior agents. Unfortunately she had died in a London nursing home in 1950, so corroboration could not be obtained.

The Security Service that Hollis joined in 1938 was tiny compared to its post-war successor. It was divided into three sub-sections – (a), (b) and (p) – headed respectively by Captain Charles Butler (assisted by Captain Herbert Bacon), Major W.A. Alexander (assisted by Captain H.F. Boddington) and Colonel John Mellor (assisted by Captain Humphrey Lloyd). The total MI5 staff counted just ninety-two: fifteen officers supported by five administrative assistants, fourteen secretaries, thirty-nine Registry personnel, two male clerks, three detectives, five photographic technicians and a 'Scientific Section' of two.*

Miss Sissmore, who later married Group Captain Archer, MI5's liaison officer with the RAF, was concentrating on the accumulation of knowledge about the Comintern and no doubt a large part of Hollis's duties during his first months in MI5 would have been learning about the Communist Party of Great Britain rather than engaging directly in anti-Soviet counter-intelligence operations. This latter field was the responsibility of Max Knight, who was based away from the MI5 headquarters' building. In other words, if Hollis had been a Soviet agent he chose a relatively unproductive area of the Security Service to work in.

On 26 August 1939 MI5 moved all their staff into Wormwood Scrubs Prison, which proved an unsuitable home, so the following May new accommodation was secured at Blenheim Palace. All the non-essential sections were transported down to Oxfordshire, while the more vital departments took over a large building in St James's Street. Hollis fell into the former category and thus spent much of the first part of the war in the country.

On Monday, 10 June 1940, the incoming Prime Minister, Winston Churchill, instructed the Head of the Civil Service, Sir Horace Wilson, to sack Sir Vernon Kell who had been MI5's Director-General since

---

* The (p) unit was not included as headquarters' staff because officially it remained the War Department Constabulary.

1909.* Kell's place was taken temporarily by Brigadier A. W. A. (Jasper) Harker, while Lord Swinton's Security Executive supervised an internal reorganization. By November 1940 Harker had been appointed Deputy D-G and Sir David Petrie chosen as Kell's successor. The Security Service was sub-divided into six Divisions – 'A', 'B', 'C', 'D', 'E' and 'F' – and by a stroke of good luck these changes heralded Colonel Alexander's retirement, along with several of the older MI5 staff. This meant new responsibilities for Jane Archer, but later in the war she decided to accept an offer of a job with MI6. Coincidental with the move to Blenheim, Hollis was appointed Assistant Director of 'F' Division, and allotted Roger Fulford and Hugh Astor as his assistants. Hollis retained his brief for monitoring the CPGB, whilst Graham Mitchell took on the extremists of the other end of the political spectrum, assisted by a recently recruited solicitor, Kemball Johnson.

After the war Hollis was, as we have already seen, appointed Director of 'C' Division and then sent on a mission to organize the Australian Security Intelligence Organization. In 1953 Dick White appointed him his Deputy D-G and three years later he became Director-General, a post he held for nine years. At no time did he head a Soviet counter-espionage section which would have been a natural target for a Soviet agent. When Blunt joined the Security Service in 1940, he deliberately obtained a transfer from his relatively dull post in 'D' Division to 'B' Division so as to be closer to the centre of MI5's operations. There are plenty of other examples of Soviet agents worming their way into key anti-Soviet counter-intelligence jobs. Philby manœuvred himself from Section V of MI6 into Section IX; Leo Long applied for but was refused a transfer from his MI3 post to MI5. In post-war Germany the examples are legion: in December 1951 Dr Otto John, a former anti-Hitler conspirator, was appointed head of the Federal Internal Security Office. In July 1954 he mysteriously disappeared from West Berlin and reappeared a month later at a press conference in the Soviet Zone. This 'defection' took a bizarre turn the following year when Dr John was driven back into West Germany by a Danish journalist and announced his escape from his KGB abductors. He was arrested and sentenced to four years' hard labour. When Heinz Felfe was arrested on 6 November 1961 he was the head of the West German *Bundesnachtrichtendienst's* counter-intelligence department, entrusted by its chief, General Gehlen, with special responsibility for investigating Soviet infiltration of the German intelligence services. In fact Felfe had worked for the Russians for more than ten years, supplying them with no less than 15,661 photographs of secret documents on 300 rolls of Minox film. He also admitted

* Kell retired to the tiny village of Emberton in Buckinghamshire and became a Special Constable at Olney police station. He died on 27 March 1942.

betraying ninety-four agents. The head of the counter-espionage division of the West German Military Intelligence Service, Dr Peter Fuhrmann, had been blackmailed into supplying the Soviets with secrets for seven years. Denounced by Guenther Maennel, Fuhrmann was sentenced in September 1962 to ten years' imprisonment.

In all of these cases, the individual Soviet agent made deliberate attempts to infiltrate especially sensitive positions which would have enhanced their value to their Russian controllers. This scenario certainly does not fit Hollis, who would have learned little of value to the Soviets in terms of MI5's anti-Soviet counter-intelligence operations until he was appointed Deputy D-G. Indeed, Hollis was certainly not a 'favourite' for high office in the Security Service. He was lacking in experience in MI5's most important area of interest and was not a very popular figure in the office. On a social level he was fearfully ill at ease among other senior Whitehall officials and an invitation to lunch with an MI6 executive at White's Club would reduce him to an extraordinary state of nervousness. His own London club was the Travellers'. His promotions were in the main fortuitous: the resignation of Colonel Alexander and the transfer of Jane Archer; Guy Liddell's transfer to the Atomic Energy Authority which left open the post of Deputy D-G to Dick White who, although a year younger than Hollis, had rather longer service in MI5 and and in any case had spent his entire career dealing with counter-espionage. Having achieved the rank of Deputy D-G there was no prospect of Hollis taking over the top job until, that is, Anthony Eden asked White to run MI6. Hollis's choice of Graham Mitchell as his Deputy D-G illustrates the point about his own relative lack of counter-espionage experience. Mitchell was virtually the same age but with rather less service in the office. Nevertheless, he was a highly experienced counter-espionage officer, having been Director of 'D' Branch.

As well as covering Hollis's career in the Security Service the mole-hunters examined his operational performance and subjected all of his traceable executive decisions to the hypothesis that he was indeed a Soviet agent. It will be remembered that Gouzenko's case had initially been given to Kim Philby, when he was head of MI6's Section IX, but that he had had to leave for Ankara to see Volkov, so he had handed the case over to Hollis. The letter confirming this transfer of responsibility had gone on file. In the light of Philby's confirmed treachery, was this now evidence that Hollis was in league with Philby? Did Philby pass on Gouzenko to a trusted confederate so the defector's evidence might be suppressed? Superficially this might appear the case, but the fact of the transfer was on official record. No doubt either Philby or Hollis, or any other Soviet mole, could have removed the relevant letter from Gouzenko's personal file but neither even attempted to do so. The conclusion is inescapable: Philby had received an, albeit hasty, Soviet briefing about the consequences of Gouzenko's defection before he left London for Ankara to handle the pressing business of Volkov. Having been assured that Gouzenko had never had access to material that might endanger him, Philby turned the situation to his advantage by giving the Gouzenko file to MI5 ... and putting it on the record that he had done so. This meant that if he failed to silence Volkov, he might at least be able to gain some support by pointing out that he had been originally responsible for giving Gouzenko to Hollis. If Philby and Hollis had been collaborating, it would surely have been dangerous for the Philby/Hollis letter to go on the file. A telephone call would have sufficed, or even an emergency rendezvous with the Soviet intermediary. In retrospect the letter paid an extra dividend: it was a tangible piece of evidence to be used against Hollis.

The interviews Hollis conducted with Gouzenko were inevitably inconclusive because Gouzenko's value lay in the documents he removed from the Soviet Embassy in Ottawa, not in his own first-hand experience. There was, however, one unexpected surprise. Before his posting to Canada, Gouzenko had served in GRU headquarters in Moscow. His position had been a junior one, but one of his best friends had confided to him that the head of a British counter-intelligence department was actually a Soviet agent. Certainly the GRU could not have known of this indiscretion and no doubt there were some anxious moments when Gouzenko relayed this to MI5 and the Royal Canadian Mounted Police. To whom was he referring? In fact there were several candidates, not the least of whom was Philby himself. The translated description included the vital words 'counter-intelligence', so the field was not limited to the Security Service. Section IX, headed by Philby, was a counter-intelligence department. Before taking up that post he had been head of Section V's (counter-intelligence) Iberian sub-section. Anthony Blunt had been in MI5 when Gouzenko had noted the comment and there were several other possibilities. To interpret the remark as evidence against Hollis would be to ignore the more obvious candidates who are now known to have fulfilled such roles.

The MI5 mole-hunters delved further into Hollis's work. They noted that he had retained several subject files himself, including the Suppell/Hemner–Scales Report on Soviet espionage and several other personal files which might ordinarily have been considered 'open' for general availability within the office. Instead individual officers had to apply to Hollis for access. Was this evidence of a guilty conscience or excessive secrecy? If Hollis had been worried by the contents of a particular subject file, it would have been easy for him to doctor the contents or simply have it destroyed. To hold it and control its circulation might equally be considered prudent behaviour given the suspicion that there was a Soviet agent around.

The one MI5 officer who was convinced that the office had been penetrated during the war by the Russians was Max Knight. Furthermore, he could prove it. Tom Driberg had been Knight's informant inside the Communist Party of Great Britain, but one day Driberg had suddenly been expelled from the Party by the General Secretary, Harry Pollit. Pollit denounced Driberg as being 'agent number M8'. Driberg naturally denied the accusation, never having heard his own code-name before, and duly repeated the charge to his case officer, Max Knight. Knight realized that this amounted to direct evidence that the CPGB had a source within MI5. Only a limited number of officers received M8's reports on the CPGB and even fewer knew his real identity. When Anthony Blunt was interviewed by the mole-hunters in 1963, he filled in the missing pieces of the jig-saw: he was not on the list of those authorized to see Knight's reports, but one day he had read one which had been left unattended in someone else's office in St James's Street. A reference in the report to a book recently published by M8 betrayed to Blunt the informant's identity, knowledge that he had passed on to his Soviet case officer. Blunt recalled the incident vividly because Pollit's action in expelling Driberg had, he felt, endangered him unnecessarily and he had made an appropriate complaint.

Knight had not known about Blunt, but he had remained convinced that the office had been penetrated. Now the above incident acted in Hollis's favour. Hollis had routinely received Driberg's reports from Knight, yet M8 had remained undiscovered until the moment that Blunt had spotted the particular document which enabled him to identify M8.

Those officers who had hardened in their suspicions of Hollis saw Blunt's testimony as being incomplete and possibly the attempt of a fellow spy, anxious to clear a co-conspirator. Blunt's debriefer, Peter W., remained convinced that Blunt was being completely co-operative, but others were not so sure. In any event Blunt denied all knowledge of a further Soviet agent inside MI5 but, in so doing, appeared to make a contradiction. He agreed that because his Soviet case officer had not attempted to persuade him to stay in MI5 after 1945 it might be reasonably concluded that the Russians enjoyed an alternative source. On the other hand Blunt was very close to Guy Burgess, whom he regarded as his organizer, and he believed that Burgess would have confided in him if he had been running a further agent inside the Security Service. His testimony was regarded as inconclusive.

Once all the files had been checked and Hollis's performance assessed, the investigators were left with the last remaining 'acid test' used to determine retrospectively the loyalty of a particular double agent. The method is quite simple and is known as a profit and loss account. All the cases handled by an individual are totted up and an opinion formed about which side did best overall, MI5 or the opposition. Such an exercise can sometimes produce some surprises, and the profit and loss account on Hollis did just that.

The mole-hunters' investigation into Hollis was necessarily inconclusive and left many questions unanswered. This, of course, was inevitable without the testimony of Philby, Burgess, Agnes Smedley or even SONIA. And yet even if they had been available, as Blunt was, would their evidence have been believed? Or was there an explanation which, though reflecting no credit on Hollis, would clear him of the suspicion of treachery?

There was indeed one, and one that could also be interpreted as serving the KGB's purpose. To analyse that motive it is necessary to turn to the case of a Soviet defector which began on 8 June 1959 in Sweden. On that date a Soviet naval officer, who gave his name as Nicolai Fedorovich Artamonov, was found on the beach with his Polish girlfriend and a bewildered Russian naval rating. Artamonov and the girl claimed they had escaped by small motor boat from Poland and asked for political asylum. The sailor asked to be repatriated to the Soviet Union.

The Artamonov case was assigned to Commander Sven Ryderstrom, a former Swedish Naval Attaché in Moscow. He questioned Artamonov closely and learned that he held the rank of Captain in the Soviet Baltic Fleet and, indeed, was the youngest captain of a destroyer in the entire Soviet Navy. His name was passed to the British and the CIA, who both confirmed that Artamonov's name appeared in their Nominal Indices. His various appointments had been gazetted by *Red Star* and the Soviet Navy, and British Naval Intelligence knew Artamonov to be the commander of a *Skoryi*-type destroyer that had twice entered British ports on goodwill visits.

Artamonov spent the rest of June and July being questioned by the Swedes, who were somewhat sceptical about the defector's claim to have crossed nearly 150 miles of open sea, successfully evading the Polish patrol vessels. In spite of these doubts, both the CIA and MI6 were anxious to debrief Artamonov and made him offers via the Swedish authorities. Eventually Artamonov accepted an American offer of asylum and was flown, on 1 August, to Frankfurt for detailed debriefing at Camp King. He went, in spite of his stated objection to disclosing information of an intelligence value and despite warnings from the Swedes that this would be the price for a future in the United States. At Camp King he underwent routine polygraph tests and failed at least one. In fact the lie-detector operator reported that Artamonov was observed (through a concealed one-way mirror) to be grinning broadly soon after failing, as though he believed he had fooled the machine.

The American Director of Naval Intelligence, Rear Admiral Lawrence Frost, recommended that Artamonov be allowed to continue to the

United States, and he duly arrived in Washington on 22 August, where he was met by two CIA Soviet Russia Division officers, Walter Onoshko (using the cover-name 'Benson') and Walter Sedov. Artamonov then underwent nine months of intensive debriefing during which the defector described his meteoric rise through the Soviet Navy. He had joined the Communist Party shortly after graduating from the Frunze Naval Academy and had attended a special atomic weapons course in 1954. In September the following year, aged twenty-seven, he had been appointed commander of a *Skoryi*-type destroyer and had been to highly secret briefings given by Admiral Sergei Gorshkov, the architect of the modern Soviet Navy. His information was rated as so good, and his knowledge apparently so wide-ranging, that the American Office of Naval Intelligence offered him a five-year contract as a special adviser, albeit against the advice of a civilian counter-intelligence official, William Abbott. After three months in his new job he was considered sufficiently safe to be allowed to give evidence to the House Committee on Un-American Activities. In October the following year he lectured at the American Naval War College and, in his spare time, began a four-year engineering course at George Washington University.

During his initial nine months in the United States, the Americans put Artamonov through every test they could conceive. On one occasion they gave him command of a destroyer during an anti-submarine exercise to see if he really could command a ship. He passed every test and filled many gaps in the West's knowledge of the Soviet Navy.

In October 1962 Artamonov, who had by this date adopted the identity of 'Nicholas Shadrin', first came into contact with the world of counter-intelligence. KAGO had become increasingly difficult to handle at this time and his CIA benefactors proposed a meeting between Artamonov and KAGO. In spite of their different backgrounds they both got on well together. Artamonov's Polish girlfriend (who later became his wife, after a Mexican divorce had freed him of his wife in Leningrad) became firm friends with Svetlana Golytsin and it appeared that Artamonov had become completely rehabilitated. When KAGO sold his house in March 1963 it was to Artamonov that he gave his dog and television set. In fact Artamonov made a number of influential friends, including Admiral Stansfield Turner, then President of the Naval War College in Washington (and later Director of Central Intelligence), Admiral Rufus Taylor (Deputy Director of the Defence Intelligence Agency until October 1966 and thereafter Deputy Director of the CIA), and Admiral Sumner Shapiro, then Director of Naval Intelligence. All had a high regard for the defector and his contribution to the West's knowledge of Soviet naval strategy.

In spite of all these well-placed friends Artamonov was unable to obtain full security clearance and when his naval intelligence contract ran out in June 1965 he was without a job. In November he became a US citizen and for the next four months attempted to get re-employed by the Office of Naval Intelligence. Instead he was offered a low-grade post at the newly formed Defence Intelligence Agency which he accepted.

Before he joined the Defence Intelligence Agency in March 1966 Artamonov had had only routine contact with the CIA on a business level although he had struck up friendships with several CIA personnel, including Peter Sivess who ran Ashford Farm, the debriefing centre in Virginia. Artamonov shared a keen interest with Sivess in hunting and shooting and they both roamed the estate after duck whenever the Farm was not occupied by a defector. His only conflict with the CIA had occurred in November 1960, shortly after arriving in the United States when Artamonov refused to help recruit a recently appointed Soviet Naval Attaché in Washington, Lieutenant-Commander Lev Vtorgin. Vtorgin had apparently known Artamonov at the Frunze Naval Academy, so the CIA's Soviet Russia Division suggested that the defector would be in a good position to suborn him. Artamonov excused himself saying that Vtorgin was the finest pistol shot in the Baltic Fleet and had probably been sent to Washington to assassinate him. The CIA had pursued the matter no further.

Shortly after Artamonov had joined the Defence Intelligence Agency, he was drawn into a counter-intelligence maelstrom. One Saturday morning the Director of Central Intelligence, Dick Helms, had received a telephone call from a Washington-based KGB officer who volunteered his services to the CIA. Helms immediately contacted the CIA Office of Security and arranged a lunchtime rendevous with the Soviet informant. Helms's reason for assigning the case to the Office of Security was an attempt to keep the offer from the Soviet Russia Division which, according to Angleton, as we have seen, harboured SASHA's protector.

The Office of Security's representative at the lunch was Bruce Solie, an experienced CIA officer who code-named his informant KITTY HAWK. KITTY HAWK himself turned out to be a middle-ranking Soviet diplomat (and covert KGB officer), who said that with American help he was set to climb into a really senior position at Dzerzinsky Square. In order to prove his bona fides he reeled off a wealth of extraordinary information, including a confirmation of AE/FOXTROT's credentials as a genuine defector and confirmation of Igor Orlov's role as SASHA.

Not surprisingly the Counter-Intelligence Division were at first sceptical of KITTY HAWK although the FBI case officer present, Bert Turner, felt his story rang true and should not be ignored. In any event KITTY HAWK was accepted and arrangements were made to build up his status with the KGB before his tour of duty was scheduled to end.

One part of this plan was the recruitment of Nicolai Artamonov as a double agent.

According to KITTY HAWK the KGB felt that Artamonov would be susceptible to pressure because of his family in the USSR. Artamonov had apparently been rehabilitated by the Americans; if he was to change his mind and re-defect to Russia, it would be a considerable Soviet propaganda victory. The CIA and the FBI examined the idea and decided to go ahead. Artamonov was warned by the FBI that he was so highly regarded in Washington that they suspected he had become a target for the KGB. He was instructed not to rebuff the Soviet approach, but simply to pretend to co-operate and then report the incident to the FBI's Washington Field Office, which was conveniently located in the same building that housed Artamonov's Defence Intelligence Agency section.

Artamonov complied with the FBI's request and, in the summer of 1966, reported an approach by a Soviet diplomat matching KITTY HAWK's description. By the time KITTY HAWK had returned to Moscow at the end of 1966 he had received the credit for successfully recruiting Artamonov and had passed him on to a replacement KGB case officer, Oleg Kozlov.

Artamonov's exact role in this double-agent game remains unclear, but both sides appear to have been confident of his loyalty. The only person who had serious doubts was KAGO who, the previous year, said he had suddenly discovered that Artamonov had been a 'plant' right from the beginning. As soon as he realized he had been duped, KAGO broke off all contact with the naval 'defector' and denounced him to the CIA's Counter-Intelligence Division.

If KAGO was right, then it illustrated the extraordinary lengths that the Soviets were prepared to go to in order to deceive the West. It would also justify the Swedes' suspicion of him and explain his polygraph failure at Camp King. And, if he had been a plant, then it followed that KITTY HAWK was also a plant; that in turn would once again throw doubt on AE/FOXTROT and lead to the need for a reassessment of SASHA.

When the Artamonov case was viewed through the jaundiced eyes of the Counter-Intelligence Division, it certainly took on the shape of a giant deception. Artamonov was in all probability the real Artamonov, for it was argued that no KGB trainee could convincingly take command of a destroyer during an anti-submarine exercise. Not only had Arta-monov achieved this, but he had also impressed his observers. His background had made him irresistible to the West, and no doubt the KGB had little preference about who took the bait, MI6 or the CIA. The briefings by Gorshkov, the meteoric career, the atomic weapons course and the detailed knowledge of the *Skoryi*-type destroyer all combined to make the defector a sensational prize. It also guaranteed a direct influence on the West's assessment of Soviet naval strategy and tactics. Given the build-up in Soviet sea power in the late 1950s and early 1960s, was it not prudent to carry out a deception operation to distract the opposition?

There were more sinister aspects to the operation, if indeed that is what it really was. Artamonov had made a point of developing friendships with numerous highly placed intelligence officers who might have unwittingly imparted significant information. For example, his connection with Peter Sivess allowed him to know whenever a defector was occupying Ashford Farm. Whenever that happened Sivess was obliged to isolate the estate and refuse Artamonov access to the duck. His dual role would explain his disappointment at leaving the Office of Naval Intelligence and his reluctance to take up the low-grade Defence Intelligence job; his constant requests for security clearance; the speed with which he mastered the English language (he was sufficiently fluent to graduate with a Masters degree in engineering five years after arriving in the US); his anxiety to leave the CIA's custody and take up his job; his apparent fearlessness of KGB retribution (unique among defectors, then and now); his reluctance to contact Vtorgin (who may have been his Soviet case officer all along; he had arrived in Washington from Buenos Aires where he had been posted as Assistant Naval Attaché after Artamonov's escape to Sweden).

Artamonov might also have had the opportunity to make contact with a Soviet case officer whilst on a holiday he took, soon after his release from CIA custody in 1960. He had driven himself and his girlfriend around the United States unsupervised and, apparently, without a schedule. If the KGB had wished to confer with him in secret, this long vacation would have provided excellent cover.

It might also be said that KITTY HAWK's recruitment of Artamonov coincided with his new job in Defence Intelligence. This might indicate that the KGB had judged his operational usefulness to have come to an end. The double-agent approach would prove to the Americans that (a) he was evidently considered important by the Soviets (and thus merited a better position), and (b) that he was not a plant.

The Artamonov case continued for some years under joint FBI and CIA control and the information supplied to the KGB was accepted by the Soviets without demur. The defector either handed his messages to his Soviet case officer in Washington or the Russians met him when he went abroad. In 1969 he made a brief visit to England on his way to the Continent and two years later was used to test Jim Bennett, the high ranking Royal Canadian Mounted Police Security Service officer who had fallen under suspicion of being in Soviet pay. In September 1971 Artamonov was scheduled to meet his KGB case officer in Montreal. At the very last moment the CIA told Bennett, apparently as a courtesy, that a trusted double agent was meeting his Russian contact on Canadian territory and that there would be no surveillance for fear of scaring off the opposition. The CIA then waited to see if Bennett warned the Soviets that Artamonov was a CIA double agent. Under normal circumstances the KGB would undertake elaborate measures to detect hostile surveillance and, if warned of surveillance, would either cancel the meeting or simply fail to turn up at the appointed time.

On the occasion that Artamonov was used, the meeting went ahead smoothly, significantly in the absence of the KGB's usual precautions. The almost reckless behaviour on the part of the Soviets showed their supreme confidence that there was no team of watchers in the vicinity; it was completely out of character for them. This could have been interpreted as circumstantial evidence of Bennett's duplicity. If, however, Artamonov had always been loyal to Moscow, the Soviets' behaviour was only explicable as a remarkably devious attempt to discredit a senior counter-intelligence officer. It would appear that this was indeed the case.

On 15 March 1972 Bennett underwent four days of interrogation by the RCMP's Security Service and a few months later was given a medical discharge. He retired to South Africa, but returned to Ottawa five years later to bring a libel action against Ian Adams, the author of S, *Portrait of a Spy*,* who had described Bennett's ordeal in fictional terms. The action was settled out of Court and the Canadian Solicitor-General cleared Bennett publicly.

Artamonov was last seen on 18 December 1975 in Vienna, shortly before a scheduled rendezvous with the KGB. KITTY HAWK, who had returned to Moscow shortly after 'recruiting' Artamonov, was never heard of again.

The net result was the loss to the West of a senior counter-intelligence expert, Jim Bennett, in much the same way as Britain was later to 'lose' Hollis.

Jim Bennett was not the only Western security chief to be the subject of a smear. Jim Angleton himself was denounced as a probable Soviet mole in an official CIA report written in 1974 by Clare Edward Petty, an experienced counter-intelligence officer who had investigated Heinz Felfe, the traitor. Petty totted up the Angleton profit and loss account and theorized that both AE/FOXTROT and KAGO might have been plants. He also pointed to Angleton's obsession with KAGO's Byzantine conspiracy ideas as circumstantial evidence of his wish to disrupt the West's counter-intelligence effort. After all, it was argued, Angleton and KAGO together had voiced suspicions of, and launched inconclusive investigations into, virtually every security service in the West.

* Ticknor & Fields, NY, 1982.

The KGB, of course, had much to gain from such disinformation tactics. A carefully planted idea that a particular officer is in reality a Soviet mole has the effect of turning the entire organization upside down and distracts it from its day-to-day activities. As well as undermining it operationally, the exercise can also force a reappraisal of a suspect's entire career. This happened in the cases of PETERS and Hollis in England, Angleton in the United States and Bennett in Canada. Many other countries suffered the same experience. It could always be argued that by promoting such mole-hunts the KGB risked exposing their genuine assets, but in practice it would seem that the investigations have generally resulted in taking attention away from the real spies and focusing it on the innocent. The links between the Artamonov-KITTY HAWK-AE/FOXTROT-SASHA-Bennett cases demonstrate how a skilled disinformation manipulator can totally paralyse a Western intelligence organization's operational capability.

Virtually the only consolation that can be drawn from this state of affairs is the prospect of the KGB believing that they too are the victims of similar exercises. There is a certain amount of evidence for accepting this to be the case. When Otto John had been interrogated by the Russians in East Berlin in 1954 he could not understand why so much attention was paid to his wartime dealings with the head of the Iberian section of MI6's Section V, Kim Philby. Otto John had originally defected to the British in July 1944 in Portugal, after the failure of the assassination attempt on Hitler. The KGB appeared most anxious to determine the exact nature of his dealings with MI6. They wanted to know everything about the MI6 officers he had met in neutral Lisbon, whilst plotting Hitler's death, and the exact details of any negotiations that might have taken place.

At the time Dr John could not have known the significance of the questions put to him and he replied truthfully with the names of the MI6 officers he had been in contact with. None of them had been Philby. He also maintained, to the evident satisfaction of his Russian inquisitors, that the British government had steadfastly stuck to its agreed line of unconditional surrender. There was never, he assured them, any suggestion from the British side that they might ditch their Soviet allies in the event of a successful anti-Nazi coup in Berlin. This, of course, had been the intention of the plotters, for such an undertaking would have encouraged more senior German officers to participate in the plot. Dr John's answers unwittingly confirmed Philby's status to the Russians as a loyal agent at a time when he was incommunicado. If Dr John had told them a different story then they would, no doubt, have abandoned Philby as a double agent.

In this connection it is worth noting another example of Soviet suspicion of hostile disinformation: Burgess, on his death-bed, had denounced

Philby as a British agent! No wonder the KGB were so uncertain when George Blake escaped from prison and turned up in East Germany in December 1966.

Blake's escape from Wormwood Scrubs Prison occurred within a year of Martin Furnival Jones's promotion to Director-General of the Security Service. It was arguably one of the most disastrous lapses in security ever. It also gave credence to the popular myth that the Soviets never forget the welfare of their agents.

If prison sentences are an indication of a spy's relative value then Blake was the most important Soviet agent under lock and key. The Lord Chief Justice, Lord Parker, had sentenced him to a total of forty-two years' imprisonment, rather more than double the sentence he had given to Peter and Helen Kroger a few weeks earlier, in March 1961.

Blake himself was totally unprepared for the severity of his sentence and two days later collapsed in his cell at Wormwood Scrubs suffering from delayed shock. In stark contrast to Lonsdale, who had received twenty-five years after a plea of not guilty, Blake had pleaded guilty to all five of the charges that had been brought against him under the Official Secrets Acts. Blake's Defence Counsel, Mr Jeremy Hutchinson QC, was later to argue that the sentence was 'inordinate, unprecedented and manifestly excessive', but his client was still prepared to co-operate with MI6 and continue his debriefings.

As is customary, these sessions were discontinued during the trial itself and were not resumed until after Blake's appeal had been dismissed on 19 June. The three judges who considered the defence submissions, Mr Justice Hilbery, Mr Justice Ashworth and Mr Justice Paul, upheld the conviction and agreed with Lord Parker's remark that 'Blake's case was one of the worst that can be envisaged in times of peace'. Blake was not in Court to hear the dismissal because he was too ill to attend.

Between June and September 1961 Blake underwent detailed interrogation at Wormwood Scrubs. At one of these sessions Blake identified a photograph of his London-based KGB case officer, Sergei Kondrashev, to Tony Healey and Terence Lecky who, as we have seen, had been seconded to the Security Service from MI6. As Blake was considered to be a likely candidate for escape he was housed in a special security cell in 'D' Hall, which was subject to frequent searches. A light remained on all night and Blake was obliged to leave all his clothes outside his cell.

On 20 September 1961 MI5 informed the Prison Governor, Mr Thomas Hayes, that Blake's continued presence in London would soon no longer be required and preparations were made to move him to Winson Green Prison in Birmingham. This transfer was specifically requested by the Security Service because they wished to avoid Blake coming into contact with Gordon Lonsdale who was also serving his sentence in 'D' Hall. In the meantime, at the discretion of the Governor, Blake's name had been removed from the list of those most likely to escape.

Incredibly, the Prison Commissioners refused MI5's request on the grounds that a transfer to Birmingham would create hardships for Blake's wife and mother. During the next two years the letters went to and fro between Room 055 and the Commissioners, but they refused to budge. Blake, of course, was completely oblivious to this correspondence and was concentrating on his own, which consisted in the main of a postal course in Arabic. He had been granted permission to begin his studies in the autumn of 1961, and MI5 were obliged to read every one of his papers, and those of his teachers, so as to ensure that the model prisoner was not hiding messages in his work. This caused such long delays that, after protests, MI5 agreed that they would in future only examine photostats of Blake's mail.

Early in 1962 MI5 were involved in further deliberations concerning Blake's outside visitors. Like any other prisoner, he was entitled to receive regular visits in the presence of a prison officer. Blake only ever saw his wife and mother, whom the Security Service regarded as safe, so MI5 declined an offer to station a watcher in the room when the visits took place.

Virtually from the day that Blake began his sentence, rumours abounded that his escape was being planned. Recently discharged prisoners, who had met Blake in the Scrubs, sometimes managed to sell plausible 'rescue plans' to Fleet Street journalists and from time to time successful prison escapes brought renewed interest in Blake. In December 1963 MI5 proposed a transfer to Wakefield Prison in Yorkshire, but again the Commissioners vetoed the idea.

On 6 June 1966 four prisoners escaped from 'D' Hall of Wormwood Scrubs and the investigation that followed highlighted a number of lapses in the physical security of the prison. Various measures were recommended to improve security but, before they could be completed, Blake had vanished. He made his escape, with outside help, shortly after 6pm on Saturday 22 October. The alarm was not called until 7.20pm, by which time his absence from his cell had been reported and a home-made rope-ladder had been found hanging over the main perimeter wall. Shepherd's Bush police station was notified of the escape immediately and Special Branch at Scotland Yard a short while thereafter. The 'K' Branch Night Duty Officer at Leconfield House was telephoned with the news some time before nine o'clock by the Commander of Special Branch, Evan Jones, but by that time the prison authorities had established that none of their staff had seen Blake since half-past five. In all probability Blake had a three-hour lead over the Security Service. This depressing news was given to the Home Secretary, Roy Jenkins, and to the Prime Minister Harold Wilson, who was spending the weekend at Chequers.

'K' Branch's static observation posts around Soviet offices and homes in Kensington and Highgate were alerted, but none were issued with an up-to-date photograph of Blake for the simple reason that none existed in official files. The most recent official picture of the escapee had been taken before his trial and showed him sporting a beard. In fact a portrait had been taken of him in prison the previous year, and it was this which was hastily reproduced and distributed to Fleet Street and the police forces.

The clues left at the scene of the escape were minimal. Apart from the rope-ladder, which was found to be constructed of knitting needles, the police had only come up with a vague scratch mark on the outside of the prison wall, some tyre marks on the kerb of Artillery Road (which ran directly alongside the wall) and a pot of chrysanthemums. The explanation for the pot of flowers was ingenious: Blake's accomplice had been obliged to wait around for him and, in order to allay any local suspicions, he had carried the flowers as though he was visiting the neighbouring Hammersmith Hospital.

The knitting-needle ladder suggested an amateur effort, so the police concentrated on tracing and interviewing recently released prisoners. One such prisoner, a former RAF clerk named Sean Bourke, was already on the run from the police and within twenty-four hours he had become Special Branch's candidate for Blake's outside accomplice.

Bourke had been released from the Scrubs on licence the previous November, after completing a seven-year sentence for sending a bomb through the post to a police officer, who had arrested him earlier on. Once Bourke had gained his final release (with full remission for good conduct) on 4 July, the police officer started receiving threatening letters and telephone calls. Bourke was wanted for questioning for these offences, but it was learned that he had given up his job at CAV Limited on 23 September and had not been seen since. Chief Inspector Stephen Cunningham of Special Branch visited Bourke's home in Limerick, in Eire, and learned from his mother that he had returned to England on 15 October.

It was not until 26 October that any further progress was made. On that evening the information room at Scotland Yard received an anonymous telephone call to say that Blake's getaway car, a 1955 Humber Hawk, index number 117 GMX, was parked in Harvist Road, Kilburn. When the car was found every inch of it, inside and out, was examined by Home Office forensic scientists. They reported that its tyres corresponded exactly to the marks found in Artillery Road. The vehicle was registered in Bourke's name at 26 Perryn Road, almost a mile from the prison. There the landlord's resident representative, Mrs Smith, said that Bourke had not been seen for at least a week.

The manhunt team were inundated with tips from the public and from informants, but surprisingly it appeared that the Soviets had not to date played a direct role in the affair. A former prisoner in the Scrubs, named John McGrath, reported that the Soviet Assistant Air Attaché, Colonel Mekhonoshin, had expressed an interest in Blake's welfare but nothing further had developed. Telephone taps indicated that the Russians appeared to be as bemused by events as everyone else, although 'D' Branch naturally assumed that the KGB had at least financed the operation, even if they had not actually directed it. This later turned out to be the case.

No further progress was made by the police until 15 January 1967 when a newspaper informed Scotland Yard that they had received a photograph of Bourke through the post with an address scrawled on the reverse: 28 Highlever Road, W10.

The address was that of a house of small furnished bed-sits. The landlady, Mrs Heveringham, showed the police to the small two-roomed flat of one of her tenants, Mr Sigworth. According to Mrs Heveringham, Mr Sigworth was a journalist who spent much of his time away on newspaper assignments, but when the flat was searched the police discovered the fingerprints of both Bourke and Blake. Apparently Bourke had lived there continuously since the previous October, but had left on 10 January. The rent, however, was paid up to date and was usually paid by postal order. Bourke had found the flat through a Paddington letting agency and had given his former address as 5 Bank Road, Croydon. No such address existed.

Bourke did eventually turn up ... at the British Embassy in Moscow on 4 September 1967. He claimed to have arrived in the Soviet Union the previous January on a forged British passport. He had, he said, taken a scheduled flight from Heathrow to West Berlin, via Frankfurt, and had spent the last eight months in Moscow. Now he wished to return home. It seemed that he had been sharing a flat in the Russian capital with Blake and he had overheard a conversation in which his future was being discussed. He would either be free to leave the Soviet Union in a minimum of five years' time, or he might be liquidated.

The First Secretary of the British Embassy in Moscow, Peter Maxey, had advised Bourke that the Irish Republic was not represented in any communist countries and certainly the British Embassy had no responsibility for him, even if he was wanted by the police in London. Nevertheless, they asked him to return a week later while London was contacted. On 20 September, the Foreign Office broke the news in London of Bourke's presence in Moscow. This effectively prevented the KGB from killing Bourke, if that was indeed one of their plans. Shortly afterwards the Russians responded by announcing officially that Philby was living in Moscow.

The next chapter in the Blake story began the following summer when Sean Bourke's brother Kevin, who had been working in Scotland, asked the *News of the World* to finance a trip to Moscow so he could see his brother. The trip went ahead as planned on 12 August, but on his return a manuscript of Sean Bourke's memoirs was removed by the KGB at Sheremetenvo Airport. On his return to England Kevin arranged for the Irish Embassy in London to issue his brother with an emergency travel document valid for one journey between Moscow and Eire. This was received in Moscow on 10 October, and ten days later Sean Bourke flew on the first leg home to Amsterdam, where he stayed overnight to give a television interview. Bourke finally arrived at Shannon on 22 October 1968 in a blaze of publicity, but within the week he was arrested by the Irish Special Branch in Dublin after the Metropolitan Police had made a request for his extradition.

He was released on 4 February 1969 after the President of the Irish High Court had ruled Bourke's offence had been of a political nature. He subsequently remained in Eire and, on 27 January 1982, he succumbed to a heart attack.

The first government enquiry Martin Furnival Jones had to deal with in his capacity as Director-General was the Mountbatten Report into prison security and, in particular, the circumstances of Blake's escape. The full details of the escape only became known after Bourke had been released from custody, when he published his version of events.* MI5's conscience was clear, although considerable press attention was paid to the lack of an up-to-date official photograph of Blake or, for that matter, of Vassall or the Krogers.

If the KGB had engineered the escape, and even today there is no conclusive evidence, it is unclear why. Naturally the propaganda value should not be ignored, and Ronald Biggs's dramatic escape from Wandsworth Prison in July 1965 had proved how much publicity could be generated. But against that is the fact that the KGB must have known that Blake was something of a broken reed. He had confessed, pleaded guilty and co-operated with Lecky by being debriefed. His deliverance, more than five years after his arrest, must have been of only the most marginal operational interest in terms of MI6's current activities. Furthermore the Soviets had invariably shown minimal concern when one of their agents had been arrested, contrary to myth. The spy swaps that had taken place to date had all involved Soviet nationals: Rudolf

---

* *The Springing of George Blake* (Cassells, 1970). Blake's own account, entitled *No Abiding City*, although written, has not yet been published.

Abel in February 1962 and Gordon Lonsdale in April 1964.* The Soviets had never even brought up the subject of such British nationals as Vassall, Houghton, Bossard or Blake. The Krogers were not to be exchanged for some time. If the KGB financed Bourke, as the Security Service later came to believe, then their motives were less than obvious.

The Mountbatten Report absolved MI5 of blame for Blake's escape, but there was, no doubt, a residual sensitivity in Curzon Street about such escapes. This may have contributed to the Kachenko fiasco of September 1967, which will be described shortly. But first we should catch up with two cases which occurred earlier in the year.

The first began on 2 May 1967 with a telephone call to Curzon Street from the security unit attached to the American nuclear submarine base at Holy Loch. A United States Navy rating had reported being approached for information in the local American Services Club by a Dunoon book-maker named William MacAffer. The rating, Gary Lee Ledbetter, was a shipfitter on the USS Simon Lake, a depot ship with the 14th Polaris Submarine Squadron. According to the Americans, MacAffer had offered to buy any official documents Ledbetter cared to sell, as there was, apparently, a lucrative market for them. 'K' Branch immediately contacted the Chief Constable of Argyll, Kenneth MacKinnon, and arranged for Ledbetter to be kept under surveillance when he handed over some documents. On 28 May MacAffer was arrested in Argyll Street while receiving classified information from Ledbetter. MacAffer promptly made a statement implicating his contact, an East German agent named Peter Dorschel.

Dorschel now became the centre of MI5's attention. He turned out to be a twenty-six-year-old seaman who had, in January, married an English model and set up home in Manchester. He was arrested on 18 June and taken to Edinburgh to face charges under the Official Secrets Acts. He pleaded guilty the following day and was sentenced to seven years' imprisonment by Lord Grant, the Lord Justice Clerk of Scotland.

The second case, which ran in parallel with Dorschel's, was that of Helen Keenan, a twenty-year-old girl from Halifax, who had unwittingly been recruited as an agent for the Rhodesian Special Branch. That such an organization, or its collaborator, the South African Bureau of State Security (BOSS), should have operated against the UK would have been considered unthinkable in the days of Sillitoe who, after all, had advised on BOSS's formation after his retirement from MI5. Indeed, MI5 had long enjoyed good relations with South Africa and had stationed a Security Liaison Officer there before South Africa's departure from the Commonwealth. One such officer had been the Director of 'K' Branch.

* Lonsdale was reported dead by the Soviet press on 14 October 1970.

Helen Keenan was a short-hand typist at the Cabinet Office, one of the famous 'garden girls' of Downing Street. In the middle of May 1967, after just nine months in the job, she had handed in her notice and had been routinely interviewed by her supervisor. In the course of their conversation the typist had complained that her work had been dull and boring. This was an extraordinary remark to make considering the run-of-the-mill paperwork most secretaries have to deal with. The supervisor suspected she might have another motive and, on her last day at work on 25 May, she was interviewed by Detective Superintendent Victor Gilbert of Special Branch. He discovered her real reason for leaving.

Miss Keenan shared a flat in Earls Court with two other secretaries and earlier in the year had been taken to the Zambesi Club, a well-known local bar frequented in the main by South Africans and Rhodesians. There, by chance, she had met a young surveyor named Norman Blackburn who happened to live in Nevern Square, virtually next door to Miss Keenan's flat in Nevern Road. He had taken an interest in her work at the Cabinet Office, saying that his father had a business in Salisbury, and asked her to give him any papers she came across which concerned Rhodesia. During this time the Prime Minister had been heavily involved in negotiations with Ian Smith's break-away regime in Rhodesia and a large amount of the Cabinet Office's work had been directly concerned with those talks. On three occasions Miss Keenan had given copies of classified Cabinet minutes to Blackburn.

Gilbert took a statement from Miss Keenan and then, after consultations, went to Earls Court to see Blackburn. After his arrest Blackburn admitted to receiving the Cabinet papers and also admitted to being a member of the South African Intelligence Service. His parents, far from being in business in Salisbury, were living on the Isle of Man, where he had been born. He was a professional intelligence officer who, he alleged, had only held meetings with his British-born case officer (and representative of the Rhodesian Special Branch) on the neutral territory of Dublin. Both Keenan and Blackburn were tried at the Old Bailey on 25 July 1967 and were sentenced by Mr Justice O'Connor to six months' imprisonment and five years' imprisonment respectively. The case was the first of its kind and led to the South Africans being treated thereafter as a hostile intelligence organization. The affair also had political consequences for MI5 because it was Harold Wilson's first major encounter with espionage. No doubt the fact that it directly concerned him and his negotiations with Ian Smith, and that it happened on his own doorstep, had its effect. Certainly he remained forever afterwards acutely aware of South African intelligence operations in England.

Almost as soon as the cases of Dorschel and Blackburn had been concluded, the Security Service became entangled in yet another case which involved the Prime Minister, as it ended with him having to seek a personal briefing from the Director-General.

Dr Vladimir Kachenko was a twenty-five-year-old Soviet physicist researching low temperature physics at Birmingham University, one of ninety Soviet scientists working in England at the time. His particular project was unclassified and he was generally regarded as brilliant. Virtually the first time he had come to the attention of MI5 was in the early hours of Saturday, 16 September 1967, when he turned up at the Russian Embassy at around 4.30am. The doorman on duty told him to come back at nine, which he duly did.

Some two and a half hours later Kachenko emerged from the Embassy and walked up Kensington Palace Gardens towards MI5's static observation post in Lancaster Gate. At the top he turned right, into the Bayswater Road, but it soon became obvious that he was being chased. Four officials from the Embassy were in pursuit in a car; they swerved into the Bayswater Road, screeched to a halt beside the physicist and bundled him into the car before anyone could intervene. One of those participating in the 'snatch' was later identified as Ivan Aleksandrovich Shischkin, the KGB officer who had negotiated Abel's exchange for Gary Powers in Berlin, five years earlier.

The Soviets' behaviour was extraordinary, especially as it had been in full view of Saturday morning strollers. 'K' Branch were informed and at about the same time Aeroflot announced that their scheduled flight to Moscow that morning would be slightly delayed. The next development was a convoy of diplomatic cars to Heathrow where a Tupolov-104 was waiting, with passengers aboard, for permission to taxi to the runway. A group of Soviet diplomats ushered an apparently dazed Dr Kachenko past the formalities and placed him in a seat. As soon as he was safely aboard, the aircraft began moving away from the departure gate. The plane had just reached the end of the taxi path when the pilot was ordered to stop by the air traffic controllers, and seven police cars surrounded it. Special Branch officers from the airport swarmed aboard and tried to talk to Kachenko. The physicist was hardly conscious, but he did say he wished to talk to the British authorities in private. He was carried off the plane and placed in an ambulance which, later that morning, took him to a flat rented by MI5.

At that stage it seemed that Kachenko was being forced to leave the UK against his will, and a puncture mark on his arm proved that he had recently received some medication, presumably at the Embassy. By Monday morning, however, the position had altered. Kackenko had been examined by Dr William Sargent, one of Britain's eminent psychiatrists, who diagnosed acute schizophrenia. He advised against further chemotherapy because it was not known what drug had already been administered, but he remarked on the patient's rapidly deteriorating condition.

The physicist was thoroughly confused and had changed his mind about staying in England. It appeared to MI5 that, because they had been unable to administer an antidote to Kachenko, he was in grave danger of dying. They therefore surrendered him. At half-past ten on Monday morning Dr Kachenko was returned to the Russian Embassy and, later the same day, was flown to Moscow. That, however, was not the last of the affair. Kachenko's wife, Galina, accused the British of trying to kidnap her husband and wrote to the Prime Minister. Mr Wilson consulted the Director-General of MI5 and then answered with a suitably curt reply, pointing out that there would have been no drama if the Soviets had asked for British assistance in the first place, instead of pushing people into cars in broad daylight. He was, he said, perfectly satisfied that the authorities had acted correctly and that no attempt had been made to persuade her husband to remain in England.

A far more serious case, which only came to light in 1968, concerned an amateur radio enthusiast called Douglas Britten, a Chief Technician who had been in the RAF since 1949. When he was arrested in September 1968 he was stationed at RAF Digby in Lincolnshire, an extremely sensitive RAF signals unit. His detection came about from both technical and physical surveillance on the Soviet Consulate in Kensington Palace Gardens.

Britten had been recruited in 1962 by a man known to him simply as YURI. The Russian had approached him while he was strolling through the Science Museum in South Kensington, and had addressed him as 'Golf Three Kilo Foxtrot Lima', his amateur call-sign. It was later assumed that the Soviets had made a study of radio hams who were servicemen and had selected Britten as a target. When the conversation turned to Britten's job, YURI asked him to obtain a wireless transmitter known as the 1154. In fact this set was considered obsolete by the RAF and it was generally available to radio enthusiasts on the open market. YURI pretended not to know this and paid Britten well for this piece of equipment. When Britten was posted to Cyprus shortly after this encounter, the Russians appointed a local case officer who had the RAF technician photographed receiving money in exchange for local gossip. Thereafter Britten was constantly blackmailed. In October 1966 Britten was transferred back to England and came under the control of a Soviet intelligence officer, later identified as Alexsandr Ivanovitch Borisenko, who had been First Secretary at the Embassy since May 1966. In January the following year Britten held a meeting with Borisenko at Arnos Grove station, in north London. Pressure was reapplied on Britten and he continued to supply the Russians until February 1968, when he was photographed hand-delivering a message to the Consulate, after his case officer had failed to turn up for a rendezvous.

At his trial on 4 November 1968 before the Lord Chief Justice, Lord Parker, Britten pleaded guilty and was sentenced to twenty-one years' imprisonment. He too had been subject to the Positive Vetting procedure but, as it was later pointed out, this merely screened individual candidates, it did not detect traitors. Britten's activities had been highly damaging and, in military terms, were of much greater significance than previous post-war cases. Nevertheless, Britten fully recognized the extent of his treachery and co-operated, both with the RAF police investigators who had arrested him, and the Security Service.

The Britten case attracted only the minimum of publicity because of the defendant's plea of guilty. Another minor case, which was also wrapped up with the minimum of fuss about this time, began on 14 August 1968 when the Deputy Director of Naval Security, Captain Frederick Stephenson RN, was told of an interview that had been conducted that afternoon aboard the anti-submarine frigate HMS *Duncan* between Able Seaman Robin Cloude and Lieutenant Brian Sieff RN. Cloude had confessed to having twice visited the Soviet Naval Attaché whilst absent without leave on 8 May. Sieff promptly reported this to Lieutenant-Commander Andrews, the officer in charge of security at Portsmouth, and he in turn had contacted Stephenson.

The following day Cloude was brought up to the Admiralty security office in Spring Gardens and repeated his confession. Apparently he had been told that he was ineligible for a housing purchase scheme and had decided to sell some information to the Russian Embassy. In the event the Soviet Naval Attaché had told him to come back in a fortnight. MI5 advised that Cloude's case should be given to Special Branch, and on 21 August Detective Superintendent Beaton of Special Branch formally arrested him and he appeared at the Old Bailey the following month charged with committing Official Secrets Act offences the previous May. He was sentenced to five years' imprisonment.

While MI5 were investigating this relatively minor case, the Russians launched their 1968 invasion of Czechoslovakia. In so doing the Soviets sparked off an unprecedented series of defections. The first was that of their Deputy Minister of Defence, Major-General Jan Sejna, who had escaped to the United States the previous December. He was followed after the invasion by Captain Marous and Major Ladislav Bittman, who both underwent CIA debriefing. As a direct result Rear-Admiral Hermann Luedke, SHAPE's logistics chief, shot himself. On the following day, 9 October, Horst Wendland, the Deputy Chief of the West German intelligence service, shot himself in his office at his headquarters at Pullach in West Germany. On 14 October Hans Schenke of the Ministry of Economics hanged himself. He was followed, four days later, by Colonel Johann Grimm of the West German Ministry of Defence. Three days later Gerhard Boehm, also of the Ministry of Defence, was found drowned in the Rhine near Cologne.

All these individuals had been identified as moles by Bittman, but it was Josef Frolik who was to cause the sensation in England. Frolik had not survived the post-invasion purge of the Czech Intelligence Service and was told that after August 1969 he would be required no longer. He promptly contacted the CIA in Prague and made a deal: full details of the operations he had run in exchange for asylum for himself, his wife and his son. The Americans agreed the terms and, on 14 July, the Froliks left a Czech holiday camp near Byela in Bulgaria, feigning illness, and announced their intention to motor back to Prague. According to Frolik,* they then drove south to the Gulf of Burgas on the Black Sea, where they were picked up off the beach by a specially converted launch. In reality the Frolik family kept a rendezvous in quite a different location and were then spirited to Istanbul, 120 miles away. As soon as they reached Turkey they had been driven to the United States Air Force base outside Istanbul and flown, via Trieste, to Washington and Ashford Farm.

Frolik had joined the Czech Ministry of Security in December 1952 and eight years later had been put to work on the British desk supervising Czech operations in England. Like Bittman before him, who had worked against West Germany, Frolik had an unrivalled knowledge of Czech espionage and subversion in England, and had spent two years, from 1964 to 1966, on a tour of duty in London, nominally as a 'labour attaché'.

The first consequence of Frolik's revelations was a visit paid to the home of a Labour Member of Parliament, on 14 January 1970, by Commander John Wilson of Special Branch. The MP was the sixty-nine-year-old Member for Morpeth in Northumberland, Mr Will Owen, who, according to Frolik, had been a useful source and had been code-named LEE. Apparently Owen, a former miner, had been recruited during a 1957 visit to Czechoslovakia and had been supplied with his 'travel expenses'. Thereafter he received regular cash payments from the Czechs. He had been elected to Parliament in November 1954 and in February 1960 had been appointed to the Defence Estimates Committee. He served on Sub-Committee B, which dealt with Admiralty matters, and Frolik alleged that Owen had supplied a mass of important military information. When Owen was questioned about his relationship with Colonel Jan Paclik and Robert Husak of the Czech Embassy, he flatly denied ever receiving any money from them. At a later interview Owen admitted having lied, but claimed he had taken £2,300 in total.

An examination of Owen's tax returns revealed dozens of examples of undeclared income and he frequently inflated his expenses or claimed them several times over. He was informed that he was going to be

* *The Frolik Defection* (Leo Cooper, 1975).

prosecuted and, in April 1970, after further evidence against him had been obtained by another Czech defector, Major Frantisek August, he resigned his seat.

Owen's trial opened at the Old Bailey the following month before Mr Justice Stephenson, with Edward Cussen appearing for the prosecution. It lasted for thirteen days, during which the defence successfully argued that, whilst Owen had indeed been the subject of blackmail, he had never had access to military information that could not be freely obtained elsewhere. The former Secretary of the 'D' Notice Committee, Colonel Sammy Lohan, confirmed this when he appeared as a witness for the defence. The jury accepted this view and cleared Owen on all eight charges. Frolik himself never appeared in Court as a witness because he had not personally run LEE and therefore had no first-hand evidence to give. All the information that he had given to the Security Service would have been classed as hearsay.

Owen himself was greatly surprised by his acquittal and feared retribution by MI5 who were anxious to identify all his Czech contacts, even if he had been cleared. Eventually Owen agreed to a meeting at Room 055 of the War Office, provided another Labour MP, Leo Abse, was present to act as an independent observer. At this interview Owen spoke freely about the Czechs, safe in the knowledge that he could not be charged again with the same offences.

One amusing incident relating to the LEE case occurred when Martin Furnival Jones had to visit the Prime Minister to tell him that, according to Frolik's American debriefers, there was a Labour MP named Owen in the pay of the Czechs. Apparently Mr Wilson first thought he meant Dr David Owen, then a junior Defence Minister. The misunderstanding was quickly rectified.

Will Owen's name was not the only one given to the Prime Minister. According to Frolik, two other MPs were supplying the Czechs with secrets. The first, code-named GUSTAV, was the late Sir Barnett Stross, the Labour Member for Stoke-on-Trent who had died in May 1967. The second MP was John Stonehouse, then Labour's Minister for Posts and Telecommunications.

Frolik had identified Stonehouse as the victim of a sexual entrapment operation in Prague some years earlier. When the Prime Minister confronted Stonehouse with Frolik's allegations, he denied them and no further action was taken against him.*

Early the next year, in 1971, Frolik and 'K' Branch eliminated another Czech agent, but on this occasion the defector was able to provide the prosecution with damning details of the spy's activities. Code-named

---

*On 6 August 1976 Stonehouse was sentenced to seven years' imprisonment after being found guilty on eighteen charges of theft and fraud. After his release from prison he published a novel describing an entrapment and blackmail operation run by the East Germans, *Ralph* (Cape, 1982).

MARCONI, Frolik's man was a former RAF technician named Nicholas Prager.

The 'K' Branch investigation of Prager deeply disturbed MI5 for two reasons. One was the very high quality of information betrayed by him, another was the fact that he had undergone Positive Vetting and had been cleared, even though his Stage 1 security questionnaire contained several lies.

Prager had been born in Czechoslovakia in December 1928, the son of a clerk in the British Consulate. Shortly before he retired in 1948 his father had become a naturalized British subject, which automatically enabled his son to claim British citizenship. This he did, and the following year he travelled to England with his wife, Jana, and their baby. Soon after arriving Prager joined the RAF, stating on his application form that he was British by birth and that he had always lived in England. He made no mention of the fact that he was married and claimed his father had also been born in England. Within five years of joining the RAF, Prager had become an extremely proficient radar technician and had been posted to Fighter Command's headquarters at Stanmore. There he worked on several secret projects before transferring to RAF Wittering in 1956. It was while he was there that Prager underwent Positive Vetting and obtained clearance to top-secret defence information. Two examples of the top-secret material to which he had access, and which he passed to his Czech case officer, were the BLUE DIVER and RED STEER radar jamming devices then being fitted into the V-bomber force.

BLUE DIVER was one of several electronic counter-measure projects on which Prager worked, both at RAF Wittering and the radar development unit at Finningley near Doncaster. Enquiries at the Passport Office showed that Prager had submitted an application for a passport in January 1959, stating that he wished to visit Hawaii. When his passport was examined in January 1971 it showed a number of Continental entry stamps, but there were none for the United States. The first visa stamped in his passport was a Czech one, and it had been issued by Bohumil Malik, a known Czech intelligence officer.

Prager had left the RAF in August 1961 and had joined English Electric. In the ten years between his leaving the Services and his arrest, Prager had spent a considerable amount of time in his home country and, at one point, was engaged on the installation of an English computer at a Czech steelworks. 'K' Branch assumed that Prager had given up his espionage activity when he left the RAF, but when his home at Bramley, near Rotherham, was searched on 31 January 1971, the West Yorkshire police discovered several one-time pads and other clues which indicated that he was about to resume intelligence gathering. Prager was questioned for more than five hours, first by Detective Superintendents John

Domaille and Ronald Sills, and then by Detective Chief Superintendent Donald Craig, head of the West Yorkshire CID.

Prager's trial opened at Leeds Assizes before Lord Justice Widgery on 14 June 1971, and the prosecution was remarkable because the offences with which he was charged were all alleged to have taken place more than ten years earlier. His defence claimed blackmail and threats to his wife's family in Czechoslovakia, but half way through the proceedings he blamed his wife for everything and denounced her as a Czech agent. This, in fact, was not so far from the truth, for she had been introduced to Prager by Robert Husak who had been Will Owen's case officer. Mrs Prager had disappeared shortly before the trial although her lover, another RAF technician, gave evidence of her pro-communist sympathies.

Prager was found guilty on all charges by a majority verdict and Lord Justice Widgery sentenced him to twelve years' imprisonment.

The Prager case was the last to have originated from the Czech defectors Frolik and August, but it was not for want of their allegations or, for that matter, pressure from the Americans. For example, one person named as having been in touch with the Czech intelligence service was Edward Scott, a former Chargé d'Affaires at the British Embassy in Prague, who had resigned from the Diplomatic Service in March 1961 after an incident involving a Czech housemaid. Scott, who had previously served as Britain's wartime Military Attaché in Kabul, had also shared an office with Guy Burgess at the time of the latter's defection. He was interrogated at Littlehampton police station, near his home in Sussex, but he consistently denied having passed classified information to the Czechs. He did, however, admit to having held illicit meetings with Czech agents in London after his recall from Prague, while he was still employed at the Foreign Office. Once again, no further action could be taken, although Scott himself told the *Sunday Times* in December 1981 that he had been surprised not to have been prosecuted.

There is, of course, a built-in disadvantage in accepting defectors; the opposition recognize that they will invariably denounce as many hostile agents as they can. Unfortunately such practice also neutralizes friendly double agents, as Frolik was to discover. He was anxious to expose the Soviet and Czech agents who had been recruited from the British trades union movement. However steps were taken to ensure that the names of several senior figures in the British trades union movement were deleted from the final manuscript of his memoirs. Among them was Ted Hill, then President of the Boilermakers Union, and a covert member of the Communist Party of Great Britain. Frolik also claimed that two other prominent trades union leaders were Soviet recruits.

Frolik's defection directly resulted in Prager's arrest and conviction, but he also alerted 'K' Branch to the extent of Soviet Bloc subversion operations in London. Frolik went through the entire Diplomatic List ticking off the names of those he knew to be active intelligence officers and also produced a list of Soviet Bloc 'agents of influence'.

As the Czech Labour Attaché in London, Frolik's main task had been to mix with and recruit useful trades union members. He had been accredited to most of the major trades union conferences and had been provided with a lavish expense account with which to entertain key trades union officials. 'F' Branch had monitored such activity for years, but the defector's first-hand account of his work was chilling. The Czech Embassy was perfectly willing to create any kind of social function at the shortest possible notice, just so a target might be entertained. When Frolik compared notes with 'F' Branch and calculated the number of trades union officials receiving such attention, the totals appalled them. The options available to the Czechs ranged from a casual drink after a conference dinner to the offer of a bargain holiday, at a price subsidized by the intelligence organization. On a very few occasions, Frolik reported, he had been warned off a particular target on the grounds that the person concerned was already in harness. The Czechs specialized in the recruitment of agents of influence for several reasons. Firstly, even the most leftist union members were wary of being cultivated by Soviet officials. The Czechs, however, capitalized on their traditional good relations with the British, combined with an element of playing the underdog, stirring up memories of Britain's pre-war abandonment of Czechoslovakia to Nazi Germany. The Czech intelligence service became so adept at this role that in the late 1960s the KGB deliberately delegated to it responsibility for this type of subversion in England.

Frolik's colleagues had virtually unlimited reserves of cash at their disposal and homed in on Members of Parliament with unstable financial backgrounds and civil servants with weaknesses which opened them to blackmail. Their success rate was limited, with several such victims reporting approaches to the Security Service, but according to Frolik a much larger number of influential figures fell, possibly unconsciously, into KGB control. Both Martin Furnival Jones and Harold Wilson held strong opinions on the subject of these agents of influence. The Director-General regarded them as potential spies, whilst the Prime Minister suspected MI5 of over-reacting.

This conflict had in fact been in existence long before Frolik's categoric allegations against certain members of both the Parliamentary Labour Party and the trades union movement. A case in point was that of Bernard Floud, the Labour MP for Acton since 1964.

Floud was the son of Sir Francis Floud, a former Permanent Secretary to the Ministry of Labour and pre-war High Commissioner in Canada. Bernard had been recruited as a Soviet agent whilst at Wadham College, Oxford, and had served in the Intelligence Corps during the war.

Another of those associated with Floud was Jenifer Hart, wife of Herbert Hart, the Professor of Jurisprudence at Oxford, and himself a wartime MI5 officer. Mrs Hart was one of the five daughters of a prominent international lawyer, Sir John Fischer Williams, and had worked in the Home Office. She in turn had come to MI5's attention after being denounced by Mrs Flora Solomon, the Marks & Spencer executive who had offered proof of Philby's duplicity in 1962.

Mrs Hart had never made any secret of her strong leftist sympathies and, when interviewed by MI5, denied ever having committed an offence. She did, however, confirm that she had been a member of a Fabian-style discussion group of civil servants. One of their number was Sir Dennis Proctor, the recently retired Permanent Secretary at the Ministry of Power.

Furnival Jones had authorized an interview with Sir Dennis at his home in the South of France, but the results had been inconclusive. He admitted having been a member of The Apostles, the intellectual group of the Cambridge Left (which, incidentally, numbered Blunt, Burgess and Long amongst its members), while he was up at King's, and also agreed that he might have inadvertently provided Burgess with useful information, but he too categorically denied having committed an offence.

The dilemma facing the Director-General in 1967 was complex. Neither Mrs Hart nor Sir Dennis constituted a threat to security, but Bernard Floud's name had been included on a list of MPs the Prime Minister proposed to appoint as Junior Ministers. Soon after coming to office in 1964 Harold Wilson had instructed Roger Hollis to seek his personal approval for any investigation which concerned a Member of either House, Lords or Commons. Bearing this decree in mind F-J told the Prime Minister that the Security Service could not approve Floud's appointment unless he had been cleared. Wilson had therefore given his permission for Floud to be interviewed, and this had begun in the autumn of 1967. He denied ever having been a Soviet agent, but the MI5 officer who conducted the interview had been unconvinced. On 27 October Floud gassed himself at his home in Albert Street, north London, so no further action could be taken.

Floud's suicide, which had been motivated by reasons completely unconnected with his interrogations, ended MI5's by now long-standing enquiries into the pre-war Cambridge-orientated Soviet networks. (Although Floud had been to Oxford it was believed that he had originally been recruited as an agent by James Klugman, the veteran Cambridge activist.) MI5 had achieved confessions or defections from Burgess, Maclean, Cairncross, Philby, Blunt and Long. Several of their associates had also made statements concerning their own, albeit limited, involvement. By the late 1960s it was believed that they had virtually all been identified, interrogated and refused further access to classified information.

It should be remembered that MI5's role in the Defence of the Realm does not necessarily demand it to seek prosecutions, although this course of action has often been deemed desirable, but rather requires it to make the existing and future position secure by eliminating threats to the established order. Inevitably this has involved encouraging statements from individuals who undoubtedly would have been less co-operative if they believed they might end up in the dock of the Old Bailey.

The full extent to which the Soviets capitalized on these ideological traitors will probably never be known as the conditions which bred them have disappeared and those who did admit limited collaboration with Comintern networks have declared their remorse. Nevertheless, many mysteries continue. For example, who were the Ring-of-Five? Certainly Burgess, Maclean, Philby and Cairncross were members, but MI5 were alarmed to discover that Anthony Blunt did not fit the profile of the remaining candidate.

One person considered a possible candidate for the role of the last member of the Ring-of-Five was Dr Alistair Watson, a former Cambridge Don and Admiralty scientist. He underwent a lengthy interrogation and was once questioned in the presence of Anthony Blunt, who had been unable to confirm Watson's guilt independently. Watson admitted having met Yuri Modin and Sergei Kondrachev, two of the Ring-of-Five's Soviet case officers, but denied ever passing classified information. MI5 and Blunt were not so sure, so Watson was transferred from his defence research job to the National Institute of Oceanography.

While these enquiries were being conducted in 1967 the MI5 investigators came across the name of a senior MI5 officer. A second, though less intensive PETERS operation was launched, code-named HARRIET, which resulted in him being interviewed about certain alleged breaches of security. He satisfied his inquisitors completely and was later appointed to a senior position.

According to the then Prime Minister, Edward Heath, this in-house investigation was never reported to him. There was, however, one occasion in 1968 when the Director-General was obliged to warn Harold Wilson of a bizarre Security Service enquiry. It seems that an invitation extended by Lord Mountbatten to various public figures, to engage in talks to discuss the country's decline under Socialism, led to allegations to MI5 of an attempted *coup d'état*.

The exact circumstances of the 'plot' will probably never be made public, but it was alleged that Lord Mountbatten and Cecil King, the former Chairman of the *Daily Mirror*, had canvassed opinion on the support a military take-over might receive. One meeting, which took place early in May 1968 at Lord Mountbatten's London home, was attended by Hugh Cudlipp and Sir Solly Zuckerman, Chief Scientific Adviser to the government. Mountbatten reported that the Queen had become concerned over the very large number of letters she had received protesting about the Wilson government. According to Mountbatten, no other monarch had ever been sent so much mail on one subject. He asked, in the broadest terms, what action should be taken. Zuckerman wanted no part of it.

By the time Furnival Jones reported to the Prime Minister, the meeting had been interpreted as the first stage in a military coup, with Mountbatten and Cecil King the principal organizers. Wilson was appalled at the prospect of such a 'plot' and instructed both MI5 and the Cabinet Secretary, Sir Burke Trend, to investigate further. No doubt this action would have been enough to ensure the collapse of the 'plot', if indeed one did actually exist. Certainly no military personnel were discovered to be directly involved, although Mountbatten, having been Chief of the Defence Staff, had the very best connections.

Josef Frolik's defection (and his subsequent MI5 debriefing) left the Security Service better informed about Soviet Bloc intelligence operations in London than at any time since the war. It also paved the way for MI5's greatest post-war coup.

The operation's inauspicious start began soon after one o'clock in the morning of 31 August 1971 when Police Constables Charles Shearer and George Paterson were driving their patrol car north up the Tottenham Court Road in London. They spotted a Hillman weaving erratically across the road and decided to make a routine stop. The driver, who appeared to be drunk, gave his name as Oleg Lyalin and said he was a Soviet trade official living in West Hill, Highgate. He refused the police officers' request for a breathalyser test and was therefore arrested and taken to the police station in the Tottenham Court Road. Once in the police station Lyalin also refused to give the blood or urine sample required by law, so he was kept in a cell overnight. The next morning he appeared at Marlborough Street Magistrates Court and was remanded on bail of £50 and the surety of a representative of the London Embassy's *Sovietskaya Kolonia* security unit, Aleksandr Abramov.

If Lyalin had enjoyed diplomatic immunity, he could have escaped the appearance in Court but his conviction would have meant the end of his tour of duty in England. It might also have put to an end his career in the KGB, which would have been extremely inconvenient for MI5 as Lyalin had been recruited earlier in the year as their agent. Lyalin had been having an affair with his blonde secretary, Irina Teplyakova, even though both were married with their respective partners living in Russia. Lyalin's agreement with MI5 involved a new life for himself and Irina, and he invoked this as soon as he left the Magistrates Court. He and Irina were driven to a safe-house and their debriefing begun.

The first consequence of Lyalin's successful defection was the arrest of three of his agents. The first two, Constantinos Martianon and his brother-in-law Kyriacoṣ Costi, were Greek Cypriot tailors, aged twenty-six and twenty-nine respectively. Both were arrested at the younger man's home at 44 Upper Tollington Park Road, near Finsbury Park, on 9 September by Detective Inspector Fryer of Special Branch. Both had been members of the Young Communist League and had been recruited as KGB agents after visiting a Soviet trade exhibition in London in 1961. Both men pleaded guilty to Official Secrets Acts offences at the Old Bailey on 7 December 1971 and were sentenced to four and six years' imprisonment respectively by Mr Justice Milmo.

The arrests of Martianon and Costi were followed soon afterwards by that of Sirioj Husein Abdoolcader, a thirty-three-year-old civil servant then living in Cricklewood, who had played an extremely useful role in helping the KGB evade MI5 surveillance. Abdoolcader was the son of Sir Husein Abdoolcader, one of Malaya's most distinguished advocates. His son had come to England in 1957 to read for the Bar at Lincoln's Inn, but when he failed his exams he decided to stay in England. He obtained a job as a clerk in the Greater London Council's motor licensing department. This had given him access to the index numbers of all the Special Branch and Security Service vehicles whose registration documents had been specially 'flagged' so as to prevent details about them reaching unauthorized persons. If, for example, the police made an enquiry on a 'flagged' vehicle, they were advised that the documents were subject to a Home Office Directive which prevented information on that car being disclosed. The procedure also required the local licensing authority (in this case the Greater London Council) to report the request to the Special Branch duty officer at Scotland Yard. This would lead to the police officer who had made the enquiry being interviewed. By employing Abdoolcader the KGB had effectively obtained better access to the GLC's records than the Metropolitan Police.

Abdoolcader was arrested at his office in County Hall on 17 September by Detective Chief Inspector Fryer who searched him and found a postcard in his wallet addressed to Lyalin. On the reverse was a list of MI5's registration numbers. Abdoolcader told his interrogators that he had been recruited by a Soviet diplomat, subsequently identified as Vladislav Savin, in March 1967 and, two years later, had been handed over to a new case officer whom he had known as ALEX. ALEX, in fact, had been Oleg Lyalin. The KGB's ability to check the registration of any car they suspected of being used by MI5 watchers was extremely damaging to the Security Service's operations and its morale. There had been countless examples of the Soviets spotting even the most sophisticated of mobile surveillance operations and 'K' Branch had been aware of the possibility that their cars had been betrayed since Martelli's claim in 1963 that the Russians had lists of MI5's cars.

If anyone had been in any doubt about Soviet interest in MI5's discreetly disguised fleet of vehicles, such doubts evaporated in May 1968. In that month two Soviet Trade Delegation officials, Yuri Dushkin and Vladimir Loginov, were arrested outside the Security Service's garage in Barnard Road, Battersea, in South London. It was the sixth time the pair had been spotted in the area since 22 March 1968. When they were approached by CID officers, Dushkin 'resisted arrest' and subsequently had to visit St Mary Abbott's Hospital. Both men were carrying cameras and wireless receivers, and were later expelled.

Abdoolcader pleaded guilty at the Old Bailey and was sentenced on 8 February 1972 to three years' imprisonment. During his subsequent interrogations Abdoolcader threw some light on the 1969 case which had failed to develop. During the summer of that year the Personal Assistant to the Royal Navy's Deputy Director of Support and Transport, Miss Marie Richardson, had taken a Baltic cruise to Leningrad and on her return had reported what she believed were suspicious advances from a member of the Soviet crew who had taken a considerable interest in her job at Portsmouth. The Director of Naval Security had instructed Miss Richardson to report any further approaches, but none actually materialized. At the time there was no obvious explanation for the Russians dropping her so quickly, but Abdoolcader provided the reason: Miss Richardson was Asian in origin, so the KGB had asked Abdoolcader to recruit her, but when he tried to telephone in February 1970 he had failed to reach her. He had then given up trying and, when he got married in January the following year, had tried to reduce his work for the Russians.

Meanwhile, between Abdoolcader's arrest in September and conviction the following February, the Security Service had achieved what many of its officers regarded as their greatest post-war success.

The success was the expulsion of ninety named Soviet diplomats, and the exclusion of a further fifteen who were out of the country at the time of the Foreign Secretary's announcement early in September 1971. The Security Service had been urging the government for years to limit the ever increasing number of Soviet diplomats and trade officials accredited to London. Whenever MI5 pleaded for action, the Foreign Office would oppose them by arguing that such a step in London would only result in further restrictions on British Embassy staff in Moscow. MI5 invariably countered this with some derogatory remark about the quality of information from MI6's Moscow Station, and the debate would lapse for a further year. However, Lyalin's detailed statements on the activities of Soviet personnel in London provided the ideal opportunity to take 'once-and-for-all' action.

The climate in Whitehall also provided Furnival Jones with a unique chance to get his way. Three years earlier, in 1968, Sir Dick White had retired as the MI6 Chief and had been appointed by the Prime Minister to a newly created post, that of Intelligence Co-ordinator to the Cabinet. In 1964 he had chosen the MI6 Head of Station in Washington, Maurice Oldfield, as his Vice Chief, but Michael Stewart, then Foreign Secretary, had been unwilling to appoint either Oldfield or his successor in Washington as the new Chief of MI6. Instead he chose Sir John Rennie, a career diplomat and one-time head of the Foreign Office's Information Research Department, the propaganda organization which had inherited peacetime responsibility for what had once been termed psychological warfare.

Rennie and his Vice Chief, Maurice Oldfield, supported MI5's proposal to take firm action against the Russians, and the Director-General also found allies in Dick White and the new Permanent Under-Secretary at the Foreign Office, Sir Denis Greenhill. All agreed that Lyalin's evidence could not be ignored and that his defection would make the Soviet Embassy vulnerable for the first (and possibly the last) time. The plan was approved by Edward Heath's Cabinet and the Foreign Secretary, Sir Alec Douglas-Home, made the necessary public announcement. Without doubt the Russians were taken completely by surprise by the move. Their response was to declare just four of the British Embassy's staff in Moscow *persona non grata*.

Excellent use was also made at this time of a film which MI5 had covertly shot early in 1968 of Viktor Drozlov, a Third Secretary at the Soviet Embassy, emptying a dead-letter drop in an unidentified area of Surrey. An atomic scientist, who was also an MI5 double agent, had reported an approach by Drozlov and had allowed himself to be recruited by him. 'K' Branch had then taken the film. Now this film was shown on television, followed by an interview with the scientist. The net effect of the film was a general acceptance, in England, that the majority of Soviet diplomats were really full-time intelligence officers engaged in either espionage, sabotage or subversion. This, of course, was not news to the Soviet order of battle section of 'K' Branch, whose responsibility it had been to monitor and identify the Soviet staff; but the incontrovertible details provided by Lyalin did serve to persuade such doubters as there were, in Whitehall and elsewhere, of the Soviets' true intentions.

There was also one quite unexpected bonus to the mass expulsion: two Soviet agents suddenly volunteered confessions. The first to come forward was Sub-Lieutenant David Bingham, a Royal Navy officer based at HMS *Rothesay* in Portsmouth, who had been supplying Lori Kuzmin, the Soviet Naval Attaché, with secret documents since early in 1970. He was sentenced to twenty-one years' imprisonment by Mr Justice Bridge on 13 March 1972.

The second man to come forward was not a willing agent. He was Leonard Hinchcliffe, a thirty-nine-year-old administrative officer in the Diplomatic Corps who had joined the Foreign Office in 1964. He had been blackmailed over a friendship he had formed with a colleague's wife, whilst serving in Khartoum. They had not actually become lovers, but Hinchcliffe feared his wife discovering the friendship because she was recovering from the recent death of their son. A Soviet, he knew only as ANDREI, had paid him some £3,000 for secret documents, but on 8 October 1971 Hinchcliffe explained his predicament to the British Ambassador in Algiers, Mr Ronald Burroughs. On 17 April 1972 Hinchcliffe was sentenced to ten years' imprisonment by Lord Justice Widgery.

Martin Furnival Jones was Director-General of the Security Service for seven years, during which time there had been several important cases, the majority of which originated with defectors such as Frolik and August; he had also successfully prevailed upon Sir Denis Greenhill to evict the major part of the Soviet *rezidentura* in London. Of those exposed, Douglas Britten had done by far the most damage and his arrest had helped to reduce the leakage of the RAF's signals intelligence secrets. It was only in the summer of 1982 that MI5 belatedly learned of a second Soviet source active in the same period, Geoffrey Prime, who had also been disposing of equally sensitive information from Government Communications Headquarters at Cheltenham.

The elimination of Peter Dorschel had also been something of a success for 'K' Branch's Soviet Satellites section. In political terms the case of Helen Keenan had been a mild embarrassment. It was galling to discover that 10 Downing Street could be penetrated, and it was a blow to the Prime Minister, Harold Wilson, who had been anxious to encourage the recruitment of secretarial staff from more varied backgrounds. Regrettably, Furnival Jones's retirement may well be remembered not for the achievements of his period as Director-General, but for the discreet rumpus over the choice of his successor.

10

A MATTER OF TRUST

Before Martin Furnival Jones's scheduled retirement in April 1972 he had a number of duties to perform. Some of them concerned internal appointments which would make his departure one of the milestones in the organization's history, and thus a suitable point at which to close this study.

His Deputy D-G, Anthony Simkins, had himself retired in the autumn of 1971 and, in his place, Furnival Jones appointed Michael Hanley, the Director of 'C' Branch. The Director-General's own post was going to fall vacant within a matter of months, and there was considerable speculation about his successor. The established procedure, as we have seen, was for the Director-General to recommend a name to the 'Three Wise Men', the Permanent Under-Secretaries Committee, who would either give their approval or suggest an alternative candidate to the Prime Minister. Shortly before Christmas 1971 Furnival Jones submitted the name of his newly appointed Deputy, Michael Hanley. This choice was remarkable because the Security Service had never been headed by someone who had not first served as Deputy D-G for at least two years. That had been in the unusual circumstances caused by Guy Liddell's transfer to the post of security officer to the Atomic Energy Authority in 1953, which had made it purely fortuitous that Furnival Jones had been promoted after only two years in the job. Hanley's rise to the top would have been accomplished in a matter of months, not years.

The alternative option available to the Prime Minister was the appointment of a complete outsider, or even a senior counter-intelligence officer from MI6. Surprisingly, the choice was very limited, for 1972 was indeed becoming a year of total change. Sir John Rennie had less than two years left to run as Chief of MI6 and no one would have approved his transfer to the Security Service because, in spite of his Information Research Department background, he was not a professional intelligence officer. His Vice Chief, Maurice Oldfield, might have been a suitable candidate, but this idea met with considerable resistance from within MI6. Other senior posts were also to fall vacant soon. Sir Dick White was due to retire as Intelligence Co-ordinator to the Cabinet, and he too would have to be replaced by a senior intelligence officer. Thus, if Mr Heath had been inclined to insert an outsider into the Security Service, he would had to have had convincing reasons, given the number of other important posts to be filled.

On the political side, Conservative Prime Ministers have a reputation for leaving intelligence matters to the professionals. This, of course, is in direct contrast to the Labour Party's innate distrust of all intelligence organizations. On the two occasions that Labour politicians have appointed outsiders, Sillitoe in 1946 and Rennie in 1968, the results had been considered less than desirable. Naturally the Prime Minister would not have concerned himself with the complicated background of the intelligence bureaucracy, but it must have figured in the 'Three Wise Men's' calculations. In any event, the choice of Michael Hanley was approved and Furnival Jones circulated the decision inside Leconfield House on a Friday afternoon. With that he set off to the Far East on the Director-General's traditional farewell tour of the overseas posts.

The Prime Minister then did some fast footwork to fill the other gaps at the top of the intelligence tree. Dick White was replaced as Cabinet Co-ordinator by Sir Leonard Hooper, the Director of the Government Communications Headquarters at Cheltenham who was himself due to retire in 1974. His successor was Arthur Bonsall.

Martin Furnival Jones was scheduled to retire in April 1972, but before he could hand over to Hanley he had one further duty to perform. That was to give (incognito) evidence to the Franks Committee review of the Official Secrets Acts which had been set up by the incoming Conservative administration in 1970 following the unsuccessful prosecution of Jonathan Aitken and Brian Roberts of the *Sunday Telegraph* in that year.

Aitken had published a confidential report on the state of the Biafran war which had embarrassed the then Prime Minister, Harold Wilson. A prosecution was mounted at the Old Bailey and the defendants were acquitted after a thirteen-day trial. The case itself, which did not concern MI5, has been described fully by Jonathan Aitken in *Officially Secret*,* but Lord Franks's Committee did require evidence from the Security Service. Two extracts from the Director-General's evidence are of especial interest. The first is his reply to a question concerning Soviet contacts with MPs:

I can certainly say that very many MPs are in contact with very many intelligence officers.

A little later he commented, perhaps with the Will Owen case in mind:

* Weidenfeld & Nicolson, 1971.

No doubt many MPs, many people enter the House of Commons in the hope of becoming Ministers. If the Russian Intelligence Service can recruit a backbench MP, and he continues to hold his seat for a number of years and climbs the ladder to a Ministerial position, it is obvious the spy is home and dry.

The Director-General also had an interesting remark on the question of MI5's traditional secrecy:

There has been some erosion of what was an extremely rigid position. This has not been a matter of policy, it has not been a conscious decision by myself or any of my predecessors that their identities should not be disclosed, but the identity of my predecessor was disclosed, and my own identity was disclosed to some newspapers, and to that extent there has been a change, it is no good pursuing a policy that flies in the face of the facts ... I have no direct relations with the press. Where does one stop? If my name is published, why not my deputy's name. And if my deputy's name is published, why not my directors? And before you know where you are, you are publishing the name of someone who is running agents, and his photograph appears in the press. . . . The position in a number of other countries ... is that while they do not operate in the full glare of publicity, nevertheless they do not adopt quite so restrictive an attitude to these matters as I and my predecessors have done. I doubt whether they benefit.

Certainly the climate of secrecy in which the Security Service had operated had changed. It was to change even further during his successor's time.

1972 was a year of important changes for MI5 and these changes were not limited to staff appointments, although these were contributory to the new atmosphere. The new Director-General, Michael Hanley, and his Deputy D-G were the first of the post-war intake to reach the top. The Deputy D-G, for example, had only joined the office in 1951, the year after the defections of Burgess and Maclean. There were personnel changes elsewhere: in the co-ordinator's office and at Cheltenham, as we have seen, and in Special Branch. Ferguson Smith, who had headed the Branch since 1966, retired in October 1972 and was replaced by Victor Gilbert, a career Branch officer who had handled the Blackburn and Keenan cases.

In the decade since 1972 the Security Service has undergone many further changes. It has left Leconfield House and abandoned its garages in Barnard Road. The IRA has bombed the restaurant beneath one of its out-offices in South Audley Street and an ICL computer has been installed in a data processing centre close to the new headquarters. Since the retirement of Sir Michael Hanley in 1979 two Directors-General have served in the top job. One, Sir Howard Smith, a former senior diplomat, was an outsider. His successor is a professional who joined MI5 after serving in the Malayan Civil Service.

However, even ten years later, the office is painfully aware of the trauma caused by the Hollis enquiry and the PETERS and HARRIET investigations. The Fluency Committee's review of the Hollis case left a number of officers dissatisfied and they felt duty-bound to take the matter further. With the reluctant blessing of Maurice Oldfield, who succeeded Sir John Rennie as Chief of MI6 in 1974, an MI6 member of the Committee, Stephen de Mowbray, sought an interview with the incoming Prime Minister, Harold Wilson. Instead he saw the Cabinet Secretary, Sir John Hunt, but nevertheless he persuaded Hunt to review the Fluency Committee's findings. This was carried out by Hunt's predecessor, Lord Trend.

Trend's conclusions were twofold: firstly, that the Security Service had conducted its enquiry diligently and comprehensively; and secondly, that there was no direct evidence of treachery on the part of Hollis, who had died in 1973. There was certainly a *prima facie* case to be made against Hollis, as we have seen, but there was also substantial evidence in his favour: he had none of the proven pre-war communist contacts that other ideologically motivated traitors had had; he had never been denounced by one of the several well-informed defectors who had given MI5 clues to other Soviet spies; he had pursued Philby and Blunt with vigour, and had encouraged the PETERS investigation. Perhaps, most telling of all, by accepting the clearance of PETERS he had consciously initiated an investigation into his own conduct.

There is, of course, no denying the weight of the circumstantial evidence against Hollis. Philby's letter concerning Gouzenko is crucial in this respect. But would either Philby or Hollis have left such an apparently incriminating letter on the file if they both had indeed been Soviet agents?

An alternative explanation, which would dovetail conveniently with what has been learned of Soviet strategy, raises the pertinent question: was Hollis an innocent dupe who was used to distract the mole-hunters away from the real culprits? This scenario is not unlikely, bearing in mind the cases we have examined, and it does have the advantage of invalidating the target's thirty years of counter-intelligence work. If the Soviets were anxious to find a 'fall-guy', then Hollis fitted the bill. He was unpopular in the office, being shy and withdrawn among his colleagues. He was socially ill at ease with his MI6 contacts. He had maintained an extra-marital relationship with his secretary and had relied financially on his wife's income. After his retirement he had spent all his time in the West Country and, unlike his predecessors, had dropped out of the Whitehall scene completely. His record as Director-General had come under more frequent independent scrutiny than any of his predecessors or, for that matter, his successors. Various Commissions had looked into MI5's conduct of the Portland, Vassall, Profumo, Bossard and Allen cases. The Security Service had escaped criticism for their handling of each of these cases and had invariably received praise. Indeed, Lord Denning had been obliged to educate the public about MI5's role and responsibilities so it could be clearly understood that the Security Service and its Director-General had acted entirely properly.

Hollis's unpopularity within Leconfield House does not fully explain the professional criticisms made of his interpretation of the Security Service's role. Officers in 'D' Branch felt he had minimized the risk from Soviet espionage and had not appeared to fully appreciate MI5's counter-espionage role. No doubt 'F' Branch officers felt that on occasion their needs were not always taken care of. It is inevitable that within an organization which has multiple, compartmentalized responsibilities, one branch might feel neglected. In the case of Percy Sillitoe, all the Divisions felt the Director-General had failed them, but he was the exception. The counter-espionage Division had always been regarded as the senior branch and therefore the Director-General and his Deputy had generally been drawn from it. Hollis had been the exception to the rule. He had never served in either 'B' Division or, latterly, 'D' Branch, although as Dick White's Deputy D-G he had spent much of his time dealing with counter-espionage cases. When Hollis was appointed Director-General, officers in 'D' Branch felt their value had been underestimated, even if, in Graham Mitchell, they had acquired a Deputy D-G who had spent some years as Director 'D'.

As we have seen, Hollis's experience lay in 'F' Division and then 'C' Division. If his reportedly low appreciation of the work of 'D' Branch is true, then he may have been justified. Certainly during the war there had been any number of counter-espionage cases to deal with, but most had originated from the aggressive counter-intelligence operations conducted by double-agent specialists such as Tar Robertson and John Marriott. In the post-war period none of the most serious cases had originated with 'D' Branch. Invariably their role had been to follow up leads provided by an American source and, in the majority of cases, this had meant a CIA-sponsored defector: Gouzenko provided Nunn May; BRIDE produced Fuchs and then Maclean; Tisler gave Linney; Goleniewski gave the Portland spies; Golytsin gave Vassall; Frolik delivered Owen and Prager.

These cases tend to confirm that 'D' Branch had indeed become relegated to a 'defector follow-up' service. It had only rarely initiated successful cases, the most obvious example being that of the Hanslope Park spy, William Marshall. Yet the only person who could claim the credit for his arrest had been the watcher who, fortuitously, had spotted Pavel Kuznetsov, his Soviet case officer. It was by no means a triumph of investigation. In fact the post-war cases of Russian espionage serve to raise the importance of 'C' Branch and to place extra emphasis on physical security. In almost every instance of a security breach the authorities had made it easy for the spy to walk out of buildings with classified documents. Vassall had taken papers home overnight; Bossard had photographed them during his lunch-break; Linney had actually stolen the originals. There had never been any spot-checks on Percy Allen's register of secret documents. In all of these cases straightforward physical measures might well have prevented the leak.

If Hollis had laid emphasis on the work of 'C' Branch at the expense of the counter-espionage investigators, he would seem to have had good reason for having done so. Certainly Lord Radcliffe had called for an increase in this area in his Report of April 1962, thus apparently endorsing the Director-General's viewpoint.

Another conclusion which might reasonably be drawn from an examination of MI5's post-war cases relates to Positive Vetting. The system does not generally identify spies, and it is not supposed to do so, but if applied as intended it will weed out the more obvious security risks. Of all the post-war cases dealt with here, only Britten, the RAF signals intelligence technician, and Hinchcliffe, the spy in the British Embassy in Algiers, had received a properly executed Positive Vetting clearance. There was nothing in the background of either of these two men which would have justified a Positive Vetting refusal. In every other case, including those of the defectors, the screening had not been properly executed. The Stage 1 questionnaires of Bossard and Prager contained lies, while in Allen's case a field enquiry would have identified him as someone who was living beyond his means. Furthermore, his clearance was a limited one which was not supposed to have allowed him regular access to secret documents. In practice, Allen was in charge of a registry of nine civilian clerks and was the authorized holder of the secret documents' log.

The question raised by the failure of these vetting procedures is simple: should they have been conducted by MI5 as opposed to departmental security units? The Security Service would argue against, on the grounds that security should be a departmental responsibility and the internal unit encourages vigilance. No doubt they might also fear a loss of their traditional secrecy. Others might reply that vetting checks have proved too important to be left to amateurs. In retrospect it would certainly seem that the whole Positive Vetting system has proved to be another example of Whitehall's 'too little, too late' syndrome.

Even after the elapse of ten years it is difficult to draw rigid conclusions from MI5's performance. If, according to Harold Wilson, 'a week is a long time in politics', then ten years is a mere moment in intelligence terms. Do all the security lapses described in this book infer that Britain is thoroughly leaky? Not necessarily so. The cases fall neatly into two categories. The first group are the committed, ideologically motivated spies – the moles – who are professional, cautious, and willing to go to great lengths to protect themselves and their contacts. These individuals have all been connected by the common strand of a 1930s' conversion to communism. On the way they have left a detectable spoor. The second group are the opportunists who may have also been blackmailed. When the first hand-over is accompanied by a payment there is thereafter an implicit threat of blackmail. Britten's first transactions were motivated by financial gain. Forever afterwards there was always the risk of exposure.

After the invasions of Hungary, Czechoslovakia and Afghanistan, it seems unlikely that there will still be many ideological traitors at large, but there will always be those who are susceptible to blackmail and those who are simply greedy. In the post-war period Britain does not appear to have fared much worse than, say, the United States, which has been particularly susceptible to the infiltration of 'illegals'. Even the National Security Agency, which boasted the tightest security procedures of any Federal Agency, was the subject of penetration and defections. Two homosexual cryptologists, William Martin and Bernon Mitchell, defected to Russia via Cuba in August 1960. Three years later they had been followed by Victor Hamilton. Cornelius Drummond was arrested in September 1962 for selling NSA documents to Soviet agents in London, and Jack Dunlap committed suicide in July 1963 after his espionage had been discovered.

Perhaps most embarrassing of all, the NSA's Director of Personnel, Maurice Klein, was found to have falsified his own original NSA application form, and the NSA Director of Security, a former FBI agent, S. Wesley Reynolds, admitted having discovered Klein's secret without taking action. Both men resigned, and were followed by twenty-six other NSA officials who were later described as 'sexual deviates'.

France too suffered its share of upheavals in its intelligence community. In October 1970 Alexandre de Marenches was appointed Chief of SDECE and promptly organized a purge. Two Directors of important departments accepted early retirement.

And what of the moles within MI5?

If the Security Service had escaped Soviet penetration after the war, then it would have been the only Western security agency to have done so. The evidence presented in this book argues against such an improbability. If one accepts as fact that either the KGB or the GRU employed at least one agent inside the Service, one has to ask where he was and, if possible, who he was.

The Soviet target was unquestionably 'D' Branch. A spy in 'A' Branch would have been useful but would not have been in a position to influence individual operations. Penetration of 'B' would have revealed the identities of MI5 personnel, but again would have been of little other use. 'C' Branch would have yielded few prizes, while an 'E' Branch officer would have been too far removed from headquarters. An informant in 'F' Branch would be able to assess current penetration of the Communist Party of Great Britain and, latterly, other potentially subversive groups, but would this have interested the Russians? They know that 'F' Branch have long established moles in most leftist political organizations and are kept well informed by trades union informants. But they also know that 'F' Branch have only a reporting brief and are not authorized to conduct counter-subversive operations. In other words, MI5 will monitor extremists but they will not interfere with them. This code of practice enables the Security Service to recruit agents with relative ease. If the agents or their case officers habitually tried to sabotage the activities of, say, a union's left-wing executive, there would be few recruits for the future.

There are two useful illustrations of this policy which demonstrate its practical nature. When two convicted bank robbers, the Littlejohn brothers, announced that they had been employed by MI6 to rob banks and carry out assassinations in the Irish Republic, the MI6 Chief, Maurice Oldfield, gathered all his staff into the canteen on top of Century House to refute the allegations. He gave his personal assurance to everyone present that there was no truth in the story. Another MI6 Chief told this author, while discussing Graham Greene's *The Human Factor*,* that no MI6 Chief would authorize an assassination. This was not for humanitarian reasons, but simply because such activities would inevitably lead to greater political control over the Service. He cited the CIA's experience as a case in point. In contrast, he claimed, MI6 enjoys minimal direct political control.

If it is thus accepted that 'D' Branch had been the Soviet's principal target for penetration, the question remains, who in 'D' Branch was the spy? This is a question which MI5 itself cannot answer, although certain officers may have their suspicions, just as they have had in the past. But the mole-hunting team of John Day and Ian Carrel reported that in their opinion, by the late 1970s, the senior echelons of the office were 'clean'. They could not vouch for every employee, down to the last Ministry of Defence police officer who guarded the door, but they did feel confident about the upper levels.

Their confidence has not been shared by everyone because the lack of positive identification of a Soviet spy actually leaves MI5 worse off than other security organizations which have been penetrated and have recognized the fact. Having established exactly who the spies were, they have been able to make damage control assessments. No such exercises have been undertaken by MI5 because the extent of the damage remains an unknown quantity. There are two dangerous consequences of this: firstly, by failing positively to identify the agent or agents it is impossible

*Bodley Head, 1977.

to know if further agents have been left in place; secondly, it encourages the office to seek a convenient scapegoat. Hollis fits this description neatly. But, worst of all, it may suit the Soviets to encourage this view.

It should certainly be stressed that MI5 is not the only Western intelligence agency to undergo self-destructive mole-hunts. French, West German, Swedish, Norwegian, Canadian and American organizations experienced similar traumas during the same period.

What makes the British experience so exceptional is MI5's bureaucratic reluctance to admit a problem might even have existed. The complete absence of political guidance for the Security Service means that the Director-General is burdened with awesome responsibility. By convention MI5 does not share its secrets with politicians. This has inevitably led to preposterous situations like that faced by Hollis over the PETERS investigation: his refusal to confide in the Prime Minister the fact that his own Deputy D-G was under suspicion hampered the conduct of the enquiry. Then, as today, the Prime Minister's relationship with the Director-General of the Security Service boils down to a matter of trust.

In theory the Director-General chairs the Directorate of the Security Service and can call on the collective wisdom of his senior Directors. Unlike most outside boards the Directorate does not have a non-executive Director to express an impartial outside view. All the Directors are a part of the same intelligence bureaucracy and all have a vested interest. When it comes to an internal foul-up, history tells us that their instinct is one of self-preservation. As we have seen, the structure and constitution of the organization tends to encourage, not inhibit, this behaviour. It is a flaw that can only benefit the opposition.

One does not have to be an exponent of all KAGO's theories to concede that the KGB are past-masters of the art of decoy and deception. The pages of this book are littered with examples of the Soviets discarding pawns to protect really valuable spies. Bearing this in mind, it is likely that the Russians have actually succeeded in destroying Hollis's reputation and at the same time provided their real sources with protective cover. It is not so difficult to see Philby's conspiratorial mind at work when he wrote to Hollis in September 1945 about Gouzenko. If, subsequently, Philby had come under suspicion, he could have defended himself by pointing out that he had participated in a successful defection (and at the time the Russians had good reason to believe that Gouzenko posed no threat to their British assets); if Philby was caught, or if he was obliged to defect, he could at least take the reputation of an opponent with him. This is surely exactly what has happened.

It is perhaps appropriate that the final word here on the murky world of counter-intelligence should be devoted to Yuri Nosenko, better known as AE/FOXTROT, one of the two KGB defectors who dominated the scene during the 1960s. After a third, exhaustive review of his case in March 1969 he was released from the CIA's custody and 'rehabilitated'. He subsequently got married, and the best man at his wedding was Bruce Solie, of the CIA's Office of Security. Nosenko is now employed by the CIA as a consultant.

APPENDIX I

Sir David Maxwell Fyfe's 1952 Directive

1. In your appointment as Director-General of the Security Service you will be responsible personally to the Home Secretary. The Security Service is not, however, a part of the Home Office. On appropriate occasion you will have right of direct access to the Prime Minister.

2. The Security Service is part of the Defence Forces of the country. Its task is the Defence of the Realm as a whole, from external and internal dangers arising from attempts of espionage and sabotage, or from actions of persons and organizations whether directed from within or without the country, which may be judged to be subversive of the State.

3. You will take special care to see that the work of the Security Service is strictly limited to what is necessary for the task.

4. It is essential that the Security Service should be kept absolutely free from any political bias or influence and nothing should be done that might lend colour to any suggestion that it is concerned with the interests of any particular section of the community, or with any other matter than the Defence of the Realm as a whole.

5. No enquiry is to be carried out on behalf of any Government Department unless you are satisfied that an important public interest bearing on the Defence of the Realm, as defined in paragraph 2, is at stake.

6. You and your staff will maintain the well-established convention whereby ministers do not concern themselves with the detailed information which may be obtained by the Security Service in

particular cases, but are furnished with such information only as may be necessary for the determination of any issue on which guidance is sought.

Secretary of State for Home Affairs
24 September 1952

APPENDIX II

TELEPHONE AND MAIL INTERCEPTION
WARRANTS ISSUED 1945-72

Warrants issued by the Home Secretary for the interception of telephone calls and mail. These are the totals for England, Wales and Scotland, and include those granted to the Police and Customs & Excise as well as the Security Service.

YEAR	TELEPHONES	LETTERS	YEAR	TELEPHONES	LETTERS
1945	56	90	1959	159	101
1946	74	139	1960	195	110
1947	110	212	1961	183	75
1948	103	879	1962	242	96
1949	134	644	1963	270	128
1950	179	360	1964	253	120
1951	177	492	1965	299	93
1952	173	469	1966	318	139
1953	202	459	1967	310	92
1954	222	227	1968	343	83
1955	242	205	1969	385	93
1956	159	183	1970	409	104
1957	231		1971	428	86
1958	129	109	1972	428	97

Index